M & E HANDBOOKS

M & E Handbooks are recommended reading for examination syllabuses all over the world. Because each Handbook covers its subject clearly and concisely books in the series form a vital part of many college, university, school and home study courses.

Handbooks contain detailed information stripped of unnecessary padding, making each title a comprehensive self-tuition course. They are amplified with numerous self-testing questions in the form of Progress Tests at the end of each chapter, each text-referenced for easy checking. Every Handbook closes with an appendix which advises on examination technique. For all these reasons, Handbooks are ideal for pre-examination revision.

The handy pocket-book size and competitive price make Handbooks the perfect choice for anyone who wants to grasp the essentials of a subject quickly and easily.

Other M & E books of interest:

THE M & E HANDBOOK SERIES

Marketing

G. B. GILES, B.A., Dip.Ed., F.B.I.M., M.Inst.M.

*Head of Department of Management and Communications,
Canterbury College of Technology
Adviser in Marketing Studies, University of Kent at Canterbury*

FOURTH EDITION

MACDONALD AND EVANS

MACDONALD & EVANS LTD.
Estover, Plymouth PL6 7PZ

First published 1969
Reprinted 1970
Reprinted 1971
Reprinted 1972
Reprinted 1973
Second edition 1974
Reprinted 1977
Third edition 1978
Reprinted 1980
Reprinted 1981
Fourth edition 1983

© Macdonald & Evans Limited 1983

British Library Cataloguing in Publication Data

Giles, G. B.
    Marketing.—4th ed.—(The M & E handbook series)
    1. Marketing
    I. Title
    658.8   HF5415

ISBN: 0 7121 2804 2

Filmset in Monophoto Times by
Northumberland Press, Gateshead
Printed in Great Britain by
Richard Clay (The Chaucer Press) Ltd, Bungay, Suffolk

Preface to the Fourth Edition

This HANDBOOK has been written to provide a *vade-mecum* for mature students undertaking their first formal course in marketing. It should, therefore, be of special value to those undertaking courses leading to the Diploma in Management Studies, the National and Higher National Certificates and Diplomas of the Business Education Council and Part 1 of Business Studies degree courses, as well as those preparing for the examinations of the Institute of Marketing, Certificate and Diploma courses of the Communication, Advertising and Marketing Education Foundation and certain other professional bodies. Practising businessmen may also wish to have a compact reference book of this kind.

The coverage of subject matter is extensive, but the presentation has been condensed into the form of study notes for ease of comprehension. In addition to providing a basic framework of study, the book is intended to assist the student in examination revision.

It has been gratifying to find the earlier editions read and used in so many parts of the world both in English and translated versions. As a result of this ever-growing response, I have been concerned in this fourth edition not simply with the inevitable up-dating but with extending the breadth and depth of the subject matter still further.

Additional material has been introduced on the impact of Keynsian, neo-Keynsian and monetarist economic policies and especially low-growth situations on marketing decisions. Segmentation developments in the use of Target Group Index data and Acorn classifications are introduced, as is the setting up of the Broadcasters Audience Research Board. Many new features of the battle of the distribution channels are incorporated—franchising, superstores, productivity, service and product range conflicts as well as major changes affecting advertising, including the introduction of Channel 4 television. Attention is drawn to developments in microelectronics and their impact in the field of product development and marketing information systems. There is also additional material on industrial and service marketing as well as mergers, acquisitions and portfolio management.

I should like to reiterate that marketing is a very complex field of study and that students should undertake considerable complementary reading to explore in greater depth many of the facets which require more detailed treatment. A list of suggestions for further reading is given in Appendix II.

In earlier editions I have said that, as far as possible, the subject should be studied analytically in relation to actual business problems. In this connection, it is encouraging to see the emphasis now placed by the Business Education Council on "assignments" —student activities directed towards course objectives. It is hoped that this text which is essentially practical, avoiding some of the more abstract issues developed in detail in many advanced textbooks, will assist students and teachers in their pursuit of learning, and learning transfer in terms of their experience of the real world.

1983   G.B.G.

Contents

PART THREE: *ORGANISATION FOR MARKETING*

PART ONE

What is Marketing About?

CHAPTER I

Marketing Defined

THE INCREASING IMPORTANCE OF MARKETING

1. Historical development. At the beginning of the Industrial Revolution, Adam Smith in his *Wealth of Nations* said:

> "Consumption is the sole end purpose of all production; and the interest of the producer ought to be attended to, only so far as it may be necessary for promoting that of the consumer. The maxim is so perfectly self-evident that it would be absurd to attempt to prove it. But in the mercantile system, the interest of the consumer is almost constantly sacrificed to that of the producer; and it seems to consider production, and not consumption, as the ultimate end and object of all industry and commerce."

It was not, however, until the early years of the present century that any serious thought was given by scholars to examining the activities and institutions involved in marketing processes. The practical implications of *consumption being the purpose of production* have only in the last decade or so been recognised by business organisations. As long as the sources and supply of goods were limited and customer demands were comparatively unsophisticated it was possible for a manufacturing company to make profits—and to grow—by concentrating on production efficiency. The customer came at the end of a long chain of events. He was essentially a problem solely for the sales force, whose task was to sell what had been produced. In many cases, particularly with industrial products, it was even believed that goods were bought and not sold, and a reputation built for technical excellence would ultimately lead the customer to seek out the appropriate source of supply.

As production capacity increased and competition became more intense, more attention had to be paid to the selling process. Many companies still pay insufficient attention to selling and advertising; others have been forced to devote more and more attention and money to these activities, but often the customer still comes into the reckoning only in the final stages. The disappearance of economic, social, political and technological conditions which make possible an easy sellers' market has brought about in many other companies a complete re-orientation of business philosophy. These companies have adopted or are in the process of adopting *the marketing concept which starts with the customer* in the belief that the most profitable business can come only, as Clive Barwell put it, "by identifying, anticipating and satisfying customer needs and desires—in that order": A. Wilson (ed.), *The Marketing of Industrial Products*, Chap. I. (Hutchinson, 1965).

2. Marketing and change. It may be thought surprising that a concept which was recognised from the very early days of civilisation—as soon as man ceased to be individually self-sufficient and began to make and exchange things with others—and which was enunciated by Adam Smith two hundred years ago—should have been lost sight of, and only recently emerge as new, and even revolutionary. The reason lies in the process of industrialisation itself. At an ever-accelerating rate, Adam Smith's notions of the advantages of specialisation and division of labour spread into all forms of business. The emphasis was, not unnaturally perhaps, placed almost entirely on improving the *productive efficiency* of individually specialised units. Manufacturing specialists dealt with merchant specialists.

New worlds were opened up, populations grew and communications were developed. Soon large-scale operations were needed to satisfy the expanding demand and to capitalise on scientific discoveries and technological progress, as well as to provide economies of scale. Increased output levels required increased levels of consumption. Both combined to produce social changes at an unprecedented rate.

3. Major social changes. Amongst the social changes which have been and are still spreading from the earliest Western industrialised societies to all parts of the world, these are the most significant:

(a) *The move from agriculture to industry:* the growth of trade unions and worker co-operation; the increase in white collar workers and salaried staff.

(b) *The provision of greater educational opportunities:* schools, colleges and universities for more and more people, whether rich or poor.

(c) *The raising of living standards:* greater and greater national wealth spread more and more evenly across all levels of national communities; a breakdown of traditional class barriers.

(d) *The removal of barriers of distance:* more extensive use of faster and more efficient means of communication.

(e) *The extension of the average life span.*

(f) *The population explosion.*

Sociological changes will take place over the next few decades at an even faster rate, speeded on by technological developments—new materials, the development of new energy sources, mechanisation and automation, and improved information and communication systems.

4. Marketing: a vital business philosophy. It is the greater complexity of the interaction of these various factors of change, the greater speed at which they are taking place, and the greater risks of business investment involved, which make it imperative that the factors of production be organised with as full a prior understanding as possible of the factors of consumption. Marketing thus demands the acceptance of *consumer orientation* by the boards of directors, chief executives, management and employees in every activity. The marketing philosophy then becomes the major driving and co-ordinating force of the whole enterprise.

It is important to distinguish between marketing as a concept of business management and marketing as a group of business activities undertaken by specialists within an organisation. Michael Baker, in the 1979 edition of his work *Marketing*, in considering the broad view of the marketing concept, starts with the following proposition:

> "If economies are comprised of people, and we are endeavouring to allocate scarce resources in order to maximise satisfaction, then it is satisfaction of people at which we are aiming. This being so it is essential we determine first what people want and then allocate resources accordingly. In other words, we must determine the nature and strength of demand and create supplies of goods and services to satisfy these demands."

Macro-economic planning may be viewed in this way. The micro approach is to view business organisations *as a* whole as integrated marketing organisations.

The concept constantly reiterated in each edition of this book thus involves three fundamental propositions:

(*a*) Customer orientation.
(*b*) Organisational integration.
(*c*) Mutually profitable exchange between customer and organisation.

INTEGRATION, PROFIT AND SOCIAL RESPONSIBILITY

There are those who claim that the marketing concept has failed to live up to the high expectations of its early protagonists. The concept remains valid. What is often the problem is that the practical interpretation and application are too often woefully deficient —particularly with regard to the second and third propositions set out in **4** above. Special economic factors affecting the state of demand in the eighties are referred to in paragraph **14**.

5. Integration. Too frequently, marketing departments have been set up or marketing specialists introduced to an organisation with no essential change of attitude on the part of top management or of established functional specialists. The task of integration is particularly significant in organisations in which management personnel have powerful, vested and professional interests of longstanding in production, technical research and finance.

The concept of marketing applies equally to organisations producing industrial materials, components and capital equipment, and to those providing services such as banking and insurance, as it does to companies dealing in consumer goods. Initially, some technical and professional organisations wrongly identified the concept with special offers—"three pence off" and the like, but in recent years, many have made significant steps towards the acceptance of marketing in relation to their own businesses. Nevertheless, these are often the very organisations in which traditional attitudes are firmly held by managers in various specialist functions and in which the total organisational re-orientation is difficult to achieve. The importation of marketing specialists may improve very limited parts of the operation, but there is also a danger that marketing itself may be judged to have failed unless marketing orientation truly permeates the organisation structure horizontally and vertically.

6. Profit and social responsibility. Marketing involves an exchange —and a mutually beneficial exchange. Organisations exist to achieve objectives, and a prime objective of the private sector of business must be profit. It is, however, essential that the profit be judged by customers, governments, organised labour and the public at large as a fair return achieved by fair means. Customer orientation should not be allowed to degenerate into what appears to outside interests to be customer manipulation and exploitation. Consumerism is spreading fast.

Discussions on the responsibilities of organisations to society are currently claiming more media time and space. The issues include the adverse effects on society and the environment of products, manufacturing processes, factory sites, organisational rationalisation and redundancy. The British Institute of Marketing's definition of the concept, it will be noted, refers to the involvement of "the labour force itself". Profits will continue to be fundamental to business survival, but effecting a balance between the profit requirement and that of satisfying social demands in a changing environment will call for ever more attention to the acceptance in practice of fully integrated marketing.

Amongst the increasing number of issues which now come under public investigation are such matters as pollution by product, by process and packaging; truth in advertising and in pricing, e.g. the true cost of borrowing, unit pricing.

The following bodies concerned with consumer protection now exist:

(*a*) *Local Authority Consumer Protection Departments.* These work closely with the Office of Fair Trading.

(*b*) *Environmental Health Departments.* These concern themselves with health issues such as unhygienic food shops and restaurants; consumer complaints relating to food and drink.

(*c*) *The National Consumer Council.* Set up in 1975, this body does not deal directly with consumer complaints, but represents consumer interests on various other committees.

(*d*) *Consumer and Consultative Councils of Nationalised Industries.* It has been accepted as desirable that consumers should be represented in an advisory capacity in the policy making of nationalised industries to protect consumer interests in monopoly situations. These bodies are not free from public criticism and their effectiveness is frequently questioned.

(*e*) *The EEC Consumers Consultative Committee.* Established in 1973, to follow through five basic consumer rights as laid down by the Community, e.g. protection of health and safety by means of listing of dangerous substances only to be marketed under very specific conditions, the date stamping indicating the last permissible selling date of food.

7. Legal responsibilities. Government measures to combat monopoly and restrictive practices are likely to increase as the level of market concentration increases. Before the First World War the share in net output of the hundred largest firms in the UK was under 20%, by 1970 the share had stepped up to 50%, and in particular markets near monopoly situations existed. The *Fair Trading Act* 1973 was designed to centralise the application of competition and consumer protection policies under the Director General of Fair Trading; and monopoly and restrictive practice legislation is now very detailed and comprehensive. Consumer protection as such, however, is a relatively new but important concept—the idea of looking after the consumer's economic and social interest in matters of health, safety, fair dealing, etc. The 1973 *Fair Trading Act* is almost inevitably somewhat general, but its impact is already being felt in many wider ranging areas, such as the publication of information and advice for consumers, the encouragement of trade associations to set up voluntary codes of practice to protect the consumers and the outlawing of "pyramid selling."

Attention should also be drawn to Articles 85 and 86 of the Treaty of Rome, which deal with EEC regulations on monopolies, mergers and restrictive practices. It is perhaps significant that most attention so far has been given to restrictive practices with the prohibition of price fixing and market sharing agreements, except in cases allowed for very special reasons as a result of appeals.

8. Social services: marketing and cost-benefit exchange. The concept of marketing has so far been applied mainly to business organisations providing material goods. These organisations are faced with the problem of satisfying diverse conflicting objectives, but profit remains a prime goal. However the concept applies to many other types of organisations, e.g. to central and local government services, charity groups, churches, safety councils. Kotler and Zaltman stated, in an *American Journal of Marketing* paper in 1971, that "marketing management occurs when people become conscious of an opportunity to gain from a more careful planning of their exchange relations." In his book *Basic Marketing: a managerial approach*, McCarthy refers to four key variables in marketing:

> Product
> Place
> Price
> Promotion

The provision of hospital services will exemplify the applicability of the concept. What facilities and services does the public require hospitals to provide (the product)? Where and how should particular services be offered (the place)? What is an acceptable level of cost input in return for services offered (the price)? In what way should the service communicate its services, its locations, its use (and need) of resources (the promotion)?

Referring to the three propositions in **4**, it is valid to ask:

(*a*) To what extent is the hospital service really customer-oriented?

(*b*) To what extent is there organisational integration, e.g. amongst doctors, nurses and lay administrators, in terms of customer needs?

(*c*) Could the cost effectiveness of the service–customer exchange be improved and what would be the additional mutual exchange effect of increasing or developing the level and/or nature of the resources?

THE ROLE OF MARKETING MANAGERS

9. Marketing management and general management. Edmund P. Learned, an American management expert, has stated that the minimum role reserved for the top general management in the largest firm involves the following responsibilities:

(*a*) Formulation or approval of objectives and strategy.

(*b*) Approval of major general policies in support of the strategy adopted.

(*c*) Review and approval of major capital commitments.

(*d*) Review of master plans, programmes and budgets.

(*e*) Selection and development of key executives.

(*f*) Provision for long-range planning.

(*g*) Review and appraisal of the results of operations.

The ability of one man to encompass fully all these tasks is restricted to only the very smallest organisations. As organisations grow, responsibility for specific tasks is delegated. Activities are grouped and appropriate relationships are established so as to bring about the most effective use of human and material resources in the achievement of objectives.

10. The activities of marketing groups. Activities appropriately delegated to marketing groups are as follows:

(*a*) Identification and anticipation of demand, its level, timing and character.

(*b*) Liaising and communicating with other activity groups in respect of resource allocation to provide products and/or services in line with (*a*) and company policy and objectives.

(*c*) Organising and implementing the strategy and tactics which are necessary to bring about a mutually profitable exchange between the organisation and its target markets through products and/or services, place (channels and distribution system), price, and promotion (selling, advertising and other non-personal methods).

The role of the most senior marketing executive is thus quite different from that of the chief organisational executive. It is important that this distinction should be recognised and understood, since it is not unusual to hear opponents of marketing claiming that its protagonists describe their role in such a way as to usurp the function of the chief executive.

11. Organisation of marketing activities. Marketing managers hold delegated responsibility both for staff activities, e.g. the provision of information and services, and for line activities, e.g. the implementation of a co-ordinated product/market plan. Organisation is itself a means to an end, and its efficiency—necessary for the achievement of that end—depends largely on the clear understanding by those concerned of the elements in the formal organisation structure: i.e. authority, responsibility, accountability and lines of communication.

Organisation of marketing involves both the co-ordination of individual marketing activities *and* the integration of the marketing function with the other functions in the business structure. Thus a marketing manager may have

(*a*) prime delegated responsibility for:

(*i*) sales forces;
(*ii*) advertising and promotion;
(*iii*) customer advisory services;
(*iv*) channel strategy;
(*v*) marketing research; and

(*b*) major shared involvement with other specialist groups in such critical decision areas as:

(*i*) product planning;
(*ii*) pricing;
(*iii*) physical distribution.

12. Qualities needed in a marketing director. It cannot be too much stressed that success depends on the harmonious integration of the whole, as well as on the individual parts. To achieve a profitable balance of products, price, promotion, service and other elements to meet objectives which are in line with the policy and multiple objectives of the board, marketing executives need more than a drive to achieve current sales volume targets, which is the usual objective of sales managers. They must be capable of objective conceptual forward thinking, with the ability to diagnose and analyse problems and to make plans and see that they are implemented and evaluated. Experience must be combined with an understanding of economics, behavioural sciences, finance, statistics, mathematics and operational research.

MARKETING THEORY

13. The essence of marketing theory. There are three basic approaches to the study of marketing:

(*a*) *Institutional analysis.* Marketing institutions are business organisations which are principally concerned with the distribution of goods and services, e.g. retailers, wholesalers, advertising and marketing research agencies, commodity exchanges. These institutions have developed because of the separation between producers and consumers. This separation may be one of:

(*i*) distance;

(*ii*) time (difference between time of production and time of consumption need); or

(*iii*) knowledge.

In addition, organisations such as banks and hire purchase and insurance companies function as marketing institutions when they provide services that facilitate the flow of goods from producer to consumer.

(*b*) *Functional analysis.* Marketing functions may be described as major marketing operational activities, e.g. pricing, selling, advertising.

(*c*) *Commodity or channel of distribution analysis.* A study of channels of distribution would involve tracing the passage of individual products or commodities through various marketing institutions from producer to consumer, investigating the functions performed at each stage.

It is important for students to understand the three basic approaches that are combined in this book.

14. The relevance of economics. In order to understand each of the three basic approaches and their interrelationships it is necessary to draw on relevant concepts of economics. A study of economic aggregates, i.e. total consumption, total income, total employment, is described as *macro-economics* and this branch of study has relevance to marketing, e.g. demand for goods and services may be subject to external constraints imposed by government economic policy or wage levels. A study of the economy in detail, e.g. how prices of goods are determined, what factors determine the quantity and type of goods produced, is described as *micro-economics* and has very special significance for the marketing student. The application of micro- and macro-economics may be seen in the case of the demand for television sets, which may be affected by such considerations as the price, the hire purchase facilities available, the number of producers and distributors, government taxation policy and technological development.

Up to the late seventies governments of the more industrialised nations had tended to follow Keynesian thinking in regard to total demand. Trade cycles were offset by stimulating money circulation in a recession and by money supply restriction in a boom. The process may be exemplified in simple form as follows:

Depression	*Boom*
Lower taxes (to create budget deficit)	Raise taxes (to create budget surplus)
Lower interest rates	Raise interest rates
Increase public, especially, capital expenditure	Reduce public expenditure
Encourage spending and investment	Discourage spending and investment

In the UK policies of this kind succeeded from the mid-thirties up to the late seventies in keeping employment high, inflation within reasonable bounds, expanding demand overall, and improving material living standards—even if the percentage improvement was often not so good as that of other industrialised countries. Two major considerations have in recent years, upset the economic scene, viz. oil and labour cost inflation. Recession and inflation have actually co-existed! There have been many suggested prescriptions, e.g. incomes and prices control (neo-Keynsian) and control of the money supply (monetarism). The latter attacks inflation by means of high interest rates, exchange rates, reduced public expenditure etc. Similar situations and sometimes similar measures taken by other major world powers, e.g. the USA, have led to internationally interactive effects and the marketer often now finds himself in unfamiliar low-growth situations. In times such as these it should be realised that there are still some growth areas and whether there is need for coping with demand reduction or innovation, marketing has a very vital role to play.

15. The relevance of behavioural sciences. Production, marketing and consumption are carried on by human beings whose attitudes and decisions are the result of psychological or sociological influences which may be in conflict with rational economic motives. Marketing students must, therefore, make use of relevant concepts of the behavioural sciences.

16. The relevance of statistics, mathematics and finance. Marketing is concerned with the allocation of scarce resources to achieve profit and growth objectives in the market place. The marketing student should therefore learn to assess and control wherever possible, in quantitative terms, input and output. He must consequently become familiar with the relevant branches of statistics, mathematics and finance.

17. The approach of this book. Because of the complexity of real marketing situations an inter-disciplinary approach has been taken in this text. Institutions, functions and channels will be studied against a background of interacting and changing technical, economic and cultural conditions. In the remainder of Part I we shall first look at the key figure in this complex—the customer—and examine ways of understanding him better by means of marketing research. Part II is concerned with planning, distributing and communicating in such a way that customer and company goals are satisfied. Part III is devoted to the operational strategy, organisation and control which are essential for growth, and even survival, in dynamic marketing conditions.

PROGRESS TEST 1

1. What major social changes have contributed to the need for companies to be marketing oriented? **(3)**
2. What are the three propositions contained in the concept of

marketing, and what significance do they have in the practical application of the concept? **(4–8)**

3. What tasks are appropriately delegated to marketing managers? **(10, 11)**

4. Give examples of high-, moderate- and low-growth markets in the early years of the eighties. What explanations can you offer? **(14, 15)**

CHAPTER II

Consumer Behaviour

STAGES IN THE DECISION PROCESS

1. Outline of the decision process. Consumer behaviour is determined by economic, psychological and sociological considerations. It is important to study non-economic buying motivations as these are present in the buying of industrial goods and services as well as in consumer purchases.

The process of decision may be long in duration, as in the decision to buy a computer, or short, as in the decision to buy a packet of sweets, but similar stages may be observed:

(*a*) A general or a specific need is felt (*see* **2–5**).

(*b*) A period of pre-buying activity follows, i.e. an investigation of sources of supply which might satisfy the need (*see* **6**).

(*c*) A decision is taken (what to purchase, or even to make no purchase) based on the results of the pre-buying activity and the strength of the need (*see* **7**).

2. The basic need. This may be either *general*, e.g. I need a change of environment, or *specific*, e.g. I need a holiday in Spain. The more specific need may arise spontaneously or it may be stimulated by creative marketing. The basic need is for a collection of utilities providing a psychological or social satisfaction and not for a product. Consequently, it is important that marketing programmes should be designed to identify products or services giving satisfaction of a need. A classification of basic needs relevant to marketing is set out in **3–5** below.

3. Psychological needs. These cover the following:

(*a*) *The physiological*—the need to satisfy the bodily requirements, e.g. of hunger, thirst.

(*b*) *Pleasure satisfaction*—physical and aesthetic, appeals to the senses. Certain foods have a pleasurable flavour; certain furnishings bring aesthetic satisfaction.

(*c*) *Security*—the need to protect oneself from danger or worry.

(*d*) *Ownership*—the innate drive to possess things.

(*e*) Self-esteem—the desire to satisfy the "ego."

4. Sociological needs. These include the following:

(*a*) *Love of others*—particularly those in close family relationship.

(*b*) *Social acceptance*—the need to be recognised by the many formal and informal groups to which a person belongs. This need may be to conform or to be distinctive.

5. Maslow's hierarchy of needs. Some of these needs are stronger than others at particular times, in particular people, and in particular societies. It will also be apparent that some of these needs are closely linked with others. Maslow has set out a five-stage priority of human needs, the first two of which are primary needs fundamental to existence, the last three secondary:

(*a*) Basic physiological needs (conditions affecting the human body—hunger, sleep, temperature).

(*b*) Safety needs (self-protection against present and future dangers).

(*c*) The need for recognition, for love and belonging.

(*d*) Ego-satisfying needs (desire for self-esteem, self-respect).

(*e*) Self-fulfilment needs (realisation of complete self-creativity). This need is felt and satisfied by relatively few.

See A. H. Maslow, *Motivation and Personality* (Harper and Row, New York, 1954).

6. Purchasing activity. No two people "perceive" things in exactly the same way. Past experiences, the way in which one's senses have been stimulated, condition one's attitude towards objects, words and ideas. Accumulated experience builds up, over a period of time, a perceptual framework so that one has a predisposition to see or believe what one expects or would like to see or believe. Once a buying need is felt the perceptual framework is more vigorously activated and motivated at a conscious and subconscious level. The potential buyer's ultimate decision is now more likely to be influenced by advertising, displays, or personal sales talks, or by other people's attitudes and opinions. This purchasing activity can be broken down into six stages as follows:

(*a*) Awareness.

(*b*) Knowledge.

(*c*) Liking.

(*d*) Preference.

(*e*) Conviction.

(*f*) Purchase.

7. The decision complex. The decision itself is really a result of a collection of decisions, e.g. what class of product, what type or brand, what design, what quantity, in what place, from whom, at what price, by what method of payment. One of the tasks of marketing is to communicate with the potential buyer in such a way that not only does he become aware of the existence of the product or service offered, but develops such a sufficiently strong and favourable attitude that he will go through the buying decision processes with a greater degree of confidence. Uncertainty and delay in making buying decisions are often the result of a conflict between rational economic motives and non-rational external and internal stimuli. So-called "impulse" buying is more frequently found where there is no economic anxiety—with comparatively inexpensive, frequently purchased products, for example where non-rational external stimuli (packaging, promotions, display) have a major influence.

THE INFLUENCES OF PERSONALITY AND ENVIRONMENT

8. Socio-psychological influences. Freudian psychology is based on the proposition that individuals have an "id" and an "ego," and a "super-ego." The id represents instinctive needs; the super-ego represents social values which tend to be in conflict with instinctive needs; the ego is the mechanism seeking to resolve the conflicts between the id and the super-ego.

Although there has been comparatively little development of Freudian theories in marketing practice—with the possible exception of the use of sexual imagery in some advertising—the more recent work of social psychologists has brought greater illumination to the significance and nature of formal and informal social groups in influencing, by their values and mores, individual behaviour.

While personality conditions a buyer's behaviour in an individual way according to his personal aspirations, temperament and philosophy, cultural and organisational influences also have a profound effect. Cultural differences are brought about by the sets of values to which individuals have been exposed from birth, e.g. as a child at home, as a pupil in a particular school environment, etc. Other social influences later are brought to bear. The organisation in which people work is a social institution where irrational values develop. This complex of influences is brought to bear on both consumer and industrial buying.

It would be impossible to devise a marketing programme to meet every individual circumstance and it is important, therefore, to identify significant group behavioural patterns. Consistent spending patterns may, for example, be related to the following variables:

   (a) Urban and rural communities.
   (b) Family income levels.
   (c) Occupations.
   (d) Education.
   (e) Age.
   (f) Sex.
   (g) Informal social group membership.
   (h) Race or nationality.
   (i) Religion.

9. Dangers of conventional market profiles. The problem then is to examine the behavioural patterns which emerge from combinations of those variables listed above and to uncover the underlying and not merely the superficial rationalisations of attitudes, and to determine which patterns are really significant.

10. Social grading. The most widely used scheme of grouping people for marketing purposes in the UK in terms of society divisions is based on occupation alone and is carried out on behalf of the Joint Industry Committee representing newspaper and periodical publishers, advertising agencies and advertisers. There are six categories based on the occupations of the head of the household (*see* VII, **8** (*d*)). In fact, the six categories are normally grouped into four classes—most commonly AB, C_1, C_2, DE.

Users are increasingly sceptical of these categories. The very high sales of Target Group Index data based on computerised results of many types of data are highly significant, as is the fact that "occupation" is only one of several variables used by American researchers.

Changes in purchasing behaviour may be significantly affected by such variables as household size, previous buying experience, life cycle stage, total family income and its use within the family unit. The researcher must also beware of the erosion of differentials in wages and salaries between some of the traditionally high- and low-income earning occupations.

The development of buyer classification by the ACORN technique is yet another sign of the unease felt in many quarters by conventional occupationally based data. The neighbourhood scanning technique has been used in the US for a number of years, but has only recently been researched in depth and validated in the UK mainly as a result of the work of Richard Webster at the Centre for Environmental Studies. The initials ACORN are derived from the term A Classification Of Residential Neighbourhoods and the concept derives from the notion that life styles and behavioural patterns of particular neighbourhood groups have a great deal in common. Eleven family groups are most commonly used, although these can be further subdivided and related to postcodes and census districts. As an indication of this approach which is gaining increasing favour, 7.4 per cent of households in Great Britain (classified under ACORN as groups) are living in modern, privately owned dwellings and these are mainly populated by young families living on the outskirts of large towns or in small estates in commuter areas. There is an expectation of career development and residential movement. Incomes, education and car ownership are well above average.

11. Life styles and attitudes. Two specific fields of study in relation to buying behaviour which are currently attracting the attention of both academics and practising marketers relate to life-style patterns and attitudes.

The concept of life-style patterns and their potential application to marketing decisions was brought forward by William Lazer in 1963. Since then, continuous efforts have been made to identify groups of people according to their activities, interests and opinions. If significant correlations exist between life style and product use, television programme preferences, store choice, etc., the possibilities of devising appropriate products and/or communications directed towards similar life-style groups are opened up. Life-style data can, of course, be associated with more conventional demographic information, e.g. age, education, income, family size, occupation, etc. The life-style approach has been applied during the seventies not only to the marketing of consumer goods but also to marketing service facilities such as bank credit cards and insurance.

Attitudes can be defined as predispositions to act in particular ways towards particular people, ideas or situations. They are not innate and can be changed, although it is difficult to effect changes since many attitudes have become deeply ingrained over time. Some attitudes are held with great intensity and, in general, the evidence indicates a positive correlation between attitudes of high intensity, intentions to buy or not to buy and ultimate buying action.

Until comparatively recently, attitudes have been difficult to identify and even more difficult to measure with the precision necessary for marketing application. Reference to new research techniques in this field is made in Chapter III.

INDUSTRIAL BUYING BEHAVIOUR

12. Buying motives. Many products are bought as part of a total system; for example, even a domestic detergent is part of a system involving the whole organisation of the housewife's tasks and, in particular, is related to problems of time and equipment (e.g. washing machine) available, apart from its fitness for a particular purpose.

It is more commonly *industrial products* which are consciously thought of by buyers *as part of a total system*. Materials, components and machines fit into a manufacturing process system and change will react upon the whole system. Therefore, in marketing the product it is necessary to consider not only the functioning of the whole system, but also the subjective behaviour and values of people likely to be affected by change. Constructional materials, for example, must be functionally compatible with other elements in the system and be acceptable to architects, engineers, contractors, as well as being compatible with the human and mechanical resources available. There is, indeed, a growing movement towards systems selling. This may involve a product which incorporates a number of functions, e.g. the combine harvester or the computer. In large-scale contracts it is sometimes an advantage for companies to combine to present a total system, e.g. to construct an electricity power station.

13. The industrial buying complex. Successful industrial marketing requires that very special attention be paid to discovering the following:

(a) *Who* the buyers are.
(b) *Where* they are.
(c) *How* they may be reached.
(d) *What* they really want.
(e) What *motives* will induce them to buy.

It should not be assumed that industrial products cannot be

differentiated and that success or failure depends only on a single combination of the right specifications, price and delivery. In the most non-differentiated commodity situations a whole range of differentials is possible, e.g. better technical advice, more frequent or regular delivery. The way in which buyers "perceive" a problem (*see* 6) can change. Technology changes, company policy changes, company organisation changes.

Until comparatively recently purchasing as a specialist activity had not received the attention it really merited. Expressed as a percentage of the gross output of goods in the UK, materials purchased represent some 60 per cent of the total.

14. New pressures in industrial purchasing. Classically, purchasing objectives are based on five key criteria:

(*a*) *Quantity*—ensuring availability.

(*b*) *Quality*—satisfying required purposes yet avoiding over-specification.

(*c*) *Time*—ensuring delivery.

(*d*) *Source*—evaluating possible suppliers.

(*e*) *Price*—negotiating appropriate terms.

More recently, increasingly sophisticated techniques have been applied in terms of total organisational economics, to these criteria. Quantities are related more closely to the interrelated factors of alternative use of capital and space and the requirements of particular levels of production throughput, or stock turn.

Buyers' stock and quality control procedures are becoming much more sophisticated. For example, sampling inspection alone may lead not only to faulty finished products but also to wasted costs incurred by the processing of initially unsatisfactory materials. Companies such as Ford and Marks & Spencer use intensive quality control or assurance schemes which involve inspection and approval of suppliers' quality control systems.

The increasing flow of new products is leading to a re-evaluation of existing supply sources and the exploration of new ones. In some cases, contact in the early stages of a project leads to joint development work and the establishment of relationships with a wider range of users, specifiers, financial approvers and professional buyers, each motivated in different ways.

The initial price of capital equipment is set against life-cycle cost calculations involving taxation considerations, maintenance requirements, breakdown incidence, past availability, etc.

Value analysis and brainstorming techniques are being applied more regularly and systematically. Value analysis involves the careful analysis of components and materials by cost and function, so that existing use of particular designs, materials, processes etc. can be questioned and alternative solutions advanced, which may save the company costs while taking nothing away from, and sometimes adding to, the customer's value perception. Value analysis is sometimes associated with brainstorming—a technique by which a group of people, often from a diversity of specialisms within the organisation, are stimulated to make suggestions on specific problem situations, however wild. Criticism is barred and, when carefully handled, brainstorming often produces a number of completely different, useful approaches which merit further investigation.

Increasing attention is now being paid to the process of negotiation; this is particularly important in effecting industrial deals.

15. Specific behavioural questions. Key questions to be answered when marketing industrial products are the following:

(*a*) *When repeated purchases are made, is each regarded as a major new decision* or as a re-buying situation?

(*b*) *How is a "re-buy" or a "new buy" situation handled* in terms of the decision process?

(*c*) *Who are the major buying influences* in various situations? Who plays a key role and when?

(*d*) *What are the major motivations* of these decision-makers and executives of key influence likely to be in particular situations? These motivations will not be entirely rational. There will be different formal and informal relationships, different environmental backgrounds, training and interests.

(*e*) *What is the effect of the formal and informal organisational structure on buying behaviour?* The reward system, the status system, the authority system and the communications system, the extent of centralisation—all have an important bearing (*see* X, **2,** **15**). Good industrial salesmen know intuitively that buyers are subject to normal human anxieties, frustrations, inertia. A more scientific study of behaviour would improve not only the effectiveness of the salesman, but the effectiveness of the whole consumer-oriented marketing operation.

MAJOR MARKETING STIMULI

16. The product. A product may represent economic utility to a purchaser. He may, for example, believe an electric drill will save the expense of hiring outside labour to make improvements to his house. The purchase of an electric drill, however, may not arise from purely economic motives. The prime urge may be to gain the admiration of others. Even if there are economic motives these will be modified by the system of values of the individual and of the social environment which influences his attitudes and behaviour. The more affluent the society, the greater the spread of disposable income (money available after essential purchases have been made), the greater is the problem of choice. The choice is not simply between various types and makes of drills but between drills and a whole collection of completely different items such as holidays, refrigerators, furniture, between buying now or saving. Similarly, choice between drills of different designs, performance and price depends on interacting economic, psychological and sociological motivations.

17. The package. Packaging materials, design, colour, size, illustrations, brand names and associated symbols (logotypes), type faces, copy and layout may affect to a very considerable extent a potential buyer's perception of a product. Packaging plays a vital role in stimulating memory and helping recognition, gaining shelf space and attracting the eye, providing use, storage and transportation benefits, but it has wider behavioural implications in terms of establishing customer preference.

18. Price. The level at which a firm sets its prices will affect both sales and profitability. The demand for a car at £10,000 will be smaller than that for a car at £4,000. Under certain circumstances, it may be more profitable for a particular company to concentrate on the more limited demand market. From the basic economic law of supply and demand (i.e. the lower the price, the greater the quantity of demand) it is possible to construct graphs of theoretical demand quantities in relation to price. Some products will be seen to have much greater price elasticity than others, e.g. the demand for a breakfast cereal might be reduced by one-tenth if prices were doubled, while the demand for a toilet soap might be cut by 70 per cent by a similar price change. It is important to study price elasticity considered in conventional economic terms, such as availability of substitutes, durability and ability to postpone purchase, income, population and the prices of competing products. It is also important to realise that, in developed economies, psychological aspects of pricing take on greater and greater significance.

Low price, for example, may be irrationally associated with poor quality (*see* Chapter V).

19. The promotion. Many advertising campaigns are mainly planned in quantitative terms. How many people will be exposed to what weight of advertising during what period of time? To this quantitative thinking is added a target audience defined in broad socio-economic categories. The most common measurements of effectiveness are based on recall (i.e. recollection of advertisements), but recall may be utterly unrelated to purchasing activity (*see* VII, **9–10**).

Advertising and communications must be directed towards stimulating favourable trade opinions and feelings about a company, as well as favourable customer attitudes towards product quality, price, delivery, sales and technical services. Concepts derived from clinical research and the findings of sociologists, psychologists and anthropologists may be used to determine why people buy particular products or services, and lead to advertising which appeals to needs, wants and desires, so that potential buyers may rationalise the desire to buy; e.g. a ten-year guarantee originally given with mopeds in Germany inhibited sales, since many potential customers had guilt feelings about buying a product they would expect to exchange for a car in two or three years. Advertising copy and visual elements are therefore designed in the light of anticipated connotations, i.e. the mental images aroused in the reader or viewer, beyond the superficial or explicit meaning.

In marketing a product it is certainly important that the product itself, the packaging, the price and the promotion should have a consistent appeal in terms of the attitudes and motivations of potential buyers. This calls for deliberate research and planning.

20. Distributive structure. Some products and services are bought direct from the producer; others are made available through various intermediary channels, e.g. retail and wholesale outlets, brokers, agents, mail-order houses. The producers and the "channels" are all involved in marketing operations and it is important, in considering strategy and tactics, to understand the flow of the consumption system, the motivations of buyers and sellers along the chain, the relative importance of these channels and changing customer perceptions of them.

An organisation can either effect change in an established distributive system or react to change. A number of important movements are currently taking place for both these reasons in distribution patterns, amongst which the following changes are highly significant:

(*a*) The growth of vertically integrated systems, whereby an organisation moves into ownership or special contractual arrangements with the owners of organisations which come earlier or later in the consumption system. Thus, Marley have moved strongly forward into retail outlet ownership. Marks and Spencer have developed contractual relationships with suppliers on strictly controlled "St Michael" specifications. Brewery and oil groups are strengthening their tied-house approach. New forms of franchising are developing. Franchising involves any contract under which independent retailers or wholesalers are organised to act together or with manufacturers to distribute given products or services.

(*b*) The growth of non-store retailing such as home selling, e.g. Avon, Tupperware; the use of vending machines in offices and factories; the spread of mail order.

(*c*) The growth of horizontally diversified trading. Thus, supermarkets which previously restricted their retailing activities to grocery items are now offering clothing, furniture and electrical goods. Producing organisations are also involved in acquisitions, mergers and development programmes leading in the direction of "free form" operation – a willingness to supply forward any products or services at a level which can be profitable.

(*d*) The growth of discount and cash-and-carry trading based on minimum services and decor, etc., high volume and low unit margins.

(*e*) The growth of shopping centres with parking facilities away from the high street. Banks, insurance offices, solicitors, estate agents and other services are associated with these logistic shifts.

These changes give rise to the need to consider buyer behaviour in terms of buyers' perceptions of and attitudes to organisations, products, brands, stores, suppliers.

21. The corporate image. A potential buyer's attitude to a product may be modified by his attitude to the organisation which manufactured the product. A retailer may be more ready to handle a new product from a manufacturer whose products have yielded good profits in the past. A potential user may choose a plane of a particular brand because he has had good service from a saw made by the same manufacturer. In view of the fact that most companies now manufacture and/or market a wide range of products or services, increasing attention is being paid to the development of corporate images which are aimed at creating a widespread favourable company identification or image by means of advertising, public relations, factory design, product design, stationery, transport and so on. Corporate image building is aimed not solely at potential customers but also at other individuals and institutions on which future prosperity may depend, for example:

(*a*) shareholders and potential investors;

(*b*) the government;

(*c*) employees;

(*d*) suppliers;

(*e*) the public in the immediate vicinity of company premises;

(*f*) schools and universities from which staff may be recruited.

THE BEHAVIOURAL COMPLEX

The student of buyer behaviour would be well advised to examine in greater detail the following aspects of psychology and sociology.

22. Psychology. While psychology involves the broader study of living organisms, the student of marketing will derive most direct advantage from investigation of a limited number of aspects of human behaviour:

(*a*) *Motivation*—strivings or inner states which move people towards goals whether primary and physiological, e.g. hunger, or secondary, e.g. attracting attention; the degree of individual consciousness of particular motivations; their relative strengths; their inter-relationships, etc.

(*b*) *Perception*—the way in which people interpret the information coming through the senses, e.g. words and pictures in different media.

(*c*) *Learning*—the changes in behaviour which lead to new habits or reinforcement of existing behaviour, e.g. brand switching and brand loyalty.

(*d*) *Personality*—the classification of a person's characteristic ways of reacting to situations.

(*e*) *Attitudes*—predispositions to behave in certain ways towards particular objects, ideas, situations.

23. Sociology. Sociology, the study of groups in society, tends to overlap with other sciences, e.g. the interaction between individuals and groups which is the subject matter of social psychology.

Individuals when faced with a buying decision are likely to be reflecting to some extent values and behaviour patterns derived from identification with one or a number of social systems as follows:

(a) the political system;
(b) the economic system;
(c) the family and kinship system;
(d) the educational system;
(e) the religious system.

Within these groups there will be primary groups (those who interact on a face-to-face basis); peer groups: those who have the same status in relation to a particular situation (evening class students; managers of equal level in an organisation); reference groups (groups which provide a model for an individual's behaviour, e.g. a junior clerk aiming to imitate the behaviour of works accountants).

The following simplified diagram is intended to illustrate the behavioural complex:

The Individual	Psychological Processes	The Environment
	Social	Physical
Attitudes	Primary groups	Geography
—PERCEPTION→		
Beliefs	Reference groups	Climate
Values ←LEARNING—		
Motives	Peer groups	Urban/rural

PROGRESS TEST 2

1. What is meant by "the hierarchy of needs"? (5)
2. What are some of the social and economic group factors to be considered in examining buying patterns? (8)
3. What is systems selling? (12)
4. What are the five key criteria in industrial purchasing, and how has the application of these criteria been improved by new methods? (14)
5. By what four major stimuli might a marketing organisation stimulate customer demand? (16–19)

6. Comment on the development of vertically and horizontally integrated systems of distribution. **(20)**

7. Why is it necessary to develop a corporate image? **(21)**

CHAPTER III

Marketing Research

MARKETING RESEARCH AND DECISION-MAKING

1. Decisions and risk. Marketing decisions are inevitably made under conditions of uncertainty. Uncertainty involves both risk and opportunity. The use of marketing research does not and cannot eliminate either risk or opportunity, but its intelligent use can reduce risk and indicate the degree of probability of the various possible outcomes of opportunity. Markets are increasingly dynamic and competitive; their successful exploitation calls for greater investment, and more frequent innovation. Decision-making, therefore, must be faster and less susceptible to many of the needless errors of intuitive judgment.

2. Marketing research: definition and application. Marketing research may be defined as the objective and systematic collection, recording, analysis, interpretation and reporting of information about: existing or potential markets (i.e. market research, **5**), marketing strategies and tactics, and the interaction between markets, marketing methods and current or potential products or services (*see* **4–7**). It can therefore play a major role in enabling the modern executive to apply a truly analytical approach to decision-making. It can also assist in the evaluation of the effect of decisions which have been taken.

3. Origin and development. Marketing research has a comparatively recent origin, the first formal marketing research organisation having been established in the United States in 1911. From slow beginnings, in recent years, there has been a growing sophistication in methods and methodology (*see* **17**, market research process)— in the application of statistical techniques and behavioural science concepts (*see* **34** below)— and the early scepticism of managements and the sometimes exaggerated claims of pseudo-researchers are rapidly disappearing. The use of marketing research in consumer markets is now reasonably widespread. The need for the objective evidence which marketing research as a decision-making tool can provide for management in producer goods or industrial markets is probably even greater than in consumer goods markets, but its value in these areas has been too little realised and research activity has consequently been more limited (*see* XI, **6**).

THE SCOPE OF MARKETING RESEARCH

4. Marketing research and management problems. In the following paragraphs (**5–7**) are some examples of the enormous range of problems on which management may require information, whether on the markets for their products (or services), on marketing strategy, or on the products themselves seen in this context of markets and marketing methods.

5. Markets. An up-to-date knowledge of the market is essential for successful marketing. Management must ask themselves the following questions:

(*a*) What is the *size* of a market for a product or service (in terms of volume and/or value)?

(*b*) What is the past *pattern of demand*; what factors (economic, social, political, technological) might affect future demand, and when? Is demand subject to seasonal or cyclical variations?

(*c*) What is the *market structure*; e.g. is it based on industry, on size or numbers of companies, on income groups, on sex, on age, on geographical distribution?

(*d*) What are the *buying habits*, motivations, procedures, or domestic customers, retailers, wholesalers, professional and industrial buyers?

(*e*) What is the company's *market share* and how does this compare with competitive shares over various time periods?

(*f*) What are past and future *trends*—rate of change in population, national income, retail sales, industry output?

(*g*) Which *overseas markets* present the best immediate or long-term opportunities?

6. Marketing policy and strategy. Armed with a knowledge of the market, management can consider their overall marketing policy and tactics. They will require further information about competition, costs, and the probable results of different courses of action, e.g.:

(*a*) Where, how and at what cost do competitors advertise? What are competitive pricing structures and practices?

(*b*) How do marketing and distribution costs compare, in total and by individual elements, with competitive costs?

(*c*) What are the most effective channels of distribution?

(*d*) How do sales differ by territory, industry, type of outlet, and why?

(*e*) What effect on demand will there be if a new product is introduced under an established corporate image or a separate brand name?

(*f*) What would be the effect of a change in pricing structure on the number and frequency of orders, or on factory and store inventory levels?

(*g*) What amount of service, at what cost, is it necessary to provide to maintain or improve profitability?

(*h*) What is the effect of sales promotional activity?

7. Products and services. The third factor to be considered is the product itself, in terms of suitability for the market, design and manufacture, competitive advantages and profitability, i.e.:

(*a*) What is the company reputation or image for products, presentation, technical service, delivery? What are the major weaknesses of products—own and competitive?

(*b*) How are products/services used and what characteristics are considered most important? What should be the range offered, e.g. prices, sizes, colours, designs?

(*c*) What changes will be necessary in materials used, advantages offered, functions performed, and when? Should certain products be dropped, and when?

(*d*) What is the best pricing structure for a new product? What might be the effect on the profitability of a product or volume sales of a price increase of, e.g. 4%?

(*e*) What patents, licensing agreements or other legal restrictions might affect manufacture or sale of a product?

(*f*) What do reactions to products in test markets indicate in terms of national or international operations?

8. Marketing research and company organisation. The range of studies which the marketing researcher may be asked to undertake extends across departmental or functional barriers. Examples of studies in which executives other than those in marketing divisions would be concerned are as follows:

(*a*) Plant location studies.
(*b*) Economic forecasting in connection with budgets.
(*c*) Studies of companies under consideration for acquisition.
(*d*) Analysis of transport utilisation.

In any company organisation, marketing research must therefore be placed under the control of an executive who is sympathetic to its importance, its need for adequate finance and its essential objectivity (it must be protected from personal pressures to find support for the subjective judgments of management). The data and recommendations produced should be regularly and easily available to appropriate decision and policy makers, whether they be individuals or committees. In small companies, ideally a marketing research manager should report to the chief executive. In large companies, with a marketing director at policy-making level, marketing research might report to that executive. Many companies have no marketing research staff of their own, but too frequently when specialist staff is employed, its effect is negligible because it is too remote from major decision centres. (Where company marketing research departments do exist, they are usually small and a number of projects are assigned to outside independent agencies.)

9. Dangers in use of terminology. Specialists in marketing research departments must combine skills from economics, psychology, sociology, mathematics and statistics. One of the major dangers is that these specialists should forget that their prime aim is to assist in the solution of marketing problems and become too involved in research methodology (*see* **17** (*a*), **44**) for its own sake. Personal communications with other executives and final research reports can be hampered by an over-emphasis on technical terminology. Findings and methods should be explained in language non-specialists can understand.

SOURCES OF INFORMATION

10. Data types. Data is generally classified as either primary or secondary.

(*a*) *Primary data.* This is information which has originated directly as a result of the particular problem under investigation.

(*b*) *Secondary data.* Data which already exists and may be used for an investigation but has not been collected for that specific purpose is called *secondary data*. It is usually cheaper to use this kind of data than to set up special investigations, but care must be taken to ensure that the data is relevant, can be adjusted to the problem, and is reliable.

11. Sources of secondary data. These can be divided into internal and external sources.

(*a*) *Internal.* There is invariably a mass of marketing information in a company's own records—particularly sales records. This information may not have been collected systematically or in the most appropriate form, but it is clear that marketing researchers should turn first to the sources which, properly organised, can provide continuously relevant current data as well as information for occasional and special investigations. Data-processing equipment, computers and the systems approach are making the extrapolation of appropriate information easier and faster.

(*b*) *External.* In addition there is a wealth of published information available from external sources, e.g. agencies, consultants, government departments, trade associations, banks, professional bodies, research organisations, the press. Some of these are outlined in paragraphs **12–16** below. A fuller list of various bodies and publications which provide useful information is given in Appendix I.

12. Specialist marketing research agencies. Large numbers of these agencies, varying enormously in size and specialisation, exist in the UK and in many parts of the world. The larger agencies usually offer a wide range of services but some concentrate on projects requiring more specialised skills, e.g. field interviewing in connection with industrial markets, motivation research, research connected with specific industries.

Special services offered by agencies include the following:

(*a*) The *A. C. Nielsen food and drug indices* which provide extensive data at frequent intervals obtained from a large sample (*see* **21** below) of product sales by brand, retail purchases, inventory levels and movement, retail and wholesale prices, percentage distribution, etc. Data is broken down in various ways, e.g. by geographical area, type of store.

(*b*) The advertising research services of the *Gallup* and *Starch* organisations. Gallup tests advertising research in mass circulation printed media, while Starch attempts to evaluate whether particular current advertisements are or will be read more than past advertisements or competitive advertisements.

(*c*) The *Audit Bureau of Circulation*, with a membership of 2,000 publishers, advertisers and agencies, provides certified information on the circulation of printed media. It should be noted that many specialist magazines do not subscribe to the Audit and there is no objective measurement of circulation figures claimed.

(*d*) *Measurement of television audiences.* Commercial television audience ratings are published weekly from JICTAR (Joint Industry Committee for Television Audience Research) figures. These figures are derived from statistics provided by Audits of Great Britain Ltd. (AGB), who use both paper tape recordings from set meters fitted to receivers and family diaries. A new body, the Broadcasters Audience Research Board (BARB), was set up in August 1981 to be responsible for commissioning television audience research and to rationalise the differing research methods previously used by the BBC and IBA. AGB has been awarded a BARB research contract up to 1988. Problems of more refined measurements, e.g. the numbers of persons watching particular programmes or advertisements, their actions and subsequent buying behaviour, are as yet unsolved.

13. Advertising agencies. The demands of clients for more comprehensive marketing information as part of a total marketing plan, together with the growing need for agencies to be competitive, has led to a considerable extension of marketing research departments in advertising agencies. The cost of sustaining these services is leading more often to an additional charge above the 15% commission on which agencies have traditionally operated (*see* VI, **23**).

14. Advertising media proprietors and contractors. Much of this research is basically intended to show the effectiveness of the particular media being sold and great care is needed in interpreting the studies. Nevertheless, the practice of producing such research data is gaining ground rapidly and much of the information may be free from promotional bias.

15. Trade associations. Studies are usually very limited in scope and statistics may be difficult to interpret if important companies or groups of companies are omitted. However, studies which are available are particularly useful in industrial marketing research, where there is a comparative lack of sources of secondary data (*see* Appendix I).

16. Government departments and international organisations. These are invaluable research sources; British government departments provide both annual and monthly statistics on many topics, and foreign governments provide information through their embassies or issue bibliographical lists from the appropriate trade ministries. Other statistics are published by various international bodies, e.g. UNO, OECD.

Some of the great number of reports available are listed in Appendix I.

EXECUTING MARKETING RESEARCH STUDIES

17. Steps in the market research process. Research projects are not susceptible to any one complete and inflexible sequence of steps and the type of problems to be studied will determine the particular steps to be taken and their order. The following steps provide, however, a useful procedural guide:

(*a*) *Definiton of the problem.* This step is of the greatest importance. Frequently management initially poses an ill-defined problem or one which is a superficial aspect of a more fundamental problem. Care must be taken to verify the objectivity and validity of the background facts and to agree upon the problem in writing with the executive or executives concerned with its circumstances.

(*b*) *Specification of the information required.*

(*c*) *Design of the research project*, involving consideration of:

(*i*) the means of obtaining the information;

(*ii*) the availability and skills of company marketing research staff and/or agencies;

(*iii*) methodology; i.e. a detailed explanation of the way in which selected means of obtaining information, e.g. observation studies, questionnaires, will be organised, and the reasoning leading to the selection;

(*iv*) the time and cost of the research.

(*d*) *Sample design.*

(*e*) *Construction of questionnaires* and/or preparation of briefs for field interviews.

(*f*) *Execution of the project*, with arrangement for checks on the reliability of data being collected.

(*g*) *Analysis of data.*

(*h*) *Preparation of report and recommendations.*

18. Sampling. When field studies are undertaken considerations of time and cost almost invariably lead to contact being made with a selection of respondents. The respondents selected should be as representative as possible of the total population to be investigated in order to produce a miniature cross-section. The selection process is called *sampling*. The word "universe" is often used to describe the whole population from which the selection is made. Samples are of two basic types:

(*a*) *Probability or random samples:* samples which are so constructed that every element from the total population has a known probability of selection and the limits of probable error in relating results to the whole population are thus known mathematically in advance.

(*b*) *Non-probability or purposive samples:* samples based on the choice of the selector.

19. Comparison of probability and non-probability samples. Probability samples enable experimental error to be measured but they do not necessarily provide more accurate marketing research results than non-probability samples. A small probability sample may yield a high experimental error; even with a large sample, errors may arise because of variability in the characteristics of the population being examined, e.g. attitudes, habits. Non-probability samples are subject to error in sample selection, but the risk of selection bias has to be weighed against the risk of experimental errors arising from smaller probability samples. In industrial marketing research, executive judgment is likely to be more accurate than in consumer marketing research because of a more exact knowledge of a comparatively small universe. Concepts of probability are frequently used in non-probability samples and judgment is applied to give "weighting" to factors according to their likely importance.

20. Modified probability samples. Statisticians have developed a number of specialised probability procedures which are of particular value in marketing research. The most significant are considered in **21–25** below.

21. Systematic sampling. Only the first unit of the sample is selected at random. The following units are selected at fixed intervals. If, for example, questions were to be asked of householders in a road and the 3rd house were selected randomly as the starting point, there would be systematic sampling if subsequent interviews were carried out at fixed regular intervals, e.g. at the 8th, 13th, 18th, 23rd house and so on. The cost can be controlled by the intervals selected. The basic assumption is that all elements of the population are ordered in a manner representative of the total population. A systematic sample of a list of customers arranged according to their annual purchases would meet this assumption, whereas there is a possibility that every fifth customer entering a store on a given day may be unrepresentative of the weekly clientele.

22. Stratified sampling. If there is evidence that certain elements of the population are more significant for the purpose of a survey than others it may be desirable to weight these elements in proportion to their significance. If, for example, tea consumption of a household were significantly related to family size and particular age groups, a stratified sample would give due weighting to respondents who conformed to the significant criteria. Stratified samples may be especially useful in industrial marketing research if, for example, volumes of output or number of employees are known significant factors. Interviewers are sometimes instructed to survey fixed proportions of a given population, e.g. 50% of large firms in a given geographical area. This is described as *quota sampling*. This technique is not based on probability and is susceptible to interview bias in selection.

23. Cluster and area sampling. Geographical dispersal of interviews creates cost problems. Cluster sampling reduces cost by concentrating surveys in selected clusters, e.g. particular sales areas, counties, local authority areas, towns. The principle of statistical random selection could be applied in the selection of clusters and units within the clusters. Clusters may be selected on the basis of predetermined strata, e.g. if home ownership is an important factor it may be necessary to identify clusters according to known data on home ownership.

24. Multi-stage sampling. This is a development of the principle of cluster sampling. The first stage may be to select large primary sampling units, e.g. counties, then towns and finally districts within towns.

25. Sequential sampling. This is a complex technique. The ultimate size of the sample is not yet fixed in advance but is determined according to mathematical decision rules on the basis of information yielded as surveys progress. This technique is frequently used in industrial market surveys where it is particularly difficult initially to define the universe in terms of critical criteria, e.g. turnover of companies, machine utilisation; or in order to build up to a specified quota of strata in the stratified sampling (*see* **22**).

The objective of sequential sampling is to determine the smallest sample that can be used to produce confidence intervals within given margins of error. In marketing research a confidence of 95% is commonly accepted, i.e. there is a 5% chance that the true population statistic may fall outside the margins of error indicated. The basic problem here is to determine how much extra cost should be incurred to reduce risk. In this connection it should be noted that while a high degree of precision is associated with larger samples (the size of the sample being more important than the size of the sample universe), sample size has to be multiplied by four to double the precision. For further information on sampling, readers are advised to consult Elliot and Christopher's work (*see* Bibliography), but it would be well for them to remember that more real practical problems are associated with stages (*e*) to (*g*) of the market research process set out in **17** than with sample design and sampling error.

26. Methods of collecting data. Data can be collected either through observation or through direct communication with respondents, whether by mail, telephone or personal interview. The advantages and disadvantages of these methods are outlined below (**27–30**).

27. Observation. The observation method is most commonly used in studies of consumer behaviour in stores.

(*a*) *Advantages.*

(*i*) If the observer records accurately, subjective bias is eliminated (direct communication methods bear the note of bias either in questioner or in respondent).

(*ii*) Information relates to what is currently happening; it is not complicated by consideration of past behaviour, future intentions or attitudes.

(*b*) *Disadvantages.*

(*i*) It is usually an expensive method.

(*ii*) Information provided is very limited.

28. Mailing and questionnaires. This is the method most extensively employed (*see* also **33** below).

(*a*) *Advantages.*

(*i*) Low cost even when spread widely geographically.

(*ii*) Lack of interviewer bias.

(*iii*) Some respondents are difficult to interview—particularly in industrial markets.

(*iv*) Respondents have more time to give considered answers.

(*v*) Respondents may prefer anonymity.

(*b*) *Disadvantages.*

(*i*) Limitation of information. To be successful questionnaires should be comparatively short and simple. Questions may be dichotomous (yes-or-no answers), multiple choice (alternative answers listed), or open-ended. The latter are often difficult to analyse. A specialised form of multiple choice questions involves *scaling*. For example, respondents may be asked to rank products in order of preference or to indicate an attitude according to its strength, say from "like very much" to "dislike intensely." One of the problems arising from scaling questionnaires is the difficulty of establishing the exact intervals; for example, are products 1 and 2 seen to be more equal than 4 and 5?

(*ii*) Problems of having constantly to up-date mailing lists.

(*iii*) Low rate of return and the difficulty of knowing whether willing respondents are truly representative. Sometimes a number of personal field interviews or telephone enquiries are carried out to check on the validity of the sample of questionnaires actually returned. It should be noted that the rate of return will depend on such factors as the skill of questionnaire construction and time of mailing.

(*iv*) Possible ambiguity of replies or omission of replies to particular questions.

(*v*) Inflexibility; difficulty of amending the approach once questionnaires have been despatched. Pilot testing is, in any case, very desirable to avoid question construction faults which may lead to answers which defy analysis.

NOTE: Questionnaires should contain "control" questions which indicate the reliability of the respondent. For example, a question designed to determine consumption of particular materials may be asked first in terms of financial expenditure and later in terms of weight. Again, one or two questions not directly related to the purpose of the survey may produce answers which cast doubt on the reliability of the respondent.

29. Telephone interviews. Although this method has many advantages, particularly in industrial surveys, it is not used as widely in the UK as might now be expected.

(*a*) *Advantages*.

(*i*) More flexible than mailing.

(*ii*) Interviewer can explain requirements more easily.

(*iii*) Faster than other methods.

(*iv*) Cheaper than personal interviewing.

(*v*) Ease of re-call.

(*vi*) Access can sometimes be gained to respondents who would neither be interviewed personally nor answer questionnaires.

(*vii*) Replies can be recorded without embarrassment to respondent.

(*viii*) Higher response rate than from mailing.

(*ix*) Useful for radio and television surveys when checking programmes actually being heard or viewed.

(*b*) *Disadvantages*.

(*i*) Possibility of interviewer bias.

(*ii*) Little time given to respondent for considered answers.

(*iii*) Surveys restricted to respondents who have telephones or, in industrial surveys, have easy access to telephones.

(*iv*) Personal approach can inhibit replies.

(*v*) Extensive geographical coverage may be restricted by cost considerations.

(*vi*) The number of questions must usually be limited.

30. Personal interviews. These can be carried out in a highly structured way, i.e. the interviewer follows a rigidly laid down procedure asking questions in a prescribed form and order. The interviewer may, however, be allowed varying degrees of freedom in conducting the interview. The greater the freedom allowed, the higher is the skill required in the interviewer and the more complex are the problems of analysis of the results.

(*a*) *Advantages*.

(*i*) Greater flexibility and more opportunity to restructure questions.

(*ii*) More information can be obtained—and in greater depth.

(*iii*) Resistance in respondent can often be overcome by skill of interviewer.

(*iv*) Products, advertisements, etc., can be shown or demonstrated.

(*v*) Observation methods can be applied. In addition to recording verbal answers, interviewers can physically check stocks or note reactions to questions.

(*vi*) Personal data regarding respondents can be more easily obtained.

(*vii*) Sample can be controlled more effectively. Missing returns cause obvious difficulty in analysis. A skilled interviewer can arrange calls at appropriate times or make re-calls if respondents are out, or rephrase questions to which there is initially no response.

(*b*) *Disadvantages*

(*i*) Relatively expensive if large, widely scattered geographical sample is taken.

(*ii*) Possibility of respondent bias, either to please the interviewer, to create false personal prestige image, or to end interview quickly.

(*iii*) Possibility of interviewer bias.

(*iv*) Certain types of individuals, e.g. important executives, people in high income groups, may be difficult to interview.

(*v*) If the sample is large and if re-calls are necessary, the time factor in completing a survey may be high.

31. The use of panels. Panels consist of *permanent samples* of the universe (*see* **18** above) and are most frequently used in consumer marketing research. Members of these panels agree to regular interviews and/or the maintenance of diaries; sometimes panel members are given small financial incentives in return for their assistance. Panels are used by company marketing research units and by marketing research agencies, e.g. the A. C. Nielsen company, the AGB rating system (**12** (*a*) and (*d*) above).

(*a*) *Advantages*

(*i*) Trends in attitude, usage, etc., can be observed in easily controlled situations.

(*ii*) Panel members are obviously co-operative and usually supply very complete information.

(*iii*) Panels may be divided in order to compare reactions of different groups, for example, to products or advertisements—again under readily controlled conditions.

(*iv*) Appointments can be made, thus avoiding the expense of re-calls.

(*v*) Individual behaviour can be studied over time periods. When different samples are taken only group trends can be examined.

(*vi*) Panel members learn instruction procedures and time may thus be saved in the future.

(*vii*) Conversations can be recorded on tape and played back.

(*b*) *Disadvantages*

(*i*) Willingness to co-operate in a panel may indicate certain characteristics in members which are not truly representative of any particular universe.

(*ii*) If panel members drop out from time to time it is difficult to ensure that their replacements have similar characteristics.

(*iii*) There is a tendency to develop a "panel sophistication," i.e. constant interviewing may lead to specially conditioned responses.

(*iv*) Individual responses may be conditioned by the fact that people in groups may adapt their behaviour to what is considered to be socially acceptable.

PROBLEMS OF ACCURACY

32. Response accuracy. It is clear that, if marketing research is to provide information to guide decision-making, information must be as accurate as possible, taking into account the limitations imposed by time and cost. As we have seen, sampling itself involves a calculated risk in relation to accuracy and even in probability samples confidence limits are set. This problem is intensified by the fact that the statistical confidence limit presupposes that the questions posed are those to which accurate answers can and will be provided.

33. Factors in assessing accuracy of information. The following are some of the factors which must be considered in assessing the accuracy of information:

(*a*) Questions involving opinion are susceptible to greater inaccuracy than those involving fact, but even questions of fact may lead to inaccurate answers. If, for example, a physical check of stock in a store or pantry is taken, the only problems are whether the count itself is accurate and whether all stock has been seen. If, however, one asks what programme was seen on television three days earlier, the information may be inaccurate because of faulty memory or a conscious or subconscious desire on the part of the respondent to mislead. Although most respondents do not consciously try to deceive, memory can be very fallible.

(*b*) Respondents may not understand properly what they are being asked. The difficulty may be in the phrasing of the questions and it is wise to pre-test questions to avoid widespread misinterpretation.

(*c*) Respondents may not be willing to answer certain questions.

(*d*) The appearance or manner of the interviewer may influence the answers given. A respondent may give answers calculated to please or displease.

(*e*) Where questions relate to future actions, the reliability of answers depends on the extent to which people are likely to change their minds over given time periods.

(*f*) In posing questions on attitudes there is the problem of assessing the intensity of a favourable or unfavourable response.

(*g*) If questions involve the respondent in supplying reasons for an action the reasons may be inaccurate because previously they have never been consciously analysed or because they are based on false assumptions. A housewife may, for example, indicate that she buys a certain brand of tea because of its price when in fact she always buys tea at a particular shop where many brands are not available.

(*h*) Answers on purchasing behaviour or attitudes may be supplied by persons who make only a contribution to the decision-making process. Other members of the household or company may influence the decision to a greater or lesser extent.

(*i*) Buying reasons or attitudes may be subconscious and not known to the respondent.

(*j*) Answers may be given in order to convey a false status image, e.g. newspapers read, cultural interest.

BEHAVIOURAL AND MOTIVATIONAL RESEARCH

34. Depth interview. The behavioural sciences, psychology, sociology and cultural anthropology, are concerned with investigating the reasons for human behaviour. The key word in this kind of research is *why*. An understanding of why people behave as they do in given situations or why certain statistical relationships exist leads to possibilities of planning how to effect change as well as planning to "key in" to states of mind. (*See* II, **22** and **23**.)

Specialists in these disciplines may undertake "depth" interviews. The term "depth" is used since the interviews are designed to discover underlying motives and desires. Depth interviews are usually undirected and require great skill and considerable time. There are difficulties not only in establishing the right degree of confidence and eliciting answers but in interpreting the qualitative information provided. This type of research is obviously expensive and, in practice, group rather than individual interviews are more commonplace.

35. Criticisms of depth interviewing. Among criticisms of the method the following are those most usually advanced:

(*a*) Samples are too small for meaningful conclusions.

(*b*) The findings are not quantified.

(*c*) It is difficult to know whether these investigations into the reasons for behaviour do *really* indicate a purchasing need or a motive. Attitudes revealed under research conditions may change in actual buying situations.

(*d*) Individual reactions in group situations are conditioned artificially by the structure and behaviour of the group.

36. Techniques in motivation research. Amongst the special techniques employed in motivation research are the following:

(*a*) Sentence completion tests.

(*b*) Word association tests.

(*c*) Story completion tests.

(*d*) Verbal projection tests in which the respondent is asked to comment on or explain what other people do; e.g. why do people smoke? Answers may reveal the respondent's own motivations.

(*e*) *Pictorial techniques;* e.g. the "thematic apperception" test in which the respondent describes what is happening in an ambiguous picture. One of the most common of these tests is the Rorschach test in which people are asked to describe what they perceive in two symmetrical ink blots. Another pictorial technique takes the form of a series of cartoons with words inserted in "balloons" above. The respondent is asked to put his own words in an empty balloon space.

(*f*) *Sociometry.* This is a new technique through which an attempt is made to trace the flow of information amongst groups and then examine the ways in which new ideas are diffused. Sociograms are constructed to identify leaders and followers. This approach has been applied to the diffusion of ideas on drugs amongst medical practitioners.

(*g*) *Attitude-scaling tests.* A number of scaling techniques have been developed, but perhaps the best known is the semantic differential technique developed by C. E. Osgood. Basically, the idea is simple, the respondents being invited to rate particular words in relation to objects, services, products, companies etc., along a bi-polar scale, e.g. "weak" to "strong," "cold" to "hot," "small" to "large."

(*h*) *Role-playing.* In these situations the interviewer invites the respondent to act a simple role, e.g. a person advising a friend on how to set about buying a car.

37. Successful motivation research. Despite the criticisms, motivation research has been successfully applied to problems such as product design, package design, advertising, public relations, service facilities and pricing. It should also be added that some authorities maintain that valuable motivation research can be carried out by good marketing researchers who are not expert in behavioural science provided that structured questions are used and that training and direction are given by experienced psychologists.

DATA ANALYSIS

38. Preliminary care in collecting data. The care and speed of analysing data depend to a large extent on the care which has been taken in devising and executing a research project. Attention is therefore drawn to the considerations outlined in **39–42** below.

39. Constructing the questionnaire.

(*a*) If the survey is to be conducted by means of *structured questionnaires* to which the possible answers are predetermined, data can be readily machine-processed. Questions (and possible answers) should therefore be coded.

(*b*) The *length of questionnaires* should be kept to a minimum.

(*c*) Questions should proceed in *logical sequence*, moving from easy to more difficult questions, constantly maintaining the interest of the respondent. Personal and intimate questions should be left to the end.

(*d*) *Technical terms, vague generalisations* and expressions capable of different interpretations should be avoided.

40. The answers.

(*a*) *Replies to open-ended questions* lead to difficulties in analysis, and manual methods of analysis will have to be employed. For this reason and also because respondents and/or interviewers have to construct replies rather than simply provide an answer by means of underlining, crossing out or using a symbol such as a tick or a cross, the time allocated for the completion of the survey will need to be correspondingly greater.

(b) *Adequate space for answers* should be provided for ease of editing and tabulating.

(c) There should always be *provision for indication of uncertainty*, e.g. "don't know," "no preference."

41. Scaling and non-parametric data. There are, in fact, four types of scales:

(a) *Ratio scales.* Such scales have equal intervals. Each is identified with a number. The numbers can be added, subtracted, multiplied and divided and the units are interchangeable. Speed and length, for example, are measured in ratio scales.

(b) *Interval scales.* These are similar to ratio scales but lack a true zero. The intervals are equal but the zero is fixed arbitrarily—70°F is not twice as hot as 35°F. A similar deficiency attaches to Osgood's semantic differential scale.

(c) *Ordinal scales.* These range ideas or objects in an order of priority or preference. This form of scaling is used in market research when respondents are invited, for example, to list products in order of preference. The intervals between ranks are unequal.

(d) *Nominal scales.* These are merely attempts to assign identities to words, e.g. "yes," "no," "dislike," so that it is possible for a researcher to categorise in numerical form the distribution of respondents' answers.

When data can be measured in units which are interchangeable, e.g. weights (by ratio scales), temperatures (by interval scales), that data is said to be *parametric* and can be subjected to most kinds of statistical and mathematical processes. When data is measured in units which are not interchangeable, e.g. product preferences (by ordinal scales), the data is said to be *non-parametric* and is susceptible only to a limited extent to mathematical and statistical treatment.

Unfortunately, most behavioural data comes into the non-parametric category, but some of the most promising developments in behavioural research have been associated with the development of new measurement techniques which open up completely new horizons. These techniques fall under a general classification of *multi-dimensional scaling* and include several approaches to both parametric and non-parametric data. They promise a great advance from a series of uni-dimensional measurements, (e.g. a distribution of intensities of feeling towards single attributes such as colour, taste, or a preference ranking with indeterminate intervals), to a perceptual mapping in multi-dimensional space of objects—company images, advertisements, brands, etc. Such techniques, which require sophisticated computer programmes and data generation by behavioural specialists, have already indicated surprising product gaps and promotional inadequacies.

For those who have difficulty in conceptualising the idea, imagine that you have an outline map of your own country. You then obtain data on the distances between each pair of the largest towns and/or cities (perhaps twelve or fourteen). You now convert these distances into ranks by assigning rank 1 to the shortest distance, and so on, and by the application of a computer programme a configuration remarkably close to the actual town and city locations can be revealed.

Now transfer the idea to the mapping of opinions, life styles, attitudes, etc. The argument may now be advanced that opinions, life styles and attitudes derive from a constellation of components, e.g. attitudes towards a product may derive from colour, design, country of origin and many other factors. If, of course, all these variables were discrete, the number of potential spatial maps would make their use impracticable in marketing. In fact, there are usually significant intercorrelations, so that a comparatively small number of factors appears to account for an attitude formation. This can then be mapped in a manner more akin to an actual buying situation than by examining on conventional lines single factors in isolation or in simple cross-classifications.

42. Conducting the survey.

(a) Interviewers should be carefully selected, trained and briefed.

(b) Occasional field checks should be made to ensure that interviewers are neither cheating nor deviating from instructions. Control questions should be inserted in mailed questionnaires (see **28** above).

(c) Advance provision should be made so that appropriate action may be taken if selected respondents refuse to co-operate or are not available when an interviewer calls.

43. Editing, tabulating and analysis. When the data has been edited and tabulated, analysis can begin. The type of information required for analysis should, of course, determine to a considerable extent the manner in which the survey is planned and executed, as was indicated above (**38–42**). A careful watch should, however, be kept for *unanticipated factors* of significance.

In the process of analysis, relationships or differences supporting or conflicting with original or new hypotheses should be subjected to statistical tests of significance to determine with what validity data can be said to indicate any conclusions. For example, is it more probable that differences in the buying pattern of two groups of people as shown in survey results arise from chance selection in the sample or indicate an actual difference? (*See Chapter* XIX of W. M. Harper's *Statistics* in the M & E HANDBOOK Series.)

MARKETING RESEARCH REPORTS

44. The content and layout of reports. The importance of the final report cannot be over-emphasised. This is the document which the busy executive, often unfamiliar with specialist terminology, sees and to which he looks for clearly expressed findings. The following guides to report presentation are therefore offered:

(*a*) *Layout.*

(*i*) All reports should carry a *title* and *date*.

(*ii*) There should be a *table of contents* so that information that the decision-maker wishes to examine closely can be located without difficulty.

(*iii*) The report should contain a *clear statement of the objective* of the research, and an explanation of the methods.

(*iv*) *A statement of findings and recommendations* in non-technical language should appear at the beginning. If findings are extensive they should be summarised.

(*v*) The main body of the report should be presented in *logical sequence* and broken down into readily absorbed and identifiable sections.

(*vi*) *Technical data*, e.g. questionnaires, sample information and statistical tables, should be put in an appendix.

(*b*) *General rules.*

(*i*) Reports should be written in a *concise and objective style*, avoiding vague expressions such as "it seems," "there may be."

(*ii*) The inclusion of *charts and illustrations* in the main body of the report should be seriously considered if they present information more clearly or forcibly.

(*iii*) *Any constraints* or calculated confidence limits should be stated.

PROGRESS TEST 3

1. What kind of questions on products or services might be answered by the use of marketing research? **(7)**

2. What are the main sources of secondary data? **(10–16)**

3. What are the main types of modified probability samples? **(20–25)**

4. What are the advantages and disadvantages of using mailed questionnaires? **(28)**

5. What are the advantages and disadvantages of personal interviews? **(30)**

6. What factors affect accuracy of replies? **(33)**

7. What techniques are used in motivation research? **(36)**

8. What is meant by "non-parametric data"? What is the significance of the use of this data in marketing applications? **(41)**

9. How should marketing research reports be presented? **(44)**

PART TWO

Product Policy and the Marketing Mix

CHAPTER IV

Product Policy and Planning

1. Nature and scope of product policy. Product policy is concerned with defining the type, volume and timing of the products a company offers for sale. It therefore involves both existing and new products and services, e.g. bank housing loans.

Decisions on products affect the following:

(*a*) *The company's total use of financial and manpower resources.* These resources have to be planned to meet both short-term and long-term objectives.

(*b*) *The kinds of customers or market areas* at which products are aimed.

(*c*) *The promotional methods* to be used.

(*d*) *The reputation* of the company.

(*e*) *The company's position as a leader* or follower.

THE PRODUCT MIX

2. Product lines and ranges. Few companies manufacture or handle a single item (one *line*) at a single price (one *range*). In the case of most companies there are several lines and ranges. The total assortment of products a company offers may be described as the *product mix*. In its range of assorted items a company may offer a wide variety of different items and/or a large number of quality or style variations. The product mix may be extended in various ways:

(*a*) By variations in models or styles.

(*b*) By variations in quality offered at different price levels.

(*c*) By the development of associated items, e.g. cameras and photographic accessories.

(*d*) By the development or acquisition or licensing of completely different products in terms of customer needs, manufacturing processes, etc. ICI, for example, produces industrial chemicals, household paints and plastics among its range of products.

Products policy requires continuing attention since decisions on adding or dropping products will constantly arise. The more volatile the market, the more frequently will decisions have to be made, but the speed of change even in less volatile market areas (e.g. capital goods) is such that policy decisions are equally or more important since more time and more financial and manpower resources are usually required to effect change.

3. Advantages and disadvantages of multi-product operations. The greater the variety of products offered the greater, theoretically, is the market opportunity and the less the threat of complete loss of business. On the other hand, the costs of development, manufacturing and marketing may be too high to effect economies of scale, and effort may be so thinly spread that the strategic advantages of concentration are lost. Short production runs, for example, lead to high unit manufacturing costs, while advertising and selling effort scattered across a wide range of miscellaneous products and markets may be both costly and ineffective. Unless, however, as in many fields of industrial goods, there is a British or International Standard specification laid down and simplification is forced on competitive organisations, there are advantages in expanding associated lines.

Such advantages include the following:

(a) *Increased production of minor variations* may lead to lower unit costs resulting from a greater absorption of overhead, provided that there is sufficient increase in sales revenue.

(b) *Sales force costs may be reduced* if similar outlets are involved.

(c) *Advertising of a broad range or line* may be more effective.

(d) Distribution may be more readily achieved along the channels of distribution if there is a *satisfactory range in terms of consumer choice* and in terms of buying economies.

(e) *The opportunity of short-circuiting inefficient intermediaries* and controlling sales effort directly or closer to the end user may result.

4. The product life cycle. The sales of many products appear to follow a typical pattern, showing a gradually increasing growth to maturity, a levelling-out as saturation point is reached and then a decline. This is illustrated in the diagram which follows.

(a) Prior to the introduction of a product to the market there is a *development stage* during which there tends to be greater and greater investment. This investment cost must either be charged against future earnings or be written off, and it is not unnatural to find that a company which has invested large sums in a particular development project will be reluctant to abandon the research. The product life-cycle concept is useful in determining the time and cost of development projects in relation to the ultimate pay-off. Frequently, large-scale development projects take much longer than originally expected and it is important to review at regular periods progress made against life-cycle expectations.

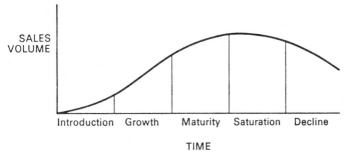

FIG. 1. *The product life cycle.*

(*b*) In the *introductory stage* costs of production and marketing will be high, but if there is a genuine product differential (an advantage not enjoyed or easily copied by other companies) a company may benefit in various ways, e.g. by high initial pricing or by rapid market penetration.

(*c*) During the *growth stage* the initial marketing efforts should lead to the greatest rate of sales expansion, but according to the rate of technical change, the rate of market acceptance, and the ease with which competitors can imitate and enter the market, buying resistance will build up. Management must therefore be ready to phase in new products and adjust marketing tactics in line with the anticipated cycle.

(*d*) The *maturity and saturation stages*, for example, may be the times for changes in pricing, in advertising and promotion, or in design or quality range.

(*e*) At the *stage of decline* profit margins become very small and every effort has to be made to reduce costs and improve distribution efficiency. Price becomes the major issue and this may, for example, lead to restriction of distribution to large outlets. A product which is at the decline stage in one country may, however, find a growth market in a country with a less highly developed economy. The cost of maintaining business at this last stage of the cycle must be weighed against the opportunity for investment elsewhere. The latest portfolio management techniques developed by the Boston Consulting Company involve sophisticated life-cycle analysis.

5. Eliminating products. Company profit contribution frequently comes mainly from a small number of items in the product mix. Dropping products which make little or no contribution can frequently make very significant improvements in overall profitability. Weak products are very costly in ways which are not readily seen in accounting returns, e.g.:

(*a*) They take up a disproportionate amount of management and selling time.

(*b*) They involve short runs and high production setting-up costs.

(*c*) They often require special warehousing and transportation consideration.

(*d*) They are incurring expense which could be directed to more profitable developments.

(*e*) They may cause customers to think of the company as being unimaginative and technically unprogressive.

6. Resistance to dropping products. Frequently resistance to dropping weak products arises, for various reasons, e.g.:

(*a*) Management is more concerned with *new product development* than with balancing the current product mix.

(*b*) There is a *sentimental attachment* to products which were successful in the past—particularly if they were part of the original mix.

(*c*) Sales forces tend to *fear loss of individual orders* without having access to the facts of the complete marketing situation.

(*d*) *Hopes of revival* tend to linger for an inordinately long time.

(*e*) Falling sales or profits are attributed to weak *advertising or selling operations* rather than to the product.

(*f*) Dropping products may lead to the assignment of personnel to new tasks and vested interests operate to resist changes of this kind.

Products must be considered truly objectively and not continued for reasons such as these.

7. The product mix and sales growth. Companies seek to achieve profitable sales growth in the following ways:

(*a*) *By increasing sales of existing products in existing markets* by more efficient or more aggressive selling and promotion, or by application to new uses.

(*b*) *By developing improved products* for *existing* markets.

(*c*) *By developing new products* for *existing* markets (but *see* **8**).

(*d*) *By offering existing products* to *new* markets.

(*e*) *By offering modifications* of existing products to *new* markets.

(*f*) *By developing new products* for *new* markets.

8. Market segmentation and product specialisation. It should be stressed that many companies seek to develop completely new products when it might be more profitable to exploit new market segments. The economies of scale possible in capital-intensive industries, e.g. chemicals, draw attention to the need to exploit markets on an international scale just as much as the need to develop new product ideas. For instance, the growth in demand for paper tissue has been stimulated not only by intoducing new use concepts, e.g. paper towels, and by extending the range in size and colour, but also by exploiting new market segments, e.g. industrial markets. The development of a segmentation strategy may:

(*a*) *Secure new user market segments.*

(*b*) Enable *concentration on most profitable buyers* by means of product design or promotion.

(*c*) *Stimulate distribution channels.*

(*d*) Build up reputation for *progressive leadership*.

(*e*) Provide sales forces with *renewed drive*.

(*f*) Force competition into defensive strategies.

(*g*) *Stretch product life cycles* at comparatively low cost.

There is a difference between product differentiation, based on such general notions as the need to offer variety and customer choice so that a wide range of needs are catered for fairly well, and *planned* market segmentation. The latter implies that a distinctly homogeneous group of needs has been identified clearly with a particular group of potential customers, and that there is a distinct demand/profit curve associated with satisfying the needs of that group. The traditional means of segmenting markets, e.g. by organisation size, geography, business classification, socio-economic grouping, age, sex, etc., are now beginning to be supplemented by behavioural research into such areas as life style, attitudes, priority spending patterns. These new approaches are often combined with more conventional data, and have been used not only in product development and promotional programmes in repeatable consumer goods markets, but also in connection with the marketing of such diverse services as bank credit cards and residential property. One other important application has been in determining the positioning of products in international markets.

NEW PRODUCT PLANNING

9. Requirements for new product planning. New product planning involves targets and timetables for:

    (*a*) research and engineering;
    (*b*) plant and equipment development;
    (*c*) commercial development;
    (*d*) staff development;
    (*e*) provision of financial resources.

10. Risks in new product planning. All new products involve risk, which is at its highest when the investment is high; the period of return on investment is long, and the product involves new areas of research, new manufacturing techniques and "know-how," and entry into new markets requiring new marketing skills and resources.

In order to reduce risk, the greatest possible care should be taken during the stages of *exploration*, *screening* and *specification*. Design testing and marketing are the really costly stages, involving many more people and greater plant and equipment resources than exploration, screening and specification.

It has been estimated that the rate of new product failure in the USA is as high as 80%. The cost of failure would probably be only one-tenth if probable failure could be detected before the design stage, by more thorough and accurate exploration and screening.

11. Sources of new product ideas. Ideas for new products can come from many sources, e.g.:

    (*a*) from research and development personnel;
    (*b*) from marketing personnel;
    (*c*) from associated companies in other countries;

(*d*) from customers;

(*e*) from outside technological or scientific discoveries;

(*f*) from employee suggestions;

(*g*) from brainstorming sessions of executives;

(*h*) from competitors;

(*i*) from knowledge of government needs;

(*j*) from individual executives;

(*k*) from a study of unused patents.

12. The screening process. Screening is the process of eliminating ideas which are out of line with company objectives or resources, or which carry high-risk cost and little profit opportunity (*see* **13**).

Screening and later stages of the product development process require contributions from a range of specialists, e.g. market researchers, engineers, development specialists, accountants. If there is no separate product-planning group—and these are becoming more common—there must be detailed arrangements for *co-ordination* (*see* **28**). In technologically based industries there is frequently too much reliance placed in the early stages on the opinions of technical specialists working in comparative isolation.

13. Screening considerations. Screening involves considerations such as the following:

(*a*) *Demand considerations.*

(*i*) What is the *potential demand* and in what markets?

(*ii*) What is the likely *life cycle* of the product? What is the *pattern of demand?*

(*iii*) What is the possibility of *substitution or product obsolescence?*

(*iv*) What are the *possibilities of modifying the product* to enter new market segments or lengthen its profitable existence?

(*v*) Will the product produce a *stable or seasonal* sales or production pattern?

(*vi*) What is the *maximum development time* for profit exploitation?

(*vii*) What are the *growth prospects* of the product in terms of the total market?

(*b*) *Considerations of resources.*

(*i*) Is the new idea in line with *company policy and objectives*, e.g. profit, image, market growth, product lines?

(*ii*) Is the new idea in line with *company resources*, e.g. capital, physical resources, "know-how"?

(*iii*) What *time, equipment and money* will be required to carry out the project and what *other opportunities* will have to be delayed or missed as a result?

(*iv*) Are sufficient numbers of *qualified personnel available* or can they be made available by recruitment or training?

(*v*) What is the *availability of materials* and bought-in components? What are the likely price variations and how will these affect final price and demand?

(*vi*) What *manufacturing problems* will arise?

(*vii*) To what extent will the product assist in *reducing production* or *marketing costs* of other products?

(*viii*) What will be the effect on *inventory levels*?

(*ix*) Can *existing distribution systems be used*?

(*c*) *Competitive considerations*.

(*i*) What *patent considerations* are involved—either the company's own or competitive patents?

(*ii*) What is the *competition*—numbers, size and resources of companies, strengths and weaknesses?

(*iii*) How do the company's likely *costs* compare with those of potential competitors?

14. Commercial evaluation. The screening process will throw up the more obvious pitfalls and opportunities which a new product offers, but desk and field market surveys will assist in defining the market or markets by size, location, structure and buying habits. Information can also be obtained on competition and other possible external factors and thus calculations can be made to indicate the share of market likely to be obtained at various time periods at various costs, and by the use of various methods of distribution, pricing and sales policies.

15. Product testing and test markets. Once the product has passed through the development and design stage full-scale production risks are avoided by building models, prototypes, or by using a pilot plant. It may also be feasible to carry out limited tests of the product in the market place. In the marketing of consumer goods a geographical area—possibly one of the smaller television areas—may be selected to test consumer and channel reaction to both product and marketing methods. A gradual extension of the test market can follow with the advantage of allowing for a gradual build-up of manufacturing capacity, inventory and selling effort.

16. Arguments for and against test marketing. The main argument against test marketing is that competitors immediately become aware of what is happening and can take steps to counter the development before national distribution or the growth stage of the product life cycle is reached.

Against this it could be argued that test markets assist in providing a realistic picture of the way in which competitors will react. The problem is to weigh the risk of failure against the advantage of a time lead—a particularly acute problem in narrowly differentiated consumer markets.

17. Operating test markets. Test markets need to be operated against controls and companies frequently use the areas on which they have previously accumulated considerable data in connection with other product launches. Competitors may, of course, react by introducing unusual variables which make interpretation of results difficult, e.g. running special promotions on a scale which would be uneconomical on a national basis.

Other problems arise in operating test markets, e.g.:

(*a*) *What should be the size and structure of the sample*—which towns, cities, rural areas, etc?

(*b*) *Over what period should a test market run* in order to obtain reliable information? What time should be allowed for initial purchase and repeat purchases, without providing invaluable cost and revenue data to competitors or incurring disproportionately heavy expenses in analysis, and production at uneconomic levels.

18. Selecting test markets. Criteria employed in the selection of test market areas have been ranked by the American journal *Sales Management* as follows:

(*a*) Typicality of distributive outlets.
(*b*) Relative isolation from other cities.
(*c*) Availability of advertising media that will co-operate.
(*d*) Diversified cross-section as to ages, religion, etc.
(*e*) Representative as to population size.
(*f*) Typicality as to *per capita* income.
(*g*) Previous good record as a test city.
(*h*) Stability of year-round sales.

19. Consumer panels. In addition to, or as alterations to, test marketing, use is frequently made of consumer panels. Consumer panels are often used at an early stage of development to determine consumer attitudes or strength of preference. In industrial markets, prototypes or limited batches may be tested in the working environment on company customers or potential customers of various sizes and types.

20. Forecasting accuracy. Product testing almost always brings about changes in production methods, in design, in packaging, in pricing or in marketing procedures. A Nielsen investigation of 141 consumer products reveals that forecasting accuracy increases the longer products are on test, up to a period of 9 months. The chances of a correct projection of sales based on limited tests were as follows:

After 2 months	.	.	.	.	1 in 9
,, 4 ,,		.	.	.	1 in 7
,, 6 ,,		.	.	.	1 in 2
,, 8 ,,		.	.	.	2 in 3
,, 9 ,,		.	.	.	5 in 6

THE BREAK-EVEN CONCEPT

21. Break-even point. It is important to calculate in advance the likely relationships between cost, volume and profit over various time periods. Break-even charts are often used for this purpose. The illustration below is based on certain assumptions:

(a) That *fixed and variable costs can be separated* clearly and meaningfully.

(b) That *variable costs change* in direct proportion to output.

(c) That *price does not change* at different levels of output.

(d) That the relationships are real only at a *particular point of time*.

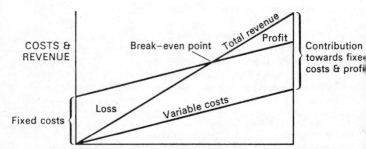

FIG. 2. *A break-even chart.*

Expressed as a formula the *volume* of output at which break-even occurs

$$= \frac{\textit{Total fixed costs}}{\textit{Margin of contribution}} \quad \frac{\text{(total in £'s)}}{\text{(£'s per unit)}}$$

The margin of contribution is derived from subtracting the unit variable cost from the unit selling price.

It is often important to know the *amount of net sales revenue* at which break-even is reached on a variety of units at different selling prices. In this case, fixed costs should be divided by the margin of contribution expressed as a percentage of net sales. The margin of contribution as a percentage of net sales may be calculated from the formula:

$$1 - \frac{\textit{Total variable costs}}{\textit{Net sales}}$$

This formula derives from the fact that it is the complement of the percentage of total variable costs of net sales, i.e. the percentage contribution margin to net sales.

22. The effect of variable factors on break-even points and profit contributions. A decision to increase volume, apart from strategic reasons, can only be justified if additional revenue is at least equal to additional variable costs, and will provide funds for contributing to fixed costs and thus add to profit.

Break-even calculations can show the likely effect of an increase in price, or increased costs arising from the purchase of additional equipment, increased wage rates, changes in material prices, and so on. It will be clear that the higher the fixed costs the more important is the volume consideration. Capital-intensive industries are particularly susceptible to volume changes and normally demand high plant utilisation. A high investment in plant, as in certain sectors of the chemical industry, for example, may lead to a situation where home markets are insufficiently large to reach really profitable volume levels, but high plant investment and utilisation achieves the enormous economies of scale which are necessary for competitive prices in internationally competitive markets.

23. Break-even and cost concepts. Calculations of profitability depend to some extent on accounting conventions and company accounting practices. Methods of assessing costs differ considerably, as will be seen from a study of the following paragraphs (24–26).

24. Fixed and variable costs. *Fixed costs* theoretically remain constant over all levels of output. *Variable costs*, e.g. direct labour or materials, vary with changes in output level.

Fixed costs per unit of output therefore decline as production increases; variable costs per unit of output may increase if there are changes in wage rates or material prices, or decrease if, for example, materials are bought at more advantageous quantity terms. Some costs, e.g. power, may be partly fixed and partly variable; power for lighting may be classified as fixed, while power for operating machines may be classified as variable.

Classification into categories of fixed and variable costs depends on accounting practice and the time over which the costs are calculated.

25. Opportunity costs. In economic terms a cost incurred for any item or project means that there is a consequent loss of the opportunity to spend that money in another way.

(*a*) *Return on investment.* The cost of development of a new product involves the loss of opportunity to use resources elsewhere and consideration should therefore be given to rates of return on alternative investment opportunities. In assessing new development possibilities the following equations are useful:

ROI = *Percentage of profit per unit of sales revenue*

$$\times \frac{\text{Annual sales revenue}}{\text{Capital invested}}$$

ROI = *Percentage profit* $\times$ *Capital turnover*

(*b*) *Discounted cash flow.* Conventional accounting procedures frequently place a penalty on new developments by ignoring the fact that marketing research, technical development, tooling up, initial advertising and similar expenses are investment costs and should be treated quite differently from normal operating costs. Cost must, of course, be recovered. The problem is to establish a relevant time base and a realistic means of allocating costs directly involved in development projects.

Projects occupy differing periods of time and bring in varying flows of profit over their life cycle. One of the techniques which is being increasingly used to cope with the problem of alternative investment decisions over varying time periods is *discounted cash flow*. This technique seeks to translate future cash flows to present values by a process of *discounting*—taking into consideration the many implications of cost of capital and the return over various time periods. Alternative investment proposals are therefore ranked qualitatively, and not purely quantitatively as in the accounting-rate-of-return method or the pay-back-period method. The notion of *opportunity cost* is involved in using discounted cash flow to decide on problems such as:

(*i*) whether to build a new factory or expand other facilities;

(*ii*) whether to replace existing plant by plant with higher productive capacity or rate of production;

(*iii*) whether to lease or buy equipment;

(*iv*) what alternative methods of financing should be adopted.

26. Incremental cost. Incremental cost is the additional total cost charge which arises from the making of a new decision. Clearly it is important to ensure that the additional cost incurred by a particular decision is more than covered by the additional revenue resulting from that decision. The concept would be particularly relevant in decisions on changes in levels of production output or in deciding whether to accept a special order at a special price. In the latter event it would be necessary to compare the outcome of acceptance against the outcome of order refusal. Consideration would also need to be given to the possible effect on other prices in the future as well as the possible loss of alternative investment (opportunity cost).

ORGANISATION FOR PRODUCT PLANNING

27. Principles of product-planning organisation. It is dangerous to generalise on ideal organisational arrangements for product planning since companies differ in so many ways. There are, however, certain important principles which should be observed:

(*a*) Product policy depends greatly on the attitude of top management and it is vital that top management should be constantly alive to change in the market.

(*b*) If product planning is to be consumer-oriented, marketing personnel should be closely involved from the earliest stages of development and throughout the life cycle of the product.

(*c*) Product planning involves the co-operation and co-ordination of specialists with different attitudes—engineers, scientists, accountants, marketing men, production specialists. It is necessary, therefore, to set up clear definitions of responsibility and authority in relation to product decision and to ensure that there are easy and known systems of communication (*see* VIII, **1**).

28. Co-ordination through groups. One of the problems of organisation for product planning is to ensure that vested interests do not dominate or produce conflicts. There will, in fact, often be a strong case for establishing a *new product-planning group, as well as product managers* responsible for co-ordination of activities and profitability of existing products or product groups. The product-planning group may consist of a committee of executives which meets at regular intervals or a permanent "staff" group freed from the problems of day-to-day line operations. The completely separate "staff" group is most commonly found in large organisations and is normally concerned with new product development. Existing products are, in these cases, under the direction of product or product-group managers, reporting in turn to the senior marketing executive. When new product planning is carried out by an independent group it is important that a mechanism exists for decision-making, so that new products can be moved over to line product managers at the appropriate time.

29. Use of networks in product planning. One of the ways in which the many necessary activities of different people at different times can be effectively co-ordinated is by the use of network analysis. A network is a graphical representation of a project showing all activities linked sequentially in such a way that interdependencies are clearly seen, i.e. when the beginning of one activity depends on the completion of other activities. Timings are shown so that it is possible to see the earliest and latest times at which an activity can begin. The shortest possible time for completion of the project can also be traced along the network. This is the *critical path*, any delay along which will cause a hold-up in the completion of the total project. Cost elements can also be built in, if desirable, as well as a range of alternative time estimates.

30. Decision tree. Another technique which may be used in product planning is the *decision tree*. It has been made clear that product planning involves a sequential decision-making process and that at various stages a decision to stop the project or to follow an alternative course of action could be taken. The decision tree is based on the notion of probability. At each decision point an estimate is made of the probability of success or failure and the

consequent effect on loss or gain. In Fig. 3 (taken from a paper by
J. F. Magge in the *Harvard Business Review*) a decision tree is used
to show the likely outcome of alternative investment decisions.

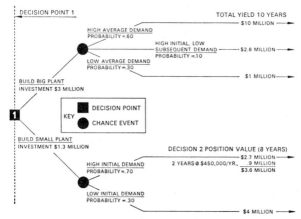

FIG. 3. *Decision tree.*

31. Cost, revenue and price. Determination of product policy and
planning the most profitable product mix are highly important
and complex areas of management. Cost and revenue considerations have to be calculated and estimated as precisely as possible.
The effect of price on costs and revenue will be examined in the
next chapter.

32. Product-market planning—recent developments. The very high
fixed levels of cost associated with single-purpose plant and equipment and the increased risk of substantial operating losses in the
product-market pioneering stage—particularly in large organisations—have led to a number of significant developments in connection with product-market planning:

(*a*) *Concept testing.* New product concepts are tested before any
money is invested in product research and development, to determine what the user benefits of projected products really are likely
to be as well as to find their individual importance and priority
rating. Pockets of potential resistance in terms of product characteristics or groups of customers can be identified and an approxi-
mation of demand structure can be made.

(b) *More development and less pure research.* More and more organisations are concentrating the greater part of their research and development investment on application research, geared towards exploiting existing "know-how." There are already signs of a greater willingness to co-operate in areas of fundamental research, to enter into research exchange agreements and to engage university researchers on a retainer basis.

(c) *More formal systematic review* of progress and expenditure on research projects set against market time-scales, by multi-disciplinary groups representing all vital functions.

(d) *The setting-up of venture groups.* These are small groups of personnel specially selected to liaise with operating functions—research, production, purchasing, industrial engineering, marketing, finance—in order to speed up the process of product development to the point of commercialisation. A prime requirement for such groups is an effective leader—one who can achieve results, working informally with a multi-disciplinary team through existing operational units with their individual priorities and vested interests. The most successful venture groups have been appointed essentially on a temporary basis for one major project.

(e) *Systems approaches and corporate auditing procedures.* Many organisations have seen the need to achieve real economies of scale through the development of "families" or "systems" of products. This approach allows all assets, e.g. finance, technical skills, productive capacity, marketing expertise, to be audited, harnessed and developed towards the fulfilment of a succession of product-market objectives over time.

PRODUCTS AND PACKAGING

33. Growth and importance of packaging. The growth of self-service stores and the importance of gaining distribution, shelf space and display have made packaging decisions in the field of consumer goods a highly important area of decision in regard to product policy and planning. Even in the marketing of industrial goods packaging is taking on increasing significance and extending beyond the obvious necessity of providing for protection, transportation and storage.

The demand for packaging has led to an enormous increase in the range of packaging equipment and materials available. There have been spectacular increases in the use of flexible packaging involving special papers, plastics and aluminium foil. New printing methods have been developed, e.g. flexography, by which process it is possible relatively inexpensively to reproduce photographs or artwork in a wide range of colours on a wide range of materials.

Packaging design is influenced by the cultural, social and political environment. In the USA, for example, the housewife buys approximately 90% of her weekly purchases from supermarkets and self-service shops in one day. In the UK the percentage of food purchases from self-service outlets is much lower and there is still a great deal of daily shopping. In Latin countries pre-packed foods are rather slow in sales growth. Attitudes to colour differ; white is symbolic of mourning in many Far Eastern countries as opposed to purple in Latin countries.

34. Factors to consider in package design. A package should be designed to perform many functions:

(*a*) *Provide protection*—at any stage in the distribution process and ultimately in the home or factory of the user or consumer (e.g. against product damage, contamination, evaporation, chemical change, pilferage): *see* **35** below. For example, surface treatment of packaging avoids deterioration of appearance after transit and/ or storage.

(*b*) *Offer convenience.* This covers handling, storage and opening of packages at all stages of distribution, and frequently in eventual use.

(*i*) *Convenience of storage in warehouse, shop and house.* In designing the package there must be a consideration of the economies of stocking large quantities of bulky, slow-moving, low unit profit-margin products, and the difficulties of stacking certain carton shapes.

(*ii*) *Convenience in use.* There must be a consideration of the development of new materials and functional designs—aerosol, containers, vacuum cans for vegetables, flip-top cigarette packets. New packaging ideas may lead to new products or product formulation, e.g. hair sprays, cheese spreads. Safety features should also be considered, as in the design of easy-opening cans eliminating the possibility of cuts and finger-nail damage.

(*c*) *Reduce transport costs.* This is achieved by the use of lightweight yet adequately strong materials, especially important when goods have to be transported by air.

(*d*) *Provide opportunity for re-use.* The package may be deliberately designed so that it can be used for the storage of other items once the original product is consumed, e.g. plastic and aluminium containers. On the other hand, some packages are designed so that refills may be bought. The design may be so differentiated that only a refill of the same product can be used in the original container.

(*e*) *Create a favourable product image*. The package has frequently to represent the product symbolically—to convey its buying advantages. The packaging "image" will be reinforced if there is a close tie-in with advertising and promotion (*see* VII, 21).

(*f*) *Establish product differences*. The package is often the major way in which narrowly differentiated products are distinguished. The difference may be in the art design, the shape or the materials used. A package can be used to convey an impression of quality differences. Gift packages are a good example of extending the range through packaging.

(*g*) *Establish corporate identity*. Some companies aim at promoting individual products in their own right. Others deliberately aim at creating a company rather than product loyalty, e.g. Heinz baby foods.

(*h*) *Gain display at retail level*. The package must be easy to arrange on shelves or racks and at the same time should attract the potential customer. Developments in printing techniques, e.g. flexography (*see* **33** above), combined with newer packaging materials, e.g. polyethylene film, have significance in this connection.

35. Packaging and protection. In considering some of the more sophisticated uses of packaging the protective aspects of packaging should not be disregarded. Attention is therefore drawn to the following hazards against which packaging should provide a defence:

(*a*) *Damage by mechanical handling*. Most damage occurs in the handling process and, the more frequently products are handled in the distribution process, the greater is the need for protection. One of the advantages of the liner train and other container transport development is that they will result in less damage through handling. Damaged goods have to be replaced and are likely to cause loss and inconvenience to seller and purchaser. Often slightly damaged products may not be returned, but may inhibit repeat purchase.

(*b*) *Product loss*. Liquids and powders are highly susceptible to loss, e.g. powder leakage, liquid evaporation.

(c) *Pilferage*. Loss through pilferage can be quite high—especially if there are many handling points.

(d) *Contamination by dust or dirt*. Clothing, food and fine machinery are obvious examples of products liable to damage in this way.

(e) *Moisture gain and loss*. Many products have an optimum moisture content, e.g. cement, ceramic paints, frozen foods.

(f) *Chemical change*, e.g. metal corrosion, coffee rancidity.

(g) *Flavour loss or change*.

(h) *Mould*, e.g. in canned foods, paints.

(i) *Insect attack*, e.g. moths in clothing.

36. Further reading. Students are strongly recommended to study the excellent Gold Medal paper included in the 1980 Institution of Marketing Author of the Year Awards: Nigel Piercy's *Marketing Information—bridging the quicksand between technology and decision making*.

PROGRESS TEST 4

1. What are the advantages and disadvantages of multi-product operations? **(3)**

2. What is meant by the "product life cycle"? **(4)**

3. Why is there resistance to dropping products? **(6)**

4. What are the main considerations in screening ideas for new products? **(13)**

5. What criteria might be used in selecting test markets? **(18)**

6. Construct a break-even chart. **(21)**

7. What is meant by (a) "opportunity costs"; (b) "incremental costs"? **(25, 26)**

8. How might networks be used in product planning? **(29)**

9. What is a decision tree? **(30)**

10. Why is more attention now being paid to packaging? **(33)**

CHAPTER V

Pricing and Demand

PROBLEMS OF PRICING

1. Perfect competition. A great deal has been written by economists on the interaction of price and demand. Much of this writing was based on a situation in which price was the dominant variable differentiating products or services. *Perfect competition* demands that goods from different producers are identical, that there are identical circumstances under which a sale takes place, that complete information on products and markets is equally available to all potential buyers, and that there are sufficient producers to prevent restriction of supply to one (monopoly) or a limited few (oligopoly) producers. Such conditions hardly ever exist and the growth of an affluent society has further complicated the quantitative assessment of elasticity, i.e. the sensitivity of demand in relation to price.

2. Imperfect competition. More recently it has been realised that in a society where everyone is living above mere subsistence and exercising discretionary spending power, with ever wider ranges of goods available from competing producers, qualitative variables take on an increasing importance. *Imperfect* markets and *imperfect* competition are a feature of a sophisticated capitalist or mixed economy. This is not to deny the existence of varying degrees of demand elasticity. Economic pricing theory has relevance to practical marketing situations. The more a product or general product category is regarded as a necessity the more inelastic is demand likely to be. If discretionary incomes fall, the demand for food will continue whereas the demand for washing machines will decline. Likewise the demand for exotic expensive foods will decline much more than the demand for bread. Again, with all products there is an upper and lower price level, outside which demand would fluctuate sharply; the problem is to determine those levels. Within a given price range some products have a more elastic demand pattern than others, but too little is known of these more subtle elasticities since there is a tendency for competitors to follow each other's pricing systems fairly closely in order to avoid the risk of the unknown. Demand is a measure of the utility that a product has for a consumer or a market and price is only one aspect of that utility.

3. Factors of demand. Factors which may affect demand can be subsumed under three broad headings:

(*a*) Market considerations (*see* **4**).

(*b*) Company and product considerations (*see* **5**).

(*c*) The demand for other products (*see* **6**).

4. Market considerations. Demand is affected by the size of the market and the needs and desires of the people constituting that market.

(*a*) *Population.* Total population in most parts of the world is growing and the size of markets is increasing. On the other hand, populations are becoming more mobile and even industrial concentrations are shifting—sometimes as a result of government economic policy. Demand for both goods and services will, therefore, depend to some extent on the direction of marketing effort to particular market sectors.

(*b*) *Disposable income.* A highly developed industrial society has a large proportion of the population with considerable discretionary incomes. Countries in early stages of development have fewer people above subsistence level but there may be a small layer of society with exceedingly high levels of disposable income. Government economic policy and especially taxation systems may affect actual and anticipated disposable income levels very considerably. Expectation of earnings or profits has a marked effect on demand for deferrable items, e.g. luxury goods, plant and equipment.

(*c*) *Customer satisfaction.* People are motivated to buy goods and services for a whole host of economic, social and psychological reasons. Current fashion, individual taste, prestige, imitation of others, the relative importance of comfort, convenience or security, may all have a bearing on buying behaviour. Some products may even sell better in certain markets because they are higher in price.

5. Company and product considerations. Demand for a product is obviously influenced by the ideas people have about that product and the company that manufactures it.

(*a*) *Company or product reputation.* The higher the price range of the product, the more it is likely to affect health or security, or the more influence it may have on the performance of other products, the more is a purchaser likely to avoid untried commodities from little-known firms.

(b) *Advertising and promotion.* A product must be known before it is bought. Selling skill or the creation of a favourable product image through advertising may have a very considerable effect on purchasing action. "Promotional elasticity" is a measure of the changes in demand relative to advertising expenditure.

(c) *Service.* The provision of pre- or post-sales advice and servicing facilities may more than compensate for an initially high price.

6. The demand for other products. The following factors are important.

(a) *Cross-elasticity.* The demand for goods may be influenced by the demand for other goods, which may vary according to price.

(b) *Competition.* Demand will depend not only on the price of competitive products or substitutes but on their reputation, availability, performance, aesthetic appeal, length of service, flexibility of use and so on.

(c) *Derived demand and choice.* The demand for almost all products is conditioned by the demand for others. Sometimes the buying problem is a question of deciding on the use of limited resources to buy one make of car as opposed to another—or to go on an overseas holiday instead of buying a car. Sometimes there is a close dependency in the demand for one product on the demand for another. The demand for nylon depends on the demand for nylon-finished products. The demand for machines depends on the demand for the goods the machines produce. It is sometimes possible for the manufacture of derived demand goods to stimulate primary demand; e.g. the promotional campaigns of manufacturers of fabrics in man-made fibres led to an increased demand for the fibres and for the raw materials and machinery.

7. The problem of changing variables. The problem of pricing is intensified not simply because of the increasing *number* of variables affecting demand, but also because those variables are in a *constant state of change.* It is a basic task of marketing to determine which of the variable factors of demand have greatest significance in particular markets at particular points of time. Attempts to determine the factors at present range from sheer guesswork or intuition to the construction of complex mathematical models.

Successful product differentiation depends on the determination of the relevant factors and the creation of some of the elements of monopoly benefits.

8. Specific problems facing the price setter. Amongst the many problems often solved intuitively or by conventional cost-based formulae are the following:

(a) Establishing an initial price structure for new products.

(b) Reacting to changes in competitive prices.

(c) Forecasting the role of price in relation to the various stages of the product life cycle (see IV, 4).

(d) Determining the sensitivity of resellers to prices and margins.

(e) Estimating the relative sensitivity to price of basically similar products or services supplied to different markets or market segments.

(f) Organising price schedules for products with inter-related production costs.

(g) Arranging prices for products differing in cost and profitability but which are purchased only in combination.

(h) Determining the appropriate timing, frequency and amount of price changes.

9. Top-level management objectives, policies and constraints. Too frequently, in practice, price setters lack clear statements by top management of the objectives and policies which must be accepted as given constraints by executives at a lower level who have to make pricing decisions in relation to specific markets, products and/or services—and indeed specific situations. Some of these top-level decision areas are set out below:

(a) Does the company intend to communicate a corporate image which is closely identified with price levels, e.g. a reputation for high quality only?

(b) Does the company have short-run and long-run objectives in terms of overall profitability, and to what extent are these objectives to be applied to individual products or product groups regardless of their stage in the life cycle? Are different criteria to be applied to different home markets, or to overseas as opposed to home markets?

(c) What is the company's commitment to market penetration or share maintenance and to what extent is it prepared to sacrifice short-run profit to gain strategic ends?

(d) Does the company seek price leadership and subsequent

competitive price stability? Is it prepared to take aggressive action against "inconvenient" price cutters?

(e) What is the company's attitude towards risk in which parts and what proportion of its business?

(f) What is the company policy on transfer pricing (see 36)?

BASIC PRICING STRATEGIES AND PRACTICES

The majority of companies have no clear pricing policies. Where these are quoted, they often cover a range of general and specific strategies, objectives and practices, such as those discussed in 10–16 below.

10. Market penetration. Low prices are set in order to penetrate markets, to gain a major market share—usually in a comparatively short time. This policy can only be valid if the market is very price-sensitive, and/or if production costs fall significantly in line with volume increase, and/or if competitors will be discouraged. If penetration targets are achieved and competitive activity has been restricted, the problem of whether to raise prices or reduce margins to intermediaries, e.g. wholesalers, retailers, might arise.

An important factor to take into account when considering market-penetration pricing is supply capacity. British Leyland launched the Jaguar XJ12 in 1972 and within a few months demand so greatly exceeded supply that second-hand models were commanding a price premium greatly above the new list price. In 1973–1974, many continental European manufacturers complained that British products were grossly underpriced in overseas markets, yet supplies were not available and there were long delays. The burden of the complaint was that the British companies were apparently unable to take advantage of their lower prices which had resulted from the advantageous currency situation, had failed to adjust upwards, and had brought customer pressure on those indigenous companies who could supply to lower their prices. In the case of British Leyland, it has been argued that price can be an important factor in segmenting markets, and so avoiding blurred product images, which can result in two models, with consequent additional costs, competing with each other for the same customers.

Another argument advanced has been that, in conditions of great demand uncertainty, provided a "satisfactory" profit is made in the short run, prices can be moved up if market demand exceeds expectation. Such an argument has no practical validity in situations where governments impose statutory price constraints—an increasingly important consideration in inflationary situations which governments attempt to control by some form of prices and/or incomes policy. Prices geared essentially to costs, lacking close analysis of short- and long-run supply/demand considerations, are particularly vulnerable in inflationary conditions.

11. Short-term profit maximisation. A policy of setting very high prices in order to make as much profit as possible in a short time is normally only valid if the producer has an innovation of such significance that there is a ready price-elastic market with virtually no immediate competition but likely competition in the near future. The producer must also normally be prepared to move out of the business when he has made his quick profits. The Reynolds International Pen Company introduced ballpoint pens at a retail price of $12.50 and in three months made a profit after taxes of $1,558,608 on an investment of $26,000. Competitive pressure forced prices down and the company closed, but the originator made a fortune. A primary objective of most companies, however, is to stay in business.

Short-term profit-maximising (or "skimming the cream") pricing objectives have sometimes been applied successfully to segment markets, to recover costs quickly in conditions of uncertainty, or to compensate for high development costs. Books are often produced first in a limited expensive edition and, in the light of demand indications, cheaper paperback editions may follow. New drugs are often extremely expensive initially but prices fall rapidly after the first one or two years of the product life.

12. Satisfactory rate of return. Some companies fix their prices on the basis of a traditional rate of return over a given time period, related to the extent of risk or investment involved. In its most sophisticated form this becomes *target pricing*. Target pricing is aimed at securing in a given period of time a predetermined rate of return on investment. The process involves the calculation of an average mark-up on average costs and at the same time projecting sales revenue at various stages of the product life cycle. Target pricing is thus directed towards the twin objectives of stabilising prices and yet achieving a given return on investment over the product life. At particular points of time the return will be high, at others low.

Target pricing demands accurate forecasting and accurate costing in terms of levels of output and marketing expenditure.

Problems lie in the fact that, despite the importance of other factors, price remains a factor of demand, and this method ignores the influence of different price levels on volume.

13. Product-line pricing. Many companies selling a wide range of products gear pricing to a range of products rather than to individual products. It may be considered that certain products yielding a comparatively low profitable return are necessary to support products which yield a high profit. At the extreme some products may even be "loss leaders"—products which are basically non-profitable or just cover cost—which stimulate buying of other profitable lines. "Loss leaders" are a feature of large retailing operations; e.g. a housewife who buys low-priced aspirin tablets may be tempted to buy at the same time a perfume carrying a high profit.

14. Variable pricing. This is most commonly applied to products or services with known variable time demands. It may be used to take advantage of extra profit at peak periods or to reduce production and overhead costs by stimulating demand in non-peak periods. Hotel rates may be high in peak holiday seasons and low in winter and autumn. Specially reduced rates for use of electricity at off-peak periods may be introduced to utilise output more effectively and even cut the production load.

Occasionally differential pricing may be negotiated with individual customers, though this is a risky practice, or disproportionately high profit margins may be demanded for unusual extras, such as a television set with a particular type of wooden cabinet or a car with special chrome fittings.

15. Competitive-based pricing. Most companies set prices after careful consideration of competitive price structure. Deliberate policies may be formulated to sell above, below or generally in line with competition. One of the problems here is that cost and profit structures and practice will differ. The more closely a company's price policy is geared to match or undercut competitive prices, the more important it is to bring cost in line, to accept a lower rate of return or to provide a product package which is really different.

Many companies attempt to keep price levels in line with an average rate for the industry (the "going rate"). The "going rate" is a valid policy where market conditions are highly competitive and where products are narrowly differentiated. This is a major problem of commodity and raw material trading, upon which many underdeveloped countries depend so much.

Close competitive pricing is also found in markets where one company or a small group of companies is in a highly dominant position and can either directly or indirectly regulate prices of materials or components used by small price-cutting organisations, or stand the strain of a price war much more readily. In some cases one company clearly emerges as a price leader.

16. Bid pricing. When contracts are awarded as a result of tender, e.g. government contracts and large-scale plant construction, companies must clearly attempt to determine the level of competitive bids. If the object is to obtain the contract, cost will be considered mainly to determine the minimum price level. Calculations of anticipated profit against probability of tender price acceptance may be undertaken. Mathematical models have recently been developed with some success especially to cater for situations in which a previous history of competitive-bid data exists, e.g. in open tender conditions. In some cases, models take account both of past data and subjective probability estimates, by knowledgeable executives, of success or failure at a range of price levels. The significant advantage of models which are in use is that the successful bid price is regularly above that which would have been the outcome of conventional methods.

THE COST BASE

In practice, the build-up of price consists of an estimate of cost and a mark-up on that cost. In determining cost, three principal approaches are in common use.

(*a*) Full, total or absorption costing.

(*b*) Direct costing.

(*c*) Marginal costing.

17. Full, total or absorption costing. The essential feature of the approach is that an attempt is made to apportion all expenses, whether they can be traced directly or not to a product. Apportionment of overheads follows some "reasonable" convention, but is of necessity arbitrary. It is claimed that this approach avoids the danger of incomplete recovery of overheads and appropriate profit. No account is taken of the fact that some products will inevitably be more price-sensitive than others, and its acceptance for all pricing decisions will normally lead to both under- and over-pricing, since market forces are ignored.

Oil has presented very special pricing problems, since, as has been stated, in power industries such as oil it is often impossible to avoid producing several products simultaneously. There are thus difficulties in allocating joint costs to particular products under reasonably stable world conditions. Between 1973 and 1975, however, the decline in demand for OPEC oil was around 20% and an overall period of general economic recession was set in train in the majority of Western industrialised countries. The recession was uneven in its effect on countries and on particular markets within these countries. Governments pursued differing policies in coping with this problem and the associated inflationary pressures. Hence the need for fundamental rethinking of pricing strategies by the oil refineries and distributors.

18. Direct costing. This approach represents an attempt to include in a product or process cost calculation only those costs which are directly incurred and which could be avoided in the medium or long term if the particular product or process were discontinued. Such costs may include factory costs, selling or other costs, e.g. research and physical distribution, which are specific to a product or product range.

Both fixed- and variable-cost elements are also included. Although organisations using direct costing methods have developed reasonably sophisticated systems of charging production cost at a given standard level of output, there is often a lack of data analysis in terms of direct marketing expenditure incurred in connection with specific product and customer market groups. As there is increasing evidence that a very high proportion of business potential is concentrated on relatively few customers, products and geographical areas, there is a need to develop more detailed information wherever possible on marketing costs directly attributable to specific product market groupings.

Perhaps the most important disadvantage of direct costing methods is that, since these ignore the distinction between fixed and variable costs, it is not possible to assess the effect of volume changes.

19. Marginal costing. The essential feature of this costing method, which is known as *variable costing* in the USA, is the emphasis placed on the separation of costs into two main sections, namely, fixed and variable. Fixed costs are those which tend to remain constant, regardless of changes in output. Variable costs are those which tend to vary with output. In accounting practice, marginal cost differs from the economist's use of the term. Marginal cost to the economist is the increment to total cost of the last unit produced. The accounting approach takes average variable costs within given ranges of output.

The method has great advantages in its ability to highlight the effect of changes in volume, price or costs. Once an appropriate price/volume relationship has been established to cover variable costs, additional revenue becomes a "contribution" towards recovery of fixed cost, overhead and profit. Profit/volume sensitivity is of particularly great importance where the level of committed fixed costs is high. Clearly, the level of committed fixed costs also indicates the level of price above which an order is preferable to having plant idle. At the same time, marginal costing methods also allow for a consideration of opportunity cost in decision-making, e.g. what would be the likely outcome of raising price on product X, with a resultant loss of some volume and revenue, if this loss could be more than offset by using the released capacity to generate additional sales revenue on product Y?

The two principal arguments against marginal costing are:

(a) There is often a practical difficulty in segregating fixed and variable expense—and such a segregation can only be valid for specified ranges of output and time.

(b) There is a danger that, if every price decision is taken on the basis of marginal cost, fixed expenses and profit will not be adequately recovered, and this situation can be intensified if short-term pressures on price become hardened in the longer term.

It is important for marketers to understand the principles, advantages and disadvantages of the main approaches to costing. Different cost conventions may be required for different decisions. Some costs bases will certainly represent the pricing floor. Total costing represents neither the true floor nor the true ceiling for good strategic decisions. Marginal and direct costing approaches, on the other hand, may both be regarded as valid—and sometimes complementary—approaches to the strategic managerial aspects of pricing decisions.

DISCOUNTS

Discounts involve the offer of reductions (differentials) from a base price and must also be considered when price policy is being determined. The following are the most usual forms:

20. Trade discounts. In areas where there is resale price maintenance

(R.P.M.), such as in some parts of the USA, the fixed retail price is usually the base. Elsewhere, as now in the UK, a suggested or expected retail selling price might be used. Prices to retailers might be at list price less a percentage discount to cover the retailer's margin. Prices to wholesalers might be at list price, less retail discount, less a discount to cover the wholesaler's margin. Although, except in R.P.M. conditions, there is no control over resale prices, discounts have some stabilising influence on final prices.

NOTE: Some companies argue that R.P.M. is itself an important stabilising influence and that marked price disparities at retail can lead to such a value uncertainty in customers' minds that demand is seriously inhibited.

21. Quantity discounts. Price advantages might be offered on the basis of order size or particular assortments.

Quantity discounts might be applied to retailers and wholesalers within their own prices structure, or there may be a general quantity rate pricing structure which gives bulk-buying advantages to retailers and wholesalers equally—size of business or order being the only criterion.

Quantity discounts may attract large buyers or induce smaller buyers to order large quantities. Most quantity discount arrangements apply to either single orders or single deliveries and these involve economies of scale in transportation and administration. Some discounts are paid retrospectively on the basis of orders received or goods delivered. In some countries there are legal restrictions on discount procedures, e.g. in the USA.

22. Cash discounts. Most business transactions from manufacturer to wholesaler and/or retailer are conducted on credit terms. The length of time allowed for payment varies considerably and payment in practice is often delayed beyond the duration of the officially stated credit terms. When this happens the supplier has the problem of deciding how rigidly to press for payment, and whether to refuse to supply further goods. Some suppliers offer a special discount for payment within a stipulated period from the date of invoice.

23. Seasonal discounts. These may be offered to stimulate sales at special times of the year or day, e.g. "off-peak" period railway tickets.

24. Geographical differentials. These are differential rates offered in relation to distance from supply base, e.g. petrol zone pricing, new car delivery.

NOTE: Transportation costs may or may not be included in the price, and this is particularly important in the import/export business. For example, F.O.B. (free on board) indicates that the vendor is selling at a price which includes all charges incurred in placing the goods on board the vessel. Once they are on board, the buyer bears the risk and any subsequent expenses. A C.I.F. price covers the cost of goods, insurance and freight, the buyer taking no responsibility until he takes the goods from the ship at their destination.

PRICE CHANGE AND CUSTOMER ATTITUDES

25. Problems of price-changing. The risks involved in price change either upwards or downwards are so great that suppliers are usually slow to act. They are particularly slow to move prices upwards, knowing that such action will affect competitors, ultimate buyers, intermediaries, and will also be subject to government scrutiny. The fact that prices of particular types of products tend to move upwards or downwards at a particular time may be the result of:

(*a*) Unofficial inter-company communications.

(*b*) Changes in cost factors which affect all suppliers, e.g. variations in material costs, new wage agreements.

(*c*) A fear of loss of business if prices are not competitive.

(*d*) Action which should have been taken previously but has been delayed in order to avoid placing the company in an isolated pricing situation.

26. Estimating reaction to price changes. Some of the methods of pre-judging reaction are as follows:

(*a*) *Attitude surveys:* field interviews based on statistical samples.

(*b*) *The use of mathematical models* constructed from significant and controllable socio-economic variable factors.

(*c*) *Statistical estimates* based on regression analysis and simple or multiple correlation (*see* **27** below).

(*d*) *Experimental pricing* in limited test markets.

(*e*) *The use of operations research techniques*, such as game theory, to anticipate likely competitive reaction (*see* **28** below).

27. Regression and correlation analysis. Regression analysis is a statistical method of examining the past trends of relationships between one variable, e.g. sales volume, and one or more than one other variable, e.g. advertising expenditure, cost of salesmen. Correlation analysis is a statistical method by which it is possible to measure the closeness of those relationships. Regression analysis will show that there is a relationship between disposable personal income and the sales of most consumer goods. Correlation analysis will show how close that relationship is in the case of specific consumer items. When an increase in one variable coincides with an increase in another, the two variables have a positive correlation. When an increase in one coincides with a decrease in the other, the variables have a negative correlation. The highest possible correlation is expressed at + or − 1. Simple correlation is restricted to the relationship between two variables. Multiple correlation takes into account the simultaneous relationship of more than two variables.

28. The use of operations research techniques. Operations research is a comparatively new science derived from many disciplines, e.g. mathematics, physics, engineering, economics. A basic concept is the building of a model, usually mathematical, i.e. sets of equations relating significant variables in a situation to the outcome. Professor Stone of Cambridge has constructed a model of the economy, for example, in an effort to study and forecast the effect of changes of variables, e.g. Gross National Product, on the whole economy and on other variables.

Operations research is essentially designed to assist in resolving complex problems and after being developed in the 1940s to tackle military problems it is now being applied increasingly to business situations.

The most familiar type of pricing model is based on multiple regression, a linear functional relationship being sought between sales and marketing input variables such as personal selling efforts and costs, level of advertising, distribution and service support, etc. Regression analysis can also be used to produce models which aim to give decision-makers the chance of experimenting with various levels and combinations of strategic input to simulate probable outcomes. Some experiments have been carried out in the application of games theory technique, by which there is an attempt to examine systematically the possible reactions of a competitor or competitors to a company's change in pricing strategy—and the consequent company outcomes (pay-off) (*see also* **16**).

In practice, few pricing models are in regular use and the use of purely historical economic data is unlikely to lead to models of predictive usefulness. Behavioural facts must also be considered.

29. Behavioural factors. Psychological and sociological factors have a considerable influence on buying decisions in both consumer and industrial markets. There is, for example, a great deal of evidence to indicate that a buying choice is influenced by a high "perceived" element of risk. Lack of confidence in assessing the relative quality of items leads to acceptance of a higher price as a quality indicator and, in many cases, to buying at a high price to avoid risk. Risk may be perceived to be low in buying some products which have come to be regarded as non-differentiated commodities, e.g. salt. Value judgment is seen to be much more difficult in the purchasing of tape recorders or carpets, and price becomes a quality indicator —particularly so if there is the reinforcing support of peer-group experience or opinion.

In industrial markets, recent research work has indicated that in cases where a product-buying situation has become a routine procedure, with an established buyer–seller relationship, it is rare for that relationship to be broken at all—and similar products and services are unlikely to be considered on a price basis unless the differential is in the order of 10% or more. Even then the risk avoidance factor is strong if other processes or products are likely to be affected, and if the decision is to be taken by a single buyer isolated from the comforting support of other executives.

Amongst other considerations are the following:

(*a*) It may be thought a product is *faulty* or comparatively unacceptable and, therefore, has to be at a reduced price. However, established price values do persist and, provided there is *quality acceptance*, reduced prices may be seen as bargains.

(*b*) Experienced buyers may anticipate *further reductions* and wait until they judge prices have reached their lowest level.

(*c*) It could be imagined that there was a *danger of obsolescence*. Price reductions sometimes precede the entry of new models.

(*d*) Buyers—especially industrial buyers—*may prefer maximum price stability* as an indication of reliable trading practice. Frequent price changes may give an imrression of financial instability.

(*e*) Many purchasers—particularly domestic consumers—are *unaware of the precise price* of a wide range of goods and only become aware if there is a change, when they tend to re-assess the values of competing products.

(*f*) Customers may not have a precise knowledge of prices of existing products but they usually have *firm ideas of upper and lower* limits or a "price zone." Prices outside the zone may have to overcome additional psychological barriers. The price zones for new products are much more vague and there is little or no opportunity to compare. This greater pricing latitude for new products is not always utilised by manufacturers.

(*g*) *Some people like to be innovators* or to be seen as innovators; others follow. Price attitudes of leaders and followers may be quite different.

(*h*) Price notions may be geared to the *coinage system.* Elementary use of this idea, such as £1.99 instead of £2, is still sometimes effective, but there may be other price barriers associated with coinage which we know little about.

PRICING TACTICS AND DEMAND

30. Pricing and research and development costs. Frequently companies set prices for new products with the objective of recovering research and development costs in a given time period. Research costs do not necessarily relate to individual product success and an attempt to recover disproportionately high research and development costs by high pricing may indeed reduce profit by inhibiting demand.

There is much to be said for covering the costs of research and development by aiming at the highest revenue above marginal cost. Consumers will not pay for research as such, but for the *distinctive utility*—economic, psychological or social—which the product offers. In the last resort, products should be measured by the contribution they make to overhead and profit. Working in reverse and basing prices on arbitrary allocation of general overheads, whether they be management, research or clerical administration, can never be justified except perhaps for a "one-off" guaranteed sale.

31. Indirect pricing differentials. Non-listed special allowances, service provision and other concessions are sometimes given (to major customers) in non-differentiated product markets. Other indirect concessions may take the form of margin guarantees, special credit terms and allowances to whosesaler, retailer or agency advertising or promotional campaigns.

Indirect price competition is openly seen in many consumer markets in offers of various kinds, e.g. the use of coupons for free trials or for purchases at reduced prices. There are, for example, banded packs with two similar products at a special price, premium offers of gifts on purchase, and "trade-in" concessions for durable items. These special offers to domestic consumers may be supported by special deals to channel intermediaries. Some offers are described as self-liquidating, e.g. goods supplied at bargain prices in return for tokens indicating product purchase. Theoretically the "bargains" are achieved by the promoter obtaining goods at bulk prices and passing on the advantages to individual customers.

32. Reasons for special promotions. In general, however, special promotions represent a temporary price cut and are used for various reasons:

(a) *Novelty appeal.* It is claimed that permanent price cuts are easily imitated and it is difficult to return to the original prices. Promotions on the other hand have a novelty appeal and can be a way of differentiating one product from another.

(b) *Psychological advantage.* Promotions, it is said, have a psychological advantage in creating a greater impression of extra value than a price cut.

(c) *New customers.* A special offer may be the means of persuading people to try a product for the first time and some of the business gained will be retained when prices are normal; loyal customers also gain the advantages of the temporary price cuts.

(d) *Opportunities for selling.* Promotions in highly competitive consumer markets provide salesmen with a series of new presentations and an opportunity for acquiring shelf space. These promotions are almost invariably supported by display materials.

(e) *Uneven demand.* Promotions may help to smooth out uneven demand.

In general, promotions are more frequent at the launching of a new product campaign.

Over recent years, as far as many consumer goods markets are concerned, the balance of power has tended to move away from the major manufacturers to the large retailing and wholesaling groups. This move is associated with two important developments which have led to greater in-store display and promotional activity. Firstly, there is the growth of private label brands; secondly there is the more intensive application—certainly at retail group HQ level —of the criterion of return on investment. To counter the first of these developments and to capitalise on the second, manufacturers are spending greater proportions of their advertising budgets on special promotions and deals, and the battle for shelf space is, in some cases, being waged in retail outlets not only by salesmen but by special teams of merchandisers.

33. Pack size and price. It is sometimes difficult for a customer to compare prices of similar products since there is often a wide range of pack size and differences in the weight of the contents. Although it may be necessary legally for the manufacturers to stipulate on a carton the weight of the contents, the purchaser may completely disregard weight–price comparison, or be unable to make the comparison, e.g. between grammes and cubic centimetres. The increase in pre-packed consumer goods has made direct price comparison much more difficult. Frequently virtual price increases are disguised by decreasing the size of the pack, e.g. in confectionery.

34. Competitive pricing and company policy. Pricing policy, as has been seen, is related intuitively or by calculation to cost, demand and/or competition. Companies should, therefore, study not only their own costs but also likely competitive cost structure. If competitors change prices it will be necessary to decide on a line of action. The more products are seen to be similar, the more likely it is that prices will move in line. On the other hand, there have been examples of a company's maintaining prices when competitive prices move up and yet successfully improving market share or profits.

If products are differentiated a company must consider what part price plays in the total marketing mix. After determining why a competitor has reduced price, for example, it will be necessary to estimate whether the price change is likely to be permanent and what the likely outcomes of various reactions might be. Competitive price cuts could be met by temporary indirect offers or a change in packaging, or an increase in advertising and sales effort. The timing of reaction will be important. It may be essential in some market situations to adjust prices immediately—in others there will be an opportunity to wait.

35. Information systems needs for pricing decisions. It is evident that there is a pressing need for more sophisticated information systems to be established, so that specific pricing decisions in rapidly changing market situations can be made reasonably speedily, easily and effectively, yet be in line with a consistent overall company policy. The following list, adapted from the work of A. L.

Oxenfeldt, covers data that might be used to design a price-monitoring system:

(*a*) Current sales in units and revenue for different product-market combinations set against previous annual sales.

(*b*) Current and previous years' sales at "off list" prices as a percentage of total company, product, product group, customer or customer group sales.

(*c*) Market shares—current and previous year.

(*d*) Current competitive prices by product and market category compared with previous year.

(*e*) Current and past marketing costs; actual production costs, and production costs at accepted level of maximum.

(*f*) Stocks of company and, where appropriate, reseller finished goods—the incidence of significantly high and low levels, including "out of stock" situations.

(*g*) Behavioural studies of customers' attitudes towards the company and its pricing practices.

(*h*) Salesmen and customer reports of price dissatisfaction.

(*i*) Incidence of new customers, lost customers and enquiries, by product-market categories.

Behavioural aspects of price must be taken into account in developing practical models which will reveal to pricing decision-makers: (*a*) the key sensitive variables in defined product-market segments to which attention must be paid; and (*b*) the likely outcomes of alternative courses of action.

36. Transfer pricing relates to the policies and procedures to be followed by determining appropriate prices for inter- and intra-company transactions where there is common ownership. A process of vertical integration, with goods being transferred from one company to another at various stages of production, is a classic illustration of the need to determine, subject to statutory limitations, a clear pricing policy. The trend towards decentralisation with, for example, divisions being treated as profit centres as a prime method of performance measurement and motivation can conflict with a requirement to optimise corporate profitability. For example, a manager who believes he is judged essentially by profitability measures may feel aggrieved if he is compelled to "sell" a substantial proportion of his output to other divisions at a price artificially depressed below that which he could achieve in the open market.

The morale problem is often mainly attributable to faulty

communications—a lack of explanation of the rationale of the system and assurance of due recognition of imposed constraints in performance assessment. It is impossible to generalise on the extent to which decentralised divisions should be compelled to supply their own company's captive markets at dictated prices. Sometimes, from the point of view of the purchasing division, there is a belief that more favourable terms could be obtained elsewhere. Therefore many economically integrated companies have introduced a degree of "arm's length" trading which has to be delicately balanced so that the main advantages of integration are achieved, but the inter-company parties to buying/selling transactions may indulge in price negotiation—and indeed, on occasion, buy or sell elsewhere. For aspects of transfer pricing in international markets, *see* Chapter XII.

37. Conclusion. Pricing is a key marketing decision area. Doing nothing, provided this is a deliberate decision, is a policy. Successful pricing decisions will always be the result of a combination of art and science, but it is increasingly possible to measure the probabilities of the effect of external forces in the environment in which a company operates. More certainly it is possible to devise pricing policies which meet company objectives. No longer should a company be in the position of effecting a hasty compromise between conflicting objectives in complete ignorance of the likely market response.

PROGRESS TEST 5

1. What are the major factors influencing demand?   (3–6)

2. What is meant by "penetration" pricing and "product line" pricing?   (10, 13)

3. To what extent do companies set prices in line with those of competitors?   (15)

4. What are the main types of discount?   (20–24)

5. In what ways can the effects of price changes be estimated? (26)

6. What behavioural factors influence the attitudes of buyers to price?   (29)

7. What are the reasons for special promotions?   (32)

8. What data might a company need to establish a comprehensive information system for pricing decisions?   (35)

CHAPTER VI

Advertising and Promotion: Objectives and Institutions

1. Definitions. *Advertising* is non-personal communication directed at target audiences through various media in order to present and promote products, services and ideas. The cost of media space, time and advertisement production is borne by the sponsor or sponsors. It should be distinguished from *publicity*, by means of which an organisation derives benefit from favourable free showings, descriptions and discussions of its products in a variety of media (*see* VII, **41**).

Retailer/wholesaler merchandising, trade shows, exhibitions, product sampling, special offers, demonstrations, etc., are classified as *sales promotion*.

2. UK media and expenditure. Over £2,500 million is being spent annually on various forms of advertising in the eighties. Of this a growing proportion goes on television advertising—and it is early to estimate properly the effect of the introduction of the second commercial channel. The press—national and regional, magazines and periodicals, trade journals, directories etc.—still accounts for more than twice the TV expenditure. In addition, sales promotions are running at 800/900 per month in the continuing retail channel battle.

Apart from the highly significant advent of the new commercial Channel 4, there are two other increased activity areas worthy of note—advertising freesheets and sponsorship. 1981 Advertising Association statistics showed that there were 434 free newspapers accounting for 30% of all weekly titles in the UK. A Verified Free Distribution audit was established in 1980 and this has, no doubt, assisted in attracting advertisers while the quality of the editorial content has improved over the years, attracting the attention of the 80% of the adult population now receiving these publications.

Sponsorship is also very much more on the increase, not only because of the very positive possibilities of TV exposure but also because of public relations advantages and buyer/executive hospitality opportunities presented. Glyndebourne Opera attracts

87

corporate membership from such companies as the Midland Bank, IBM and Costain; tents and marquees at Henley Regatta proclaim the names of the Reed Group, BOC and Norwich Union and at Wimbledon Beechams, Barclays Bank and Commercial Union backing is evident. Individual company sponsorship of sporting events, of teams and of players is increasingly to be seen but the costs are often high and the marketing results extremely difficult to identify and measure.

Direct mailing is steadily increasing but still lags behind usage of this medium in such countries as Holland, France, West Germany and the USA.

Advertising by companies marketing industrial goods and services is gaining ground and it is interesting to see that even the growth rate of TV usage by such organisations is in the order of 25% p.a.

Media availability and use differ very considerably from country to country. The differences depend on a number of factors:

(a) the technical development of communication systems;

(b) country size and cultural differences;

(c) buying power—particularly the distribution of discretionary consumer income;

(d) educational development—particularly standards of literacy;

(e) national legal restrictions on advertising;

(f) the structure of distributive systems;

(g) the relative costs of the media which are available.

Advertising is a part of total marketing communications and must be considered in terms of markets and products at very differing stages of development.

TOTAL COMMUNICATIONS AND THE MARKETING MIX

3. The marketing mix. The complex of marketing decisions which may stimulate sales is frequently called "the marketing mix" —a term originally used by Professor Neil Borden of the Harvard Business School. The marketing mix may be seen to consist of elements concerned with the product, e.g. range, price, quality, with channels of distribution, and with communications. Communications involve the whole process of communication with markets, e.g. advertising, personal selling, public relations. The sales-task approach to fixing and measuring the effectiveness of advertising expenditure depends on an understanding of the various possibilities of combinations of elements in the marketing mix. The basic elements of the marketing mix for machine tools may be products of rigid quality-control standards, high unit prices, low advertising expenditure, high personal selling cost, direct distribution from manufacturer to user. In contrast, the basic marketing mix for flour may involve greater product quality variation, low unit price, comparatively high advertising expenditure with low personal selling cost and indirect distribution through wholesalers and retailers.

Just as marketing goals and strategies depend on the formulation of corporate goals, strategies and policies, so total communication goals and strategies depend on those of marketing.

4. The integration of marketing and communication objectives. In a handbook of this kind it is not practicable to explore the great diversity of marketing goals and strategies which might be applied to specific products or services in specific situations. Fundamentally, however, a business organisation may be following an aggressive strategy to expand a total market and/or its share of that market. It may seek to achieve this by increasing the business it transacts with existing customers and/or by gaining new customers. In some circumstances, it will be pursuing basically a defensive strategy, e.g. seeking to maintain an existing market share. Advertising and promotional objectives and strategies should be integrated with marketing goals and strategies. Objectives are a prerequisite for decisions on budgets, on message strategy, media selection, timing and frequency, and the measurement of effectiveness.

5. Objectives and measurement. As advertising is one of a number of variable elements of marketing strategy, operating in a constantly shifting market environment, it is virtually impossible, except in mail-order selling or certain direct mail campaigns, to quantify exactly its contribution to profits. The more precise the objectives are, however, the easier it is to estimate the value of a campaign and to design an effective campaign.

The following are examples of objectives:

(*a*) To inform potential customers of a new product or service.

(*b*) To indicate new uses of an existing product.

(*c*) To remind customers of an existing product in order to maintain loyalty against competing pressures.

(*d*) To give information about desirable qualities of a product.

(*e*) To stimulate enquiries.

(*f*) To give reasons why wholesalers and retailers should stock a product.

(*g*) To provide technical information about a product.

(*h*) To build a corporate company image.

(*i*) To give information on price changes, special offers, etc.

Some of these objectives can be regarded as action objectives, e.g. stimulating enquiries, increasing wholesaler or retailer stock levels. Others are designed to create a mental awareness and/or favourable attitude towards an organisation, its products, services, policies, etc. Although the exact contribution to profits of a particular advertising campaign may be impossible to measure since, for example, a favourable attitude does not necessarily stimulate purchase, nevertheless communication objectives should be set and and the communication achievement measured.

6. The sales-task approach. When sales tasks can be closely defined, e.g. to increase product awareness amongst decision-makers in a given percentage of a market during a predetermined number of months, or to expand dealer stock levels by a certain percentage over a given time period, it is possible not only to direct campaigns specifically towards the achievement of stated tasks, but also to assess the contribution advertising is likely to make towards the accomplishment of those tasks.

7. Advertising and the sales process. It has been said that the sales process consists of six basic steps, *viz*.:

(*a*) making contact;

(*b*) arousing interest;

(*c*) creating preference;

(*d*) making a specific proposal;

(*e*) closing the sale;

(*f*) retaining business.

It is possible to assess the contribution which can most effectively be made by advertising towards the achievement of one or more stated objectives at each of the six stages. The justifiable cost of achieving the contribution by means of advertising can then be assessed in relation to total marketing expense. Consideration can also be given to the cost of alternative means of communication, e.g. employing extra salesmen. In this way a more realistic measurement of the economic level of advertising expenditure can frequently be made.

8. Factors influencing buying decisions. The sales-task approach to fixing and measuring the effectiveness of advertising expenditure is not always possible, and when it is used it is clear that the probability assessments of the contribution that advertising can make towards the attainment of objectives must rely on judgment as well as on facts. Apart from the problems involved in estimating the external changing market forces affecting sales (e.g. competitive activity, economic climate, customer attitudes, trade attitudes and government controls), a marketing organisation has to take into account the wide range of forces it can bring to bear in order to influence buying decisions. A potential customer may be influenced to a greater or lesser extent by any combination of the following:

(*a*) Performance of the product.

(*b*) Aesthetic design features.

(*c*) Packaging.

(*d*) Service facilities available.

(*e*) Advertising.

(*f*) Promotions which give temporary special incentives to buy.

(*g*) Personal selling efforts.

(*h*) Channels of distribution—outlet images, location.

(*i*) Margins allowed to dealers along the distribution channels.

(*j*) Distinctiveness of the product, e.g. branding, quality.

(*k*) Price to the ultimate buyer.

(*l*) Credit facilities.

(*m*) Store display.

(*n*) Convenience of handling in transportation, warehousing or end use.

(*o*) The opinions of others.

(*p*) Ready availability of goods or services.

ADVERTISING—EXPENDITURE AND STRATEGIC CONSIDERATIONS

9. Advertising expenditure. Advertising expenditures in relation to total marketing costs (costs of physical distribution and promotion as opposed to production costs) vary very widely. Sometimes they may be as high as 40% or 50%; sometimes as low as $\frac{1}{2}$%. In general, the percentage of advertising expenditure is a greater proportion of marketing costs in the case of consumer than of industrial goods and services. Regularly repeatable consumer products with mass distribution objectives, such as soap and chocolates, are particularly heavily advertised. There has, however, in recent years been a noticeable increase in marketing activity in service industries and banks, building societies, airlines, insurance companies, electricity, gas and transport undertakings have become substantial advertisers.

Too frequently the basis for an advertising budget is completely subjective. Marketing research, costing studies and operations research can increasingly assist in determining the appropriate budget to be allocated to advertising and promotion elements of the marketing mix.

Some of the attacks made on high levels of advertising expenditure take no account of the cost frequently incurred by other elements of the marketing mix. In the 1966 Monopolies Commission investigations, evidence was provided to show, for example, that, while detergent advertising and promotions accounted for 16% of marketing costs as opposed to 6% in the case of ice cream, trade margins for detergents were restricted to 19%, while they were as high as 32% for ice cream. The strategies of individual companies marketing similar products may differ considerably. The optimal allocation of funds to the various elements of the marketing mix at various times and in various product marketing contexts continues to present enormous problems. The most voluminous research activity is being devoted to the building of mathematical models. At the same time, there is a growing exploration of the use of payoff matrices based on various expectations of risk, competitive response, and marketing mix options. (See the work by Allen listed in the Bibliography.)

10. Pull and push strategies. When greater reliance is placed on the personal selling efforts of a company's sales force or of distributor salesmen than on advertising, an organisation may be said to be pursuing a "push" strategy. A "push" strategy is typical of the marketing of industrial machinery, for example. Where it is not possible to bring strong direct selling pressure to bear on the end customer a "pull" strategy may be used. Manufacturers selling grocery products, for example, usually feel that there is inadequate personal selling effort directed by wholesalers and retailers and great attention is paid to advertising and promotion which "pull" the product along the channels of the distribution and into the hands of the ultimate buyer. Push and pull strategies are therefore related to the types of products being marketed, and also to the external forces bearing on markets and company policies at particular time periods.

ADVERTISING AND THE PUBLIC INTEREST

11. Criticism of advertising. The following criticisms of advertising are frequently made:

(a) Advertising is wasteful, particularly in times of scarce internal resources.

(b) In certain circumstances heavy advertising by a dominant supplier may restrict competition by preventing new entrants to its markets.

12. Economic justification of advertising. One answer to the first charge (**11** (a)) is basically that successful companies must be profit-minded and organise their expenditure in a way calculated to obtain the best return. From a company point of view advertising may be justified when the increase in revenue is greater than the cost of advertising provided that this is the most satisfactory— and profitable—of the various possible uses of scarce resources. As far as countries are concerned, it is interesting to note that in recent years improvements in GNP per capita of individual developed countries have not been matched by relative increases in percentage expenditure on advertising. The EEC countries, excluding the UK, have relatively low levels of expenditure compared with those of the USA, the UK and Australia.

13. Advertising and the danger of monopoly. The second point of criticism (**11** (b)) implies that by means of advertising a company can create such a consumer loyalty that it can build up the level of its sales to a scale where advertising becomes a very small proportion of individual unit costs; the resulting economies of scale will provide the opportunity for pricing flexibility along the distribution chain. This pricing flexibility, it is argued, could be used to prevent the entry of competition not having advantages of large-scale production and distribution. This goal achieved, prices could be raised to a level of unethical exploitation of the consumer. A monopoly, or oligopoly, operating contrary to the public interest could thus be created.

This second criticism is based on the premise that companies lack ethical standards, a premise which could be argued at length. The larger and more successful a company becomes, the more its policies are under public scrutiny and business ethics are no longer a matter of academic discussion; they are the vital concern of boardrooms.

Accepting, however, a lack of ethical considerations, the

criticism rests upon *the mistaken notion that products and markets do not change*. Examples of companies who have been able to enter fields dominated by more powerful organisations by providing products having demonstrable technological or economic advantages are not difficult to find. Wilkinson's inroads into the razor-blade market against the powerful Gillette; Lloyd's Auto-motives' breakthrough into the car-care field against giants such as Johnson's, Simoniz and Howard's; and Damart's capture of 50 per cent of the rapidly expanding UK thermal underwear market by 1982—these are just three examples of outstanding success in the marketing of consumer goods where advertising is normally reckoned to be such a large factor in the marketing mix. It might be argued that new entrants in fields where products are more narrowly differentiated are more difficult to find, e.g. petrol, chocolate, cigarettes, but in the case of petrol there is also the important barrier of very high capital investment costs, while chocolate prices in the UK are lower than anywhere in Europe.

14. Public benefit from advertising. An argument in support of advertising and the public interest which is often ignored is that by advertising a supplier is identifying his company or his company's products. This attempt to create a distinction must be accom-panied, if it is to be successful, by the setting of quality standards. Research has shown that, while it is sometimes possible to find that the price of certain strongly advertised products may be higher than those of a random selection of non-advertised goods, the variation in quality of the advertised products is much less than that of the non-advertised products. Advertising, therefore, would appear to reduce the risk to the consumer of buying low-quality products.

CONTROL OF ADVERTISING

Advertising is subject to restrictions in various media, imposed by both internal and external bodies. Some of these voluntary and statutory controls are outlined in **15–19** below.

15. The British Code of Advertising Practice. This code is accepted by all organisations operating advertising media—press, television, cinema, posters, direct mail. The code was first published in 1962 and revisions are made from time to time, but many voluntary control systems had been applied long before that. The *Molony Committee on Consumer Protection* in its 1962 report gave support to the principle of *voluntary control* embodied in the Code. A revised, more comprehensive and detailed Code was issued in 1979.

(a) *Member organisations*. These include:

(i) the Advertising Association;
(ii) the British Poster Advertising Association;
(iii) the Independent Television Companies Association;
(iv) the Institute of Practitioners in Advertising;
(v) the Screen Advertising Association;
(vi) the Newspaper Publishers' Association;
(vii) the Newspaper Society;
(viii) the British Direct Mail Advertising Association;
(ix) the Direct Mail Producers' Association;
(x) the Periodical Publishers' Association.

(b) *Basis of the Code*. No advertisements contravening the Code may be accepted for publication (*see* **16**). The Code covers such matters as:

(i) public decency;
(ii) exploitation of superstition;
(iii) appeals to fear;
(iv) misleading descriptions and claims, including scientific terms, testimonials, price, guarantees, disparagement, imitations, medicines, mail order, advertisements addressed to children.

16. The Advertising Standards Authority. This body was established as a limited company in 1962 and is independent of the advertising industry, although it is financed by the Advertising Association. Members are appointed as individuals and not as representatives of an organisation or special group interest. There are a chairman and ten members—five connected with advertising and five entirely independent of advertising interests. The Authority, in addition to keeping in touch with the Committee responsible for the control and revision of the Code, adjudicates on general advertising issues and special disputes amongst advertising bodies. It deals with complaints from the public and investigates action or non-action on reported breaches of the Code.

17. Statutory controls. There are many Acts of Parliament restricting or controlling particular aspects of advertising. There is a growing amount of legislation aimed at protecting the consumer. Students are advised to consult a specialised text for a detailed treatment.

In addition, it should be remembered that much English law is in the form not of statutes but of "common law," which is based on the decisions of various courts since the Middle Ages. Common law is very pertinent to laws of contract and of tort—legal wrongs such as negligence and nuisance.

Examples of recent legislation that students of advertising and marketing should investigate further include the following:

Companies Act 1981.
Companies Act 1980.
Competition Act 1980.
Food Labelling Regulations 1980.
Consumer Credit (Advertisements) Regulations 1980.
Consumer Credit (Quotations) Regulations 1980.
Sale of Goods Act 1979.
Consumer Safety Act 1978.
Unfair Contract Terms Act 1977.
Resale Prices Act 1976.
Restrictive Trade Practices Act 1976. (The rules of EEC Competition Policy are contained in Articles 85 and 86 of the Treaty of Rome.)
Race Relations Act 1976.
Sex Discrimination Act 1975.

Consumer Credit Act 1974.
Fair Trading Act 1973.
Sound Broadcasting Act 1972.
Trade Descriptions Acts (1968–1972).
Unsolicited Goods and Services Act 1971.
Labelling of Food Regulations 1970.
Food and Drugs Act 1965.
Games and Lotteries Act 1963.
Weights and Measures Act 1963.
Protection of Depositors Regulations 1963.
Copyright Act 1956.
Restrictive Trade Practices Act 1956.
Food and Drugs Act 1955.
Television Act 1954.

18. The Independent Broadcasting Authority. British commercial radio came late on the scene compared with commercial television. For control purposes the role of the former Independent Television Authority was extended to embrace the new radio developments under the newly formed Independent Broadcasting Authority. Both media are strictly controlled through the IBA by Act of Parliament and must adhere to a stringent and comprehensive code of advertising standards aimed at prevention rather than prosecution after the event. These standards are regularly revised in consultation with the Advertising Advisory Committee, a Medical Advisory Panel and the Home Secretary. The constitution of the Advertising Advisory Committee, representing advertising interests and the public as consumers with an independent chairman, is laid down in the Act.

The Authority is also required to appoint or take the advice of a Medical Advisory Panel. In practice, the IBA Advertising Control Division, working closely with a specialist advertising copy group set up by the programme companies, scrutinises in advance of filming over 7,000 new television advertisement scripts per year. After enquiry and discussion some 20% are returned for amendment. Finished films are further scrutinised in closed circuit viewing sessions and some 2–3% require further revision before final acceptance. Radio commercials are also subjected to a strict copy control clearance procedure.

19. Other codes and standards. Individual organisations within the advertising industry endeavour to control advertising standards by setting their own very specific regulations for membership or for accepting advertisements. Amongst these are:

(*a*) The "Bye-Laws Relating to the Standards of Practice" of the Institute of Practitioners in Advertising.

(*b*) "Regulations covering the Acceptance of Advertisements for Display," issued by British Transport Advertising Ltd.

(*c*) "Standards of Practice Regulating Contracts for Localised Advertising," drawn up by the Advertising Association.

(*d*) "Form of Application by an Advertising Agency," for recognition by the Newspaper Publishers' Association Ltd., and the Newspaper Society.

(*e*) "Standard Conditions of Insertion of Advertisements," in newspapers in membership of the Newspaper Publishers' Association.

(*f*) "Standard Conditions of Trading," laid down by the British Poster Advertising Association and the London Poster Advertising Association Ltd.

(*g*) "Advertising Film Standard Conditions," agreed by the Screen Advertising Association and the Institute of Practitioners in Advertising.

(*h*) "Standard Conditions observed by Producer House Members," of the British Direct Mail Advertising Association.

ADVERTISING AGENCIES

20. What are advertising agencies? Advertising agencies are specialists in the planning, creating and placing of advertising. They function, therefore, between the advertiser and the media owners. An agency may assist in suggesting product features or sources of ideas. It may be asked to design trademarks and packaging, to advise on selling and promotional policy and to plan advertising campaigns. It will have artists and copywriters for creative work or will arrange for this to be done. Agencies prepare advertising schedules of media to be used and reserve and pay for the space or time (*see* **23** and **25** below).

21. Numbers and business transacted. There are over 600 advertising agencies in the UK with great variations in size of business transacted (billings), numbers employed, and range of services offered. Almost all national advertisers (over 25,000) use advertising agencies, even though they may have their own advertising departments. Many regional and local advertisers—and there are probably as many as 40,000 of these—use agencies to some extent. Some 70% of all expenditure on advertising media passes through agency hands. More than half of the agencies are members of the Institute of Practitioners in Advertising and these account for some 90% of total agency business.

22. IPA conditions. Conditions of membership of the IPA by an agency are that:

(*a*) It is equipped to provide the kind and type of advertising service and marketing advice to which the advertiser is entitled.

(*b*) Its personnel includes Fellows and/or Members of the Institute.

(*c*) It promises to observe the Institute's standards of practice.

(*d*) It is free from any vested interest in advertising media or facilities.

(*e*) It will avoid advertisements of an undesirable, unethical or offensive nature.

(*f*) It will not canvass accounts of fellow members unless at the written invitation of the advertiser.

(*g*) It will not submit speculative advertisement designs or copy to any but its own clients except on payment of an adequate fee and only after an exhaustive study of a client's problems at first hand.

23. Agency renumeration. Agencies receive from the media owners a commission ranging from 10% to 15% on time or space booked. As agencies are involved in providing marketing research, marketing and campaign plans and other services it is sometimes necessary for them to fix a minimum charge for small accounts or to ask for a special service charge. Many specialist trade and professional papers allow only 10% commission and this fact, together with the comparatively low level of advertising expenditure of companies using these publications, frequently leads to agencies specialising in mass consumer goods campaigns. It is now common practice for agencies to make arrangement for service fees to bring their minimum percentage return on turnover to 15% or more.

The agency accepts credit responsibility for its client as far as the media are concerned and media owners have, therefore, no legal right of action against an advertiser in the case of default. Agencies must, therefore, be investigated and recognised as financially sound by official media owners' organisations.

24. Creativity and campaign planners. There is a growing tendency for agencies to become involved in total marketing strategy and it is sometimes suggested that, as a result, the really major work of an agency—creativity—suffers. There is certainly considerable evidence that a great deal of advertising is dull and unimaginative. Potential customers are becoming subjected to more and more advertising and there is a need for freshness of impact if campaigns are to be effective. The constant repetition of badly conceived advertising may well create buying resistance. On the other hand, it is obviously necessary for agencies to understand an advertiser's corporate strategy and marketing objectives, and close working relationships should exist.

The increase in overheads of agencies has led to more vigorous financial discipline, and more agencies now subcontract work to freelance copywriters and visualisers. In addition, a number of "hot shops" have been set up. These organisations consist of a small number of principals who plan campaigns from modest offices and studios, sub-contracting creative work as required.

25. Agency personnel. The agency link man is the *account executive* who works with the brand manager or appropriate company advertising executive. The account executive calls upon agency or outside experts in organising the campaign in line with the advertiser's objectives. The agency, therefore, employs or engages the temporary services of specialists in copywriting, creative art, typography, printing, television and film production, as required. It has staff who specialise in, advise on and plan the use of various media, in addition to those who actually buy space or time. Larger agencies have ancillary services such as marketing research departments which may undertake tasks such as testing advertising impact or providing information necessary for campaign strategy. The large agency with high billings can afford to carry specialist staff which even the largest advertiser would find difficult to justify economically, and the constant employment of that staff—often on related products in similar markets—can provide a wealth of experience on which to draw. Conversely, it could be argued that frequently repeated narrow experience can lead to creative sterility.

Agency organisations differ enormously and so do the needs of advertisers. An advertiser with a large marketing department of its own is unlikely to require the same kind of strategic advice which is required by an advertiser with a small marketing staff.

26. Advertising organisations. The Advertising Association is sometimes described as the "umbrella" organisation of the advertising industry and has been reconstructed as a federation of the following advertising bodies covering advertisers, media and agencies:

British Direct Mail Advertising Association (BDMAA)
British Printing Industries Federation (BPIF)
Direct Mail Producers Association (DMPA)
Graphic Reproduction Federation (GRF)
Incorporated Advertising Managers' Association (IAMA)
Institute of Practitioners in Advertising (IPA)
Incorporated Society of British Advertisers Ltd. (ISBA)
Independent Television Companies Association Ltd. (ITCA)
Newspaper Publishers' Association Ltd. (NPA)
Newspaper Society (NS)
Outdoor Advertising Council (OAC)
Proprietary Association of Great Britain Ltd. (PAGB)
Periodical Publishers Association Ltd. (PPA)
Screen Advertising Association Ltd. (SAA)

The recent establishment of the Communication Advertising and Marketing Education Foundation (CAM) is of considerable significance. The Foundation, sponsored by all sections of the advertising business, has, in association with adult colleges in the public sector and correspondence schools, established a diploma course and examination of a high standard which is already making an important contribution to the advertising industry's recruitment and training programme.

27. Joint industry research. The Joint Industry Committee for Television Advertising Research (JICTAR), representing the Independent Television Companies Association, the Incorporated Society of British Advertisers and the IPA, publishes regular reports on viewing patterns and the "top twenty" programmes. For this purpose, automatic electronic meters are attached to TV sets in 2,650 homes and each household concerned in the sample completes a detailed viewing diary.

The Joint Industry Committee for National Readership Surveys (JICNARS) is formed from representatives of newspaper and periodical publishers, ISBA and the IPA. It publishes annually the results of a continuing survey based on 30,000 interviews and covers over 100 publications. The survey also includes information on Radio Luxembourg, cinema and ITV audiences.

PROGRESS TEST 6

1. Give examples of advertising campaign objectives.   **(5)**

2. What is meant by the "sales task" approach to advertising? **(6)**

3. What is the difference between "pull" and "push" strategies? **(10)**

4. Is advertising against the public interest?   **(11–14)**

5. What are the main provisions of the British Code of Advertising Practice?   **(15)**

6. What kinds of controls over TV and broadcasting advertising standards are exercised in the UK?   **(18, 19)**

7. What are advertising agencies and how are they paid?   **(20–23)**

CHAPTER VII

Advertising and Promotion: Campaign Planning and Evaluation

BASIC STEPS IN CAMPAIGN PLANNING

1. The five basic steps. There are five really basic steps in the process as follows:

(a) Objective (*see* VI, **5**).
(b) The message (copy and design).
(c) Media.
(d) Marketing co-ordination.
(e) Budget.

These are outlined in **2–6** below.

2. Determine the objective of the campaign. This is a task for company management (*see* VI, **3–7** above) and not for the advertising specialist who may, however, cause management objectives to be modified if it is felt they cannot be achieved because of copy, media, budget or other limitations.

3. The message (copy and design). Advertisements consist of verbal symbols, illustrations, colour, movement, sound, etc. Both verbal and non-verbal symbols have denotative (dictionary or literal) and connotative (emotionally associated) communication potential. It is the task of the creative personnel in advertising to achieve the mix most likely to accomplish the purpose of the advertisement. One of the big challenges of the future is to establish an appropriate balance between science and art. It is not a question of science versus art. Creativity and entrepreneurial flair will always be important in marketing. First, the advertiser has to decide which his target audience is and what message he wishes to communicate. Copy and design follow. The success rate which has been achieved in the past almost entirely by flair and chance may be substantially increased in the future as a result of behavioural research into the communication process.

Copy may clearly depend on choice of media, and this and the next step will often be considered together. An early examination of copy is necessary since the whole process of advertising is based on the ability to communicate a message to an audience which should, as a result, react favourably to the product or service. In general, the most effective copy is that which concentrates on a limited selling appeal and frequent repetition of a single appeal is a feature of many very successful campaigns. Certainly many campaigns are spoiled by the attempt to cover too many selling points in one advertisement. Campaigns may, of course, be planned to cover a number of single objectives over a given time, in line with a multiple communications strategy: i.e. to inform potential users of the company's technical achievements; to inform intermediaries in channels of distribution of a new product; to inform users of technical services offered with a new product.

Advertising can be pre-tested to determine whether the intended message is being communicated, and comparisons of the effectiveness of communication of a number of advertisements can also be made. Samples of prospective viewers or readers are exposed to advertisements and certain reactions are measured. Sometimes, tests are carried out on specially constituted panels. The tests may be conducted on the basis of aided or unaided recall of advertisements to which the panel or sample member has been exposed. It should be noted that these tests relate to the effectiveness of the communication as such and do not give a measure of sales results (*see* **9–11** below).

4. Select and schedule appropriate media. Problems of media selection include the following:

(*a*) The extent of coverage required to reach potential buyers and the effective cost of reaching them.

(*b*) The comparative communication effectiveness of various media, e.g. the compatibility of the advertising or editorial material (*see* XI, **16**) with media audiences. An advertisement designed for the popular press might be totally unsuitable in a learned journal.

(*c*) The administrative, organisational and operating requirements of the media, e.g. operating frequency of publication and length of lead time required for placing advertisements.

(*d*) Consideration of the ways in which competitors allocate expenditure to various media.

(*e*) The determination of advertising frequency—"opportunities to view."

(*f*) The size, positioning and/or timing of advertisements.

5. Co-ordinate advertising with the total promotional plan. Amongst co-ordination problems would be those of assigning tasks and expenditure to point-of-sale display, personal selling efforts, dealer-support programmes, handling and follow-up of enquiries, special promotional activity such as premium offers, contests, etc.

6. Determine and control the advertising budget. The size of the budget will, in practice, determine very largely the selection of media, but ideally budgets should be determined by companies after due consideration of the cost of achieving communication objectives.

EVALUATION AND RESEARCH

7. Advertising contribution and research. Basically management needs to know what contribution advertising makes to sales and profits. The complexity of the marketing mix makes precise evaluation extremely difficult. The sales-task method which is based on value judgment of the likely contribution of advertising (*see* VI, **6**, **7**) is gaining ground, but most attempts at evaluation are investigations into specific aspects of advertising in isolation.

8. Target audiences and media data. An advertisement has to reach a specified target audience if it is to have any chance of success at all, but no single media audience is likely to correspond exactly to the advertiser's target market.

Information on media and audience characteristics is readily available to advertisers, and the types of data may be classified as follows:

(*a*) *Data on circulation or viewing*, e.g. the circulation of newspapers and magazines, the number of people passing poster sites, the number of television sets switched on to commercial stations at given times of the day.

(*b*) *Data on total audiences*, e.g. information on the number of readers of a single copy of a newspaper or viewers of a television programme.

(*c*) *Data gained from specific studies* carried out by media owners, on, for example, incomes, spending patterns, buying habits, product usage of readers or viewers (*see* III, **14**).

(*d*) *Data on audience characteristics*, e.g. analysis of readership by social, geographical, economic groupings.

The latest JICNARS social grading categories are as follows:

Group	Adults (>15) approx. %	Men approx. %	Women approx. %
A	3	3	3
B	13	14	12
C_1	22	21	23
C_2	32	35	30
D	21	21	21
E	8	5	11
Million	42.8	20.5	22.3

Source: JICNARS National Readership Surveys, 1979/80.

Social grades used by JICNARS in the National Readership Survey are defined as follows:

	Social status	Occupation
A	Upper middle class	Higher managerial, administrative or professional.
B	Middle class	Intermediate managerial, administrative or professional.
C_1	Lower middle class	Supervisory or clerical and junior managerial, administrative or professional.
C_2	Skilled working class	Skilled manual workers.
D	Working class	Semi- and unskilled manual workers.
E	Those at lowest level of subsistence	State pensioners or widows (no other earner); casual or lowest grade workers.

Even if the objective were simply to reach on one occasion a target audience defined in basic demographic terms, there would be the problem of selecting an effective economic media mix, but there are other considerations with inevitable duplication and wastage factors (*see* **15**).

9. Media research. This is aimed mainly at:

(*a*) analysis of the *actual size of audiences* or readership of print media at particular times; and

(*b*) analysis of *attitudes* towards advertising messages.

Probability samples may be used and data may be collected by electronic devices, e.g. the television measurement system (*see* III,

12 (*d*) above). Most research is, however, undertaken at periods of time after advertisements have been seen. Postal questionnaires and personal interviewing are employed. Selected respondents are sometimes asked to maintain diaries. Researchers may use "aided recall" techniques which imply that memory is stimulated in some way, e.g. by showing a list of programmes and inviting identification of those seen or heard. None of this research gives a measurement of the *sales effectiveness* of advertising.

10. Copy research. This is aimed at assessing the differences in impact of various sizes, themes, layouts, visuals, colours, etc. Research may be carried out both before and after the appearances of an advertisement. The tests used include the following:

(*a*) *Advertisement mock-ups*, shown to consumer juries who are asked to indicate preference, usually by ranking scales or by paired comparisons. The latter method involves a statistical calculation of the number of pairs possible from a given number of trial advertisements. (Paired comparisons are also frequently used for testing reaction to new products.)

(*b*) *Eye movement analysis*, using cameras to trace not only the direction of eye movement but also the length of time spent on particular parts of an advertisement.

(*c*) *Readability studies*, aimed at assessing communication ease and effectiveness. These studies may include research into the understanding and emotional impact of words by people of different standards of education and from different cultural backgrounds as well as studies of word and sentence length, etc.

(*d*) *The use of electronic equipment* to record favourable and unfavourable responses to advertisements.

(*e*) The *Schwerin test* is a method of assessing the effectiveness of advertisements in influencing consumers to buy the product. In a theatre situation an invited audience is exposed to TV or press advertisements. Before and after exposure the audience is asked to place a number of brands in the order in which they would most like to win them as a prize in a lottery. Changes or shifts in preference are then assumed to measure the effect of the advertisement on the audience.

(*f*) *Recognition and recall tests*. These tests are widely carried out by personal interview (usually on the basis of a standard questionnaire); they vary mainly in the extent and method of memory stimulation.

(*g*) *Analysis of enquiries received* from advertisements specifically designed to elicit requests for further information. In mail-order selling and where salesmen can follow up enquiries it is possible to establish an order conversion rate. The conversion rate may, however, depend very largely on marketing factors such as price or special product features.

11. Image research. An increasing number of studies are being made to discover what buyers—whether industrial, wholesale, retail or domestic—think about products and companies. Well-planned attitude studies may lead to changes in the total marketing strategy, and often to redirected emphasis toward company or product image building. There is a growing use of psychologists to undertake this type of research by individual or group discussion methods.

12. Test markets. (*See* IV, **17**, **18**.) The effectiveness of particular campaigns is frequently judged by setting up control and test areas so that, against other known criteria, differences in sales results may be observed. The problems of establishing controls and measuring a range of possibilities, within time constraints imposed by competitive reaction, are obviously very great. The decision to buy is, however, conditioned by price, product design, personal selling efforts, advertising, promotions, user recommendations, availability display, packaging—marketing forces within the control of the seller—as well as by forces outside the seller's control. A buyer must become aware of the existence of a product or service, understand its benefits, become convinced of the desirability of those benefits and take buying action. Ranged against the buying decision are such forces as competition, sales resistance, memory lapse and alternative use of available resources. This complex of variables makes the establishment of research controls to measure the impact of advertising exceedingly difficult and progress during the next decade will depend on four main developments:

(*a*) Clear definition of *advertising goals* as part of the total communications and marketing goals (*see* VI, **4**).

(*b*) More definition of *target audiences*.

(*c*) Greater use of *behavioural science* concepts (*see* III, **34**).

(*d*) The application of *multi-variate statistical techniques*, e.g. factor analysis, with faster, more complex experimental analysis made possible by use of computers. Multi-variate techniques are necessary to examine relationships between sets of variables, e.g. attitudes on first purchase and second purchase, and advertising copy and frequency.

MEDIA AND COSTS

13. Circulation, viewing figures and media cost. The availability, cost and coverage of media differ tremendously in various parts of the world. In general, however, costs of space and time are linked to circulation or viewing figures.

Continuous monitoring of change is necessary. For example, during the ten years to 1982 peak-time viewing ratings on television declined by some 15% and adult audience groups by 25%, while some 60% extra commercial transmission time became available. Loyalty to any one programme is progressively decreasing. Contrast this with the very high loyalty to Sunday newspapers, for example. Consider that during this period people tended to live longer, to leave home earlier, to live in smaller household units (one quarter of households are single-person households; only just over one third have dependent children). New leisure activities boomed, the working week became shorter, holidays longer, more people had cars, travelled and ate out for pleasure. Advertising agencies have changed and a highly competitive field has become more so. Some programme contractors are providing in-house low-cost production, services or consultancy. More video tape is being used, also more 165 mm film. Media buying shops have been set up and these small agencies are concentrating on creativity with media contractors now taking their work through specialised media buying agencies. Computerised media scheduling is commonplace.

14. Other factors in assessing "effective cost." Many other factors enter into the calculations of the "effective cost" of media, e.g.:

(a) Circulation and viewing figures vary geographically, as do buying patterns. Television, for instance, is transmitted on a regional basis. It is therefore possible to direct advertising to specific geographical areas and this situation is frequently used to provide test market information. There is, however, an overlap situation; viewers can frequently receive more than one commercial programme.

(b) Television has a greater attention-pulling potential, especially if demonstration is needed, but social class coverage can be achieved on a more selective basis by use of press media.

(c) A single newspaper advertisement may be seen more than once by the same person. Sunday and weekly papers in particular are retained longer and provide additional opportunities to view. Some trade papers are circulated amongst several executives.

(*d*) It has been estimated that some 80% of consumer purchases are influenced by women. Regional press has an average house-wife readership of some 83%. Sixteen million women over the age of 16 read magazines—some 79% of all women in the country. *Woman*, for example, has the highest circulation amongst women of any magazine in the world. There is also some evidence that women's magazine readers are younger, more prosperous, more beauty and fashion conscious and more progressive than non-readers. The extensive use of colour in these magazines is another advantage.

(*e*) Three-quarters of the average cinema audience are between 16 and 34. Those between 18 and 24 years of age are the "heaviest viewers" representing 38% of the average audience.

Size and position of press advertisements, length, timing and programme proximity of television commercials, intensity of readership or viewership, editorial status and credibility, frequency of insertion or transmission and spread of expenditure amongst viewer media—these are all important variables to be considered in calculating advertising effectiveness in relation to cost.

Furthermore, it should be remembered that decisions to buy a product or service are almost always the result of formal and informal social interaction with a wide range of people. (This is particularly true of industrial markets.) In addition, buying attitudes and spending patterns of individuals in similar socio-economic groups vary.

The "lag" or "carry over" effect of advertising is also of no little importance. Attitudes towards companies, products, and organisations are often the result of a cumulative build-up of impressions over time.

MEDIA SELECTION AND MATHEMATICAL MODELS

15. Difficulties in building advertising models. Major difficulties in model-building are as follows:

(*a*) *The delayed sales impact* of a great deal of advertising. Advertising may often be regarded as a form of capital budgeting.

(*b*) *The importance of quality* as opposed to quantity. Creativity in content and in presentation is a highly significant feature of many of the most successful, campaigns.

(*c*) *The problem of isolating advertising* from other components of the marketing mix.

16. Media selection models. During the past ten years or so there has been a great deal of activity—notably in the advertising industry and in academic institutions—to construct advertising models. An early model (CAM—Computer Assessment of Media), developed by London Press Exchange, and still in use, is based on simulation. The model seeks to describe how a target audience is affected by a particular campaign and thus to determine how an advertising budget should be allocated amongst the various media available. The probability of a person receiving an impression (PRI) is calculated and modified by a selectivity weighting which takes into account the impact of times, days or editorial prestige.

Further modifications in accordance with, for example, the use of colour or special creative impact are made. The distribution of individual impressions can be used to arrive at a value-per-pound index.

Other models based on optimising methods, such as linear programming, are being used to arrive at media selection yielding maximum exposure subject to given constraints, e.g. a set advertising budget, maximum use of certain media, a minimum target-audience exposure rate. Optimising is the process of allocating scarce resources in such a way that an objective is reached in the most effective way. Linear programming is a mathematical technique which can be used if the relationship between the variable resources can be expressed by linear equation. The computerised model is only an aid to judgment with the great advantages of speed.

Amongst the problems are the following:

(*a*) Omission of or judgment quantification of qualitative factors.

(*b*) Lack of precise knowledge of the effect of the timing and frequency pattern of advertisements.

(*c*) Lack of precise knowledge of the effect of the overlapping of readership amongst various media.

(*d*) Changes in the interest value of editorial or programme material—a very marked problem in television advertising. An advertisement appearing alongside a press report of an international soccer match or immediately after the presentation of a sporting event on television would have a different effect from one appearing by the side of an article or after a programme with an essentially feminine appeal.

(*e*) Models which seek to determine optimal solutions cannot handle as many variables as simulation. For example, various constraints which do not apply in practice have to be built into the model, e.g. an inside front cover of a magazine may have an utterly different effect from one of the inside pages; most magazines do not sell specific inside pages. A linear programming model, therefore, taking into account any inside page as a single variable, will lack sensitivity in relation to reality.

ADVERTISING BUDGETS

17. Methods of determining advertising budgets. Some of the most common methods of determining advertising budgets are as follows:

(*a*) *As a percentage of sales.* "Sales" may relate to over-all turnover, or to revenue received for individual products or groups of products. Some companies work on current sales figures; others on projected sales.

(*b*) *On the basis of competitive advertising expenditure.* While competitive advertising must be considered, no two companies are pursuing identical objectives from an identical base line of resources, market standing, or other factors. Determination of budgets on the basis of, say, an identical percentage of gross sales revenue to that of competition is completely unrealistic.

(*c*) Both as a percentage of sales and in relation to competitive advertising expenditure.

(*d*) *As the amount remaining after deduction of other expense plus a predetermined return on capital.* This method appears to be based on the premise that it is impossible to determine the optimum level of advertising but that it is right to advertise success to almost any level. Major objections lie in

(*i*) the short-term emphasis which may lead to problems in longer-term advertising investment needs; and

(*ii*) the lack of consideration of alternative investment opportunities.

(*e*) *As a cost of achieving a given objective.* This is the most logical approach, but the difficulties of setting objectives and measuring their attainment have been previously discussed (*see* VI, **5–7**). This method may serve to determine the minimum and maximum limits, but there will usually be a considerable margin between these two. Objectives have also to be taken not only in relation to cost, but in relation to their contribution to profits.

Many companies apply information which has been developed through budgetary control systems, indicating profitability of markets, types of customers, products, etc. Problems remain in that a great deal of marketing expense is arbitrarily allocated and there is great need for improvement of cost accounting practice applied to marketing.

If the "objective" approach is used, however, the cost will be considered against other budgetary considerations, e.g. the total budget for promotion, for marketing and for the business as a whole. If budgets have to be reduced, it is vital to reconsider the advertising objectives.

Market share objectives in relation to product-profit life cycles are certainly not new to companies involved in consumer goods markets. It is not uncommon to have relatively high advertising budgets in the introductory product-market phase in order to gain high distribution and/or market penetration. The subsequent level and role of advertising is then adjusted in line with market dynamics.

18. Market dynamics and advertising models. No model has yet been developed which is of practical value in predicting share changes attributable to advertising expenditure in complex dynamic situations. Of a number attempted, *Adbudg* and variations of it are probably the most widely used. This model initially combines historical data and managerial judgment in seeking to establish four points of a potential demand curve associated with various advertising budget levels, e.g. the current level, a 50% increase, a minimum, a maximum. Carry-over effects are also taken into the reckoning, and the model has been applied with some success— particularly in those mature market situations where there is essentially an oligarchic brand-share battle, e.g. razor blades.

Empirical evidence suggests that an advertising budget must be competitive not only to gain but to maintain brand leadership. Only some 5% of brand leaders, in 30 product classes researched recently, had held their shares consistently on an advertising budget which, in relation to total product advertising, was proportionately lower than their sales revenue in relation to total product class sales.

Brand share *per se* is no justification for any level of advertising expenditure. Attempts to hold to brand shares in a declining market can lead to declining profitability because of disproportionate advertising levels, price reductions, additional service packages, etc.

Advertising is one of many variables affecting attitudes and/or sales. Many attempts to measure effect have foundered, as we have seen, because the objectives of advertising are not sufficiently specific, and/or because target audiences have not been defined adequately for meaningful analysis. One factor which has until recently been ignored is variation due to environment. Empirical validation of expenditure has generally been based on two marketing areas at most. Ronald Fisher, an Englishman, expounded the principle of replication as far back as 1925, in a book on experimental design. In simple terms, when a variable is applied to a number of environments in orderly repetition, a normal variation stemming from the environment is measurable and can be removed by statistical routines described as the analysis of variance. This principle has, since the seventies, been used by a limited number of advertising practitioners as well as academic researchers to assess the effects of given levels of advertising in several marketing areas, with very promising results.

One other development is worthy of mention—goal programming linked with sensitivity analysis. Linear programming methods, by definition, deal with uni-dimensional coverage. The goals of decision-makers are usually multiple and sometimes in conflict. Goal programming involves setting out objectives according to their priorities, together with decision variables, e.g. level of direct mailings, level of sales force incentives and assumptions such as the cost of borrowed capital, level of fixed costs, etc. The resultant simulation model is extremely flexible and allows for simulations with many variations of priorities and constraints in terms of objective outcomes.

BRANDING

19. Brand identity. A feature of advertising policy—particularly in the case of consumer goods—is to establish a brand identity. A brand identity may begin with a name, e.g. "Kleenex," "Tide," but extends to other visual features—typography, colour, package design, slogans—features which should assist in creating, stimulating and maintaining demand. It is clear that branding could have a contrary effect if either the branded product were unacceptable to the consumer or the branding image were psychologically or sociologically ill-conceived.

20. Reasons for branding individual products. Amongst arguments in favour of branding are the following:

(*a*) Memory recall is facilitated. This could lead to more rapid initial buying action or greater frequency of buying and, hence, deeper loyalty.

(*b*) Advertising can be directed more effectively and linked with other communications programmes.

(*c*) Branding leads to a more ready acceptance of a product by wholesalers and retailers.

(*d*) Self-selection is facilitated—a very important consideration in self-service stores.

(*e*) Display space is more easily obtained and special promotions are more practicable.

(*f*) The importance of price differentials may be diminished.

(*g*) Brand loyalty may give a manufacturer greater control over marketing strategy and channels of distribution.

(*h*) Other products may be introduced more readily. (The failure of a brand may, of course, lead to undue resistance to other products.)

(*i*) The amount of personal persuasive selling effort may be reduced.

(*j*) Branding makes market segmentation easier. Different brands of similar products may be developed to meet specific categories of users.

The relevance of branding does not apply equally to all products. The cost of brand advertising and promotion may be prohibitive. Again, the success of branding may depend both on the nature of the product and on the behaviour characteristics of customers. Branding, for example, demands the ability to control quality; it is also likely to be more successful where product attributes are difficult to evaluate objectively. To take extremes, it is obviously easier to brand whisky than iron ore.

21. Branding, brand names and trademarks. "Branding" is actually a very general term covering brand names, designs, trademarks, symbols, etc., which may be used to distinguish one organisation's goods or services from another. "Brand name" refers strictly to letters, words or groups of words which can be spoken. "Trademark," however, is a legal term covering words and symbols which can be registered and protected. A legally protected mark can be a very valuable asset and prevent the spread of a market leader's brand name to generic application, covering a class of products or services—as has happened, for example, with "aspirin" and "cellophane." International aspects of trademark registration require special study.

22. Corporate images: disadvantages. Instead of branding individual products, companies sometimes create product-family images or a corporate company image associated with all products. The potential cost saving of the approach is clear but certain problems arise. These include the following:

(*a*) Difficulties of marketing different quality grades.

(*b*) Difficulties of marketing a range of products which it may be undesirable to relate closely.

(*c*) The risk of damage to existing lines by the introduction of unsuccessful products.

(*d*) The difficulties of devising sufficiently clear advertising and communications objectives and assigning expenditure. Companies which pursue an individual brand policy normally have brand managers who are concerned with the marketing and profitability of particular brands, and responsibility accounting methods can therefore be employed.

23. Corporate images: advantages. More and more organisations are beginning to realise the advantages of projecting appropriate corporate images. Organisations which developed new visual corporate identities during the seventies include ICL, Shell, British Rail, the National Westminster Bank, British Steel, Air India, Lufthansa, Unilever. The visible manifestations of a corporate image programme can be very widespread. The letters, symbols, logos and other design elements associated with it, in the case of Shell, for example, appear on:

> media advertising
> promotional material
> road tankers
> sea-going tankers
> petrol pumps
> letter-headings
> sales aids
> buildings
> packaging
> uniforms

There are many reasons for developing appropriate visual corporate identities, and these include:

(a) The increasing importance of public relations—establishing the right relationships with governments, opinion-influencing pressure groups, local communities in the vicinity of offices, factories, distribution centres.

(b) The need to attract and retain investment.

(c) The need to attract labour of the right kind in the right numbers.

(d) The growing realisation of the importance of good relationships with suppliers and institutions involved in forward distribution processes—wholesalers, agents, distributors.

(e) The need to foster a feeling of belonging within an organisation; this is particularly in evidence in large, widely spread groups and/or merged or re-structured units.

(f) The realisation of the cumulative impact of multiple repetition.

(g) The need to promote new ideas, services and products linked to an established "image" for particular strengths, e.g. research, financial expertise, engineering capability—especially in circumstances where there is a broad line of services or products which could not possibly be individually promoted regularly and intensively.

(h) Growing internationalism of companies and customers.

24. Branding, corporate images, communication and change. Communication involves senders, transmitters and receivers. It is perfectly obvious that the sender's ideas must be received, understood and accepted if the sender's objective is to be accomplished. Some of the important barriers to successful communication are:

(a) The sender's message may not be received at all. Ask yourself what press advertisements you have seen today and what you can remember about them. Check on the number which actually appear in the papers you read.

(b) The sender's ideas have to be "encoded" in copy and design elements which may not, in fact, reflect his true intention.

(c) The receiver may not understand the words or symbols used. Technical details of a computer, for example, may not be understood by an accountant who is involved in authorising purchase.

(d) The medium used may have low credibility. A newspaper may, for example, be read for amusement but tend to have a disparaging effect on certain products or services advertised in it.

(e) The receiver is not just a blank screen waiting to reproduce accurately the message beamed on to it. The way in which he interprets a message will depend on many factors, e.g. the strength and nature of his needs and motivations, his past buying experience, his education, ethnic and cultural background, the influence of others to whom he looks for value standards (reference-group influence), etc.

A situation could arise in which one person is considering the personal purchase of a car and hand tools, and, at the same time, is involved in a work situation in the choice of a supplier of compressed air equipment. One large corporation could be the possible supplier in both cases. This situation illustrates the importance of thinking through, as fully as possible, the implications of the use of corporate identity and/or brand images. It is not simply a question of design and identification but of knowing what ideas can be communicated to what audiences with what effect.

Corporate and brand images take time to build and it is foolhardy to discard a valuable image which has been carefully and expensively built up. On the other hand, organisations and markets change, and regular monitoring of communication effects is necessary to avoid the modern, efficient image of a 1974 company becoming the image of an old-fashioned, slow-moving organisation in 1984.

25. Private branding and quality control. In recent years wholesaling and retailing organisations which do not manufacture have been promoting their own brands—products supplied by manufacturing organisations with special labels and packaging. The most successful operation has been carried out by Marks and Spencer, who lay down precise specifications and exercise rigid quality control over manufacturers who supply "St Michael" products. Multiple food stores are, however, increasingly involved in the branding battle—frequently without the resources to specify or control quality.

26. Reasons for the development of private brands. The major reasons for this wholesaler and retailer action are as follows:

(a) A desire to limit the control exercised by manufacturers of strongly branded products.

(b) A desire to create a company or store identity and, hence, loyalty.

(c) A desire to introduce greater price variation. Private brands are frequently cheaper.

(d) A desire to protect margins. Intensive competition amongst powerful manufacturers sometimes leads to low retail and wholesale margins.

Small manufacturers are not unnaturally attracted by what appear to be easy markets, but larger manufacturers also frequently supply private brands, both to achieve given production levels and thus absorb fixed costs, and to take defensive action by accepting business which might otherwise go to a competitor and strengthen his costing structure or trade goodwill.

PACKAGING

27. Uses of packaging. Packaging may be considered from three basic standpoints:

(a) as a protective device;

(b) as a product utility factor; and

(c) as a form of promotion.

These were discussed earlier in IV, **33–35**. Packaging is, however, a sufficiently important element in promotional communication to justify its discussion again at this point.

28. Communication and package design. The advent of self-service has created a packaging revolution. The package on the store shelf and in the housewife's pantry is a form of advertising which is attracting increasing design attention—design to be linked with other forms of advertising. A brand name on a package which cannot be reproduced effectively on television, for example, is useless to the detergent manufacturer. When buying depends to a great extent on impulse, package shape or colour may be the major means of creating product preference. Ideally, consideration of product design should include:

(a) Ease of identification in all selling situations, e.g. set against competitive products on store shelves.

(b) Appeal both in shop and in household. Contrast the likely household location of soap powders and paper tissues; packaging should appear suitable for its likely location, as well as being attractive in itself.

(*c*) Ability of cartons or outers to be quickly converted into display units.

(*d*) The impact of product visibility, e.g. use of glass containers, visi-packs, etc.

(*e*) The impact of colour and the problems of reproduction in other media.

(*f*) The pros and cons of returnable and non-returnable packaging.

(*g*) Differences in national and sometimes regional attitudes and behaviour.

29. Packaging technology. Increased attention to packaging has led to a growing use of industrial designers as well as packaging technologists. Packaging costs are rising and although the main impact of the packaging revolution has been seen mainly in the field of consumer goods its marketing potential cannot be ignored by industrial goods producers—particularly those who are tackling international markets. Packaging exhibitions in Tokyo, Copenhagen, Milan, Dusseldorf, Paris and Moscow have attracted much more than casual interest.

The growing cost, complexity and time required to develop package designs point to a greater need for top management co-ordination and direction of packaging policy as a vital factor in achieving sales.

BELOW THE LINE MEDIA

The term "below the line media" is regularly used to cover sales promotion and merchandising, sales literature, point of sale display material, direct mail and exhibitions. The commission system of payment does not apply to these media. Those to which it does apply—press, television, radio, posters and cinema— are classified in the advertising business as "above the line." A very considerable amount of the rapidly expanding "below the line" activity is handled by specialists with whom the advertiser may enter into a direct relationship.

A development worthy of special note is the marked increase in tailor-made special promotion activities designed for large retail and wholesale groups by consumer goods manufacturers. This development reflects the growing bargaining power of these buying groups.

30. Consumer promotions. Special sales promotions are part of indirect advertising programmes intended to stimulate quick action. They are a feature of packaged consumer goods selling tactics and are directed at the consumer and/or the trade. The following are examples of consumer promotion:

(a) Special price sales.
(b) Free sample distribution.
(c) Premium offers.
(d) Contests.
(e) Point of sale demonstrations.
(f) Coupon offers.
(g) Combination or banded-pack product offers.

31. Trade promotions. The following are examples of trade deals:

(a) Provision of display materials.
(b) Co-operative advertising schemes—assistance with blocks or space costs.
(c) Contests for sales staff.
(d) Special discounts.
(e) Special quantity rate terms.

32. Reasons for special sales promotions. Special promotions are almost invariably used at the time of launching a new consumer product to gain maximum dealer stocking, display space and customer attention. Costs vary from the high expense of free-sample distribution to "self-redeeming" premium offers where goods bought at special quantity terms are supplied at bargain prices to customers who return coupons or other evidence of purchase. There are so many special promotions in the more highly competitive areas of consumer marketing that it would be dangerous for a company not to be involved. Other reasons for the use of special sales promotions include the following:

(a) Stimulating a new use for a product.
(b) Encouraging more frequent use of a product.
(c) Appealing to a special segment of the market.
(d) Boosting sales in particular geographical areas.
(e) Encouraging the use of another product (combination offers).
(f) Attracting bargain-hunting non-brand-conscious buyers.
(g) Encouraging seasonal sales or stimulating off-peak period sales.
(h) Creating dealer interest and encouraging stocking.
(i) Securing shelf space.
(j) Encouraging movement of slow-selling lines.

(*k*) Offsetting price competition.
(*l*) Assisting sales force presentations.

33. Display. The importance of display in consumer selling cannot be over-emphasised. Manufacturers may have special display posters, stands, cards and other material designed for windows, counters, shelves, floors. Many manufacturers' salesmen are trained to set up displays and in new food lines there is an increase of "rack jobbing"—a jobber taking over responsibility for stock and display, with the retailer providing space at a somewhat lower profit margin.

34. Direct mail. Direct mail may be broadly defined as a method of sending unsolicited advertising or promotional material through the post to customers or potential customers at specific named addresses. It is, therefore, distinguished from house-to-house personal distribution of literature, circulars, etc. Direct mail is becoming an increasingly popular means of marketing communication. In 1982 in the UK the Post Office claimed that direct mail (commercial radio apart) was the fastest growing advertising medium. Accurate statistics seem to be difficult to obtain and even the British Direct Mail Association admitted that its estimated expenditure for 1980 of £600m was largely guesswork. Two factors have stimulated sales, namely credit cards (40% of sales financed this way in 1982) and the colour supplements. Direct marketing is likely to receive a considerable boost from selective listings of companies accessible through the Prestel system.

35. Response and cost effectiveness. Mailing may be used principally to provide information, e.g. about new savings schemes, product modifications, price changes, etc. A great deal of mailing is, however, associated with direct action on the part of the recipient. Wincanton Contract obtained a 4.4% response rate to a mailing shot aimed at managing directors and company secretaries in an early industrial marketing campaign to break into the contract hire market. This enabled highly paid sales representatives to concentrate on warm leads, rather than to be wastefully employed on cold canvass calling. It should be noted that this was an industrial marketing exercise involving high investment decisions—all too frequently direct mailing is associated with limited special ventures such as encyclopedia campaigns. Costs per 1,000 shots can be calculated against a probable percentage reply to determine the cost per response. Response rates can then be translated into sales conversion figures.

Response rates will depend on many factors, amongst which the following are very important:

(*a*) The ability to maintain accurate, up-to-date lists of potential respondents by appropriate categories. The more personalised the approach, the better. Specialist mailing-houses exist in many countries, but relevant data can often be obtained and up-dated from sales representatives, trade and professional associations, etc.

(*b*) The mailing "package" should be good enough to appeal to the respondent.

(*c*) Reply should be made easy, e.g. business reply cards or envelopes included (in the UK the Post Office covers licensing procedures in a special booklet). International regulations on mailing procedures should be checked.

(*d*) Personal and/or other forms of follow-up should be arranged speedily.

36. Exhibitions, seminars and demonstrations are essentially specialist temporary market places at which buyers and sellers meet. There are various types of exhibitions: international trade fairs; national and local trade exhibitions (usually sponsored by a trade association); indoor and outdoor public exhibitions and shows, e.g. for cars, agricultural and business equipment. In addition to these shows at which competitor vies with competitor, there is a growing use of individual company exhibitions, seminars and demonstrations where there can be greater selectivity of audience—and often at a lower cost. Sometimes the private exhibitions are mobile, and can be readily moved from one location to another by special vehicle or rail car.

37. Examining the reasons for involvement. Very careful consideration should be given to determining objectively the real reasons for entering any general exhibition. The following considerations may weigh heavily:

(*a*) A new product is being launched. It is the kind of product which cannot be physically demonstrated by sales personnel, but can be shown at an exhibition, seen by many potential customers and reported by the press, TV, etc.

(*b*) A new market is to be developed rapidly. Contacts can be made with potential customers—an image created with considerable speed.

(c) It is important to maintain or gain the goodwill of sponsoring trade or professional organisations.

(d) It is the only way to make initial contact with professional personnel buying on behalf of foreign governments, e.g. the Eastern bloc.

38. Cost effectiveness—some pointers. It is particularly difficult to assess the cost effectiveness of other than private exhibitions. Some sales may result, but these are rare, and in those cases where large orders are announced the deals have usually been virtually concluded in advance. Nevertheless, the following cautionary points should be noted:

(a) Steps should be taken well in advance to invite to an organisation's particular stand important customers and potential customers. Sales force reminders pay off.

(b) If the objective is to build prestige, the reverse effect may be obtained by having a stand which because of size, position, lighting, exhibits etc., compares unfavourably with key competitors. Missing the exhibition can be less damaging—and less costly.

(c) Staffing arrangements should be organised well in advance so that there are reasonable individual duty rosters, an avoidance of under- and over-manning, adequate briefing to competent personnel who will reflect the organisation's image effectively, suitable hotel reservations, a stand co-ordinator, etc.

(d) Less costly literature should be provided for the "free loaders," who attend for entertainment, than for the serious prospects and customers.

(e) Attention should be paid to eye-catching stand design and exhibits in terms of the particular target groups. Working models and dynamic exhibits are invaluable. Interested parties should feel attracted to enter a stand, to examine exhibits and ask questions.

(f) Staff should be trained to obtain sufficient information from interested potential buyers for speedy follow-up to be made.

(g) Close attention should be paid to press relations, with suitable news releases and visual material arranged before and during the exhibition.

39. Audio-visual aids for sales forces. In general, inadequate attention is paid to the communication process in person-to-person selling situations. It is known that over 70% of our knowledge is acquired by reading and seeing; that only some 20% is acquired through hearing. It is also well-known that a selling call should be a two-way communication process in which the potential buyer should play a positive role. In spite of this, many salesmen rely almost entirely on verbal communications dominated by themselves. The scope for visual material of all kinds in person-to-person communications is enormous. Many companies supply their sales forces with illustrated "sales presenters," and more attention is now being given to attractive sample presentation kits, but there is comparatively little use of portable overhead projectors, of sound tapes, video-tape recordings, film strips, or desk-top 8 mm films with back-projection equipment. All these methods can also be used for small group presentations. This is a field which calls for intensive investigation. Recent video disc developments seem highly promising both for sales force use and point of sale activity.

40. Publicity. Publicity may be defined as news about products or companies appearing in the form of editorial material, without cost to the sponsor, in the press, on radio, television, stage, etc. "Without cost" refers to space or time costs, since good publicity programmes depend on the skill of publicity specialists. Activities range from recipes appearing with brand names in women's magazines to City-page comment and corporate company image-building. Publicity in this sense is one specialised aspect of the wider role of public relations, which is defined by the Institute of Public Relations as "the deliberate, planned, and sustained effort to establish and maintain mutual understanding between an organisation and its public." Publicity activities may, therefore, be carried out by company marketing personnel or public relations officers, by advertising agencies or by public relations consultants.

Organisations often complain about bad publicity or the tendency of the media—press, television and radio—to concentrate on the bad news. Very often the complainants have never properly investigated the ways in which they may have their "good news" included. The requirements and workings of particular media must be fully understood if good publicity is to be gained.

The most common forms of publicity are:

(*a*) the press release or news item;
(*b*) photographs;
(*c*) feature stories;
(*d*) news conferences;
(*e*) works visits.

All of these require special handling and planning. Most press releases, for example, are thrown away because they do not fulfil the basic technical journalistic requirements of news agencies, regarding such matters as number of words, headline writing, opening paragraphs, development and final paragraphs, abbreviations, capital letters, etc. Many others fail because of a failure on the part of writers to distinguish between press releases and advertising. The release has to be factual and newsworthy to the particular readership. Some companies, on the other hand, are able to handle press releases most adroitly and it is interesting to note those companies concerned with industrial markets which not only secure favourable mentions, but have regular full-length articles by their production, research, or engineering personnel featured in authoritative journals.

41. Some useful sources of advertising data.

(a) *British Rate and Data* (*Brad*). A monthly publication giving detailed information on media facilities and charges.

(b) The Evening Newspaper Advertising Bureau (ENAB). There is a considerable amount of regionally researched data available.

(c) The Audit Bureau of Circulations (ABC). A body established by agencies, media owners and advertisers issuing audited figures at six-monthly intervals. Audits show net sales, distribution, audience statistics etc.

(d) *Nielsen Researcher*. Free publication by world-wide independent market research organisation based, in UK at Headington, Oxford

(e) Media Expenditure Analyses Ltd. (MEAL).

(f) Legion Publishing Co. Ltd.

PROGRESS TEST 7

1. What are the five basic steps in campaign planning? **(1–6)**
2. How are readership classes normally defined? **(8)**
3. What methods are used in copy research? **(10)**
4. What are the main problems in assessing "effective costs"? **(13–14)**
5. What are the most usual ways of determining advertising budgets? **(17)**
6. What are the reasons for the development of private brands? **(26)**
7. What are the main reasons for special sales promotions? **(32)**
8. What are the advantages of direct mailing and what factors condition response rates? **(34, 35)**

PART THREE

Organisation for Marketing

CHAPTER VIII

Organisation and Control

1. Organisation structure and control systems. There is no model organisation structure which will meet the requirements of all types of business. Organisation structures depend on many factors, e.g. the size of the business and its industrial classification, the markets it serves, its stage of growth, and the skills and experience of its people. There are, however, three distinctive features of the organisation of truly marketing-oriented companies:

(*a*) Certain specific marketing tasks, e.g. marketing research and information, product-market planning, advertising and promotion, sales and distribution, are co-ordinated under a single executive.

(*b*) Clear formal communications are established between the chief marketing executive and executives responsible for development, design and manufacturing and finance.

(*c*) Marketing performance is judged by profit and return on investment—not by volume of sales.

The number of marketing executives employed will vary. Small companies may not be able to justify the employment of specialists for every marketing task. A marketing orientation does not depend on the number of people employed in particular marketing specialisms but on conformity with the principles listed under (*a*), (*b*) and (*c*) above.

There are six important factors which have to be taken into account when considering a marketing organisation to fit a particular situation:

(*a*) The number, diversity and specialist needs of products and services.

(*b*) The number, diversity and specialist needs of customers.

(*c*) The geographical spread of customers and products.

(*d*) The economies of scale which are feasible in terms of central-ised specialist marketing services, e.g. marketing research, product-market planning, advertising and promotion.

(*e*) The extent and nature of specialist-service support required by decentralised operating groups.

(*f*) The extent to which it is considered important to separate overall strategic planning and co-ordination tasks from on-going operational tasks.

Some of the traditional concepts of organisation such as single lines of reporting are disappearing in new matrix-type organi-sational patterns. For example, a marketing manager may directly control some functional activities, e.g. selling, local intelligence and advertising, in a decentralised unit where he reports to a general divisional manager, while at the same time reporting to a marketing manager at headquarters who may be responsible for co-ordinating total marketing operations and services.

This chapter is concerned with the establishment of the inform-ation evaluation and control systems which guide a company towards the achievement of its marketing objectives and plans. This implies that appropriate information systems should be developed both for the planning objectives (long- and short-term) and for the monitoring of performance achieved against objectives. The particular routing, form and frequency of the information will depend upon the organisational position, responsibility and authority of line marketing decision makers and on the position and role of staff specialists. Contrast, for example, the information required for new product planning (*see* IV, **13**) and that required by a sales manager (*see* X, **11** et seq.).

EVALUATION AND CONTROL

2. Evaluation and control mechanisms. A marketing system must have evaluation and control mechanisms built into it in order that actual performance may be measured against objectives and fore-casted performance. Information indicating significant variances from plans must be fed back speedily to relevant decision points so that corrective action may be taken. Organisational structures with clear definitions of *authority, responsibility* and *lines of com-munication* are, therefore, an important element in any control system.

3. Reasons for variations from planned performance. Variations from planned performance will always arise because of the following factors:

(*a*) All plans are built on *imperfect information.*

(*b*) *Marketing decisions are complex* and there will usually be a large number of interacting objectives—failure to reach any single objective may have a bearing on the attainment of other objectives; e.g. in attempting to gain a given share of a market, profits may fall below target because additional sales expense has been incurred.

(*c*) *The marketing environment is constantly changing* and it is impossible to predict every eventuality.

(*d*) *Organisations are becoming bigger.* This leads to the involvement of more and more people who are linked by information systems rather than by personal contact; the range of products extends; the location of factories, offices, warehouses, becomes more diffuse.

(*e*) *Variations in performance in other systems*, such as production, personnel or finance, affect marketing performance.

(*f*) *Performance depends not only on the company employees* but on the performance of wholesalers, retailers, advertising agencies and others, who can never be subject to the same degree of control.

4. The importance of targets. An effective control system depends on the setting of realistic goals or targets. Targets should be quantified whenever possible. It is almost impossible to evaluate performance against general statements of objectives. However, it is also more difficult to communicate intelligibly non-qualified objectives. Numerical targets make practicable the fixing of tolerances—the extent of permissible variance. It is only by establishing control limits that management by exception can be applied; otherwise every minor deviation at every point of time at which information is received will throw up problems of decision.

5. Marketing plans—reasons for their development. During recent years there has been a very big move towards the construction of formal, written, annual marketing plans. These plans should ideally evolve from the medium- and long-range plans of the organisation and thus avoid entirely short-term considerations which are inappropriate in dealing with product-market dynamics. Nevertheless, they will inevitably be matched to the annual corporate objectives and co-ordinated with the plans and budgets of other resource facilities, e.g. personnel, purchasing, finance, manufacturing, etc. The advantages of a formal planning process are:

(a) Diverse marketing activities can be co-ordinated into effective total action with authority, responsibility, timing and communication networks known.

(b) Non-specialist marketing activities can be more effectively examined and co-ordinated to meet marketing objectives.

(c) Crisis management can be reduced to the minimum.

(d) Measurements of performance can be more readily set against known standards.

(e) Corrective measures can be applied in time at appropriate decision points.

(f) Participation in planning can be encouraged and delegation can be more effectively practised, with resultant improved motivation.

6. Marketing plans—structure. In practice, marketing plans vary in detail and sophistication, but there are detectable common elements in the structural pattern which tend to follow the following sequence:

(a) *The information base.* This is an analysis of the present position of the organisation, e.g. its profits, revenues, product-market shares, strategy and tactics, weaknesses and recent trends—economic, social, technical and competitive.

(b) *Environmental assumptions.* On the basis of the best evidence available, the effect is assessed of significant economic factors likely to affect the forthcoming year's programmes, e.g.: government measures; economic factors affecting, for example, labour or material costs; spending capability or propensity; social and technical shifts influencing demand; known or probable competitive activity.

(c) *Basic overall objectives, policies and strategies.* In a business organisation, these include profit and investment goals and product-market priorities or emphasis, as well as strategies relating to product quality, leadership, etc., pricing, distribution, promotion.

(d) *Specific goals and programmes of action.* These cover product-market segments, but are detailed in terms of specific sub-programmes for product planning, selling, promotion, distribution, after-sales service, etc. Responsibilities and task achievement timings are set out and agreed.

(e) *Planned expenditures.* The overall marketing budget is broken down into sub-group budgets and set against (f).

(f) *Quantitative and qualitative measures of performance.* Revenues, costs, market shares, etc. are readily quantifiable, but some important tasks, e.g. the development of personnel, the change of a company image, are not so readily susceptible to direct quantitative measurements. (*See* **12–13**.)

THE PROFIT-CENTRE CONCEPT

7. Responsibility or profit centres. The increasing complexity of organisations and multiplicity of products are leading to devolution of responsibility. Closely controlled centralised operations are giving way to decentralised systems with greater emphasis on delegation. *Responsibility* centres are often set up, the responsibility for making a profit on particular operations being delegated to particular executives.

8. Types of profit centres. The whole marketing department may be treated as a profit centre. This would imply that goods are really being purchased from manufacturing departments and profits result from the difference between the cost of purchase plus sales expense and the revenue obtained from the market place. In this way, the chief marketing executive becomes responsible for achieving a given return on investment and will think in terms of *cost* and *revenue* rather than in terms of volume.

Profit centres may similarly be established for individual product lines or groups of products.

Sometimes, the profit-centre concept is applied to types of customers or market segments, to branch offices or geographical sales or to channels of distribution.

9. Information and distribution costs. There is certainly a great need to pay more attention to the costs of distribution which, in many cases, are not only higher than the cost of manufacturing but represent more than half of the final selling price. Many existing accounting systems could be extended to provide more significant information on cost; sales representatives, for example, are frequently unaware of the cost of their calls, or the cost of providing special deliveries and services. Marketing management certainly needs to consider the various combinations of channels, products, promotional and sales effort, which will yield satisfactory return at the least cost. Information collection and distribution can itself be an unnecessary cost, however, and it is important to establish what information is needed, for whom, when, where and in what form. The speed of information output from computers makes it all the more necessary to determine information flow and needs precisely.

THE MAJOR BASES OF PERFORMANCE EVALUATION

10. Sales targets and budgets. These are both fundamental to overall performance evaluation.

(*a*) *Sales target.* Based on market evaluation and resources available, overall targets should be set which lay down what is to be achieved in both the short and the long term.

(*b*) *Budgets.* A marketing budget agreed by top management should be drawn up to show the permissible cost in relation to achieved target. The budget is the major means of evaluating profit performance.

11. Long- and short-range budgets. A distinction should be made between *long-range budgets* covering 3, 5 or 10 years ahead in order to determine long-range capital, facility and manpower needs, based on an assessment of long-range plans for business growth, and *annual budgets* which are a control device for the year ahead.

Long-range budgets are very necessary if companies are to plan for growth and change. These budgets require an evaluation of the likely effect of external and internal events over the forward period, against the background of which new products will be launched. The budget will indicate the likely profitability of new and existing products, as well as market shares. Products which are likely to fall below given company profit objectives have to be analysed so that decisions may be taken on appropriate action —to modify, to increase sales effort, or to drop.

12. Quantifiable overall objectives. The company must establish clear long- and short-term objectives so that these may be incorporated in the overall budgets as well as in departmental budgets.

Important quantifiable objectives may be:

(*a*) gross and net sales figures;

(*b*) market shares;

(*c*) profit expressed in monetary terms and as a percentage of sales;

(*d*) turnover of capital, inventory, and accounts receivable;

(*e*) return of investment on capital employed.

Profit on sales reflects performance in maintaining cost control; turnover reflects the speed at which capital in the business is being worked. Return on investment—a most important yardstick—can be improved by reducing costs or using capital more effectively.

13. Other overall objectives. Other important objectives may not be so easily quantified, e.g.:

(*a*) providing for manpower training and development;

(*b*) providing for effective plant and manpower utilisation;

(*c*) avoidance of excessive variations in level of business transacted;

(*d*) maintenance of and/or improvement of market standing against competition;

(*e*) providing for a satisfactory level of shareholder dividends in both short and long term;

(*f*) providing for employee job satisfaction.

14. Responsibility budgeting. If profit, expense and revenue centres are established, and managers at various levels of an organisation are accountable for their performance in relation to budgets, it is important that the following conditions are observed:

(*a*) The executive concerned should understand and agree the particular budget. Pursuing the notion of management by objectives, the executive would not only agree, he would participate in the decision and perhaps even construct his own objectives in line with major company objectives.

(*b*) An executive who carries a responsibility for profits must have the authority to make necessary adjustments to programmes in order to reach the profit target.

(*c*) Adequate information on performance should be available in the right form at the right time.

INFORMATION FOR MARKETING EVALUATION AND CONTROL

15. Reasons for information. The provision of relevant information at the right time to the right people is the basis of an evaluation and control system. Information is required to:

(*a*) provide for evaluation and control of overall marketing performance;

(*b*) provide for evaluation and control of subfunctions and individuals within marketing departments or divisions;

(*c*) provide specific data for any necessary action in relation to products, marketing programmes or prices;

(*d*) provide information for salesmen.

16. Main types of marketing control analyses. The most commonly analysed information supplied for overall marketing analysis falls under six headings described in subsequent paragraphs:

(*a*) Sales analysis (**17**).

(*b*) Product share analysis (**19**).

(*c*) Distribution analysis (**20**).

(*d*) Sales force activity analysis (**21**).

(*e*) Cost and profit analysis (**22**).

(*f*) Advertising analysis (**25**).

17. Sales analysis: information. Sales managers tend to judge current performance by the volume of business and size of individual orders. Difficulties arise if the only information available regularly is aggregate orders. Information needs to be broken down much further for evaluation and control. Possible breakdown categories in terms of unit volume and sales revenue are:

(*a*) by products; these can be further separated if necessary into particular styles and sizes;

(*b*) by customer type or size;

(*c*) by sales territories;

(*d*) by channels of distribution;

(*e*) by terms of sale;

(*f*) by key outlets.

18. Sales analysis: standards. Information received must then be set against standards, e.g. annual forecasts, previous month's performance, last year's performance. It is also important to measure performance against opportunity and not just against the company's own past record. This requires supplementary information from the field and marketing research reports. Regular reports on marketing expenses by various categories will also be required if profit targets are to be met.

One of the problems frequently encountered in actual operations is that sales analysis data arrives too late for effective action. In volatile consumer markets, for example, detailed analysis six weeks after events may be much too late to enable effective corrective action to be taken.

19. Product share (brand position) analysis. Regular information on a company's own as well as competitive brand shares of the market is extremely valuable. Growth in volume of business—or indeed in profits—is no guarantee of complete realisation of opportunities. A 3% improvement in volume is unsatisfactory set against an overall market growth of 15%. Apart from immediate lost profit opportunities, loss of market share may reflect on future business prospects. A change in brand leadership may mean considerable modification of plans. In certain fast-moving consumer markets, e.g. pharmaceutical and grocery, regular audits of brand share positions are undertaken by the A. C. Nielsen Company and other specialist agencies (*see* III, **12**). In industrial markets and consumer areas where the information is not readily available a company may have to devise its own arrangements for taking stock checks. High sales stocks in the warehouse of an agent or intermediary may indicate a high level of anticipated demand *or* a decline in demand at the next point along the chain. Stock-level information must, therefore, be supplemented by data on the estimated usage level and flow of products; a stock-piling of all brands, for example, may indicate a general recession, either cyclical or permanent.

20. Distribution analysis. It may be comparatively simple to codify outlets to reveal statistics on actual company transactions, but where products are transferred, say from wholesaler to retailer, it is more difficult to evaluate performance of particular links in the distribution chain. Information on stock levels, stock condition, order sizes, and selling effort at outlets where sales calls are not regularly made may be necessary. Again syndicated information is sometimes available from outside sources, but the sales force may be required to check on display activities or to ensure that inefficient systems of withdrawal from stock do not mean that the newest stock is used first. Old or damaged stock reflects more on the manufacturer than on the final supplier.

One of the great problems in distribution evaluation is to establish standards of performance. As in other forms of evaluation, reliable standards are needed for really effective control. The problem of measuring the performance of distribution points with which the company is not in direct contact is obvious, but comparison of performance of wholesalers and agents on the basis of one year's figures against another's is also inadequate. Does a 20% increase by one wholesaler represent a greater effort than a 10% increase by another? More attention should sometimes be paid to establishing standards in relation to potential and constraints. It may, for instance, be possible to measure performance of various overseas agents by establishing relative potential indices based on such information as total population, rural and urban population, degree of industrialisation, educational standards, and extent of communications and transport systems in each region. Similar indices could, of course, be developed for home markets.

21. Sales force activity analysis. Some of the previous analyses give an indication of salesmen's performance, e.g. sales by products in a particular territory. There are other measurements which may be necessary. A salesman may have tasks other than actually effecting a sale, such as display and service. Again, if action is to be taken to raise the level of sales performance it may be useful to have information on the following:

(*a*) Number of calls per day.
(*b*) Number of different calls per month.
(*c*) Ratio of orders to calls.
(*d*) Value of sales per call.
(*e*) Time spent on non-selling activities.
(*f*) Mileage covered in given periods—mileage per call.
(*g*) New accounts opened.
(*h*) Expenditure and cost of obtaining sales.

22. Cost and profit analysis: difficulties of allocation. Company costs might be said to cover basically manufacturing costs and marketing costs. Allocating manufacturing costs raises problems but they are nothing like so great as those of allocating marketing costs. Marketing, like manufacturing, has the problem of overhead allocation, e.g. for managerial salaries, but manufacturing costs are allocated to processes and things manufactured, however arbitrary the allocation may sometimes be in practice. The ultimate output of marketing is a sale, but it is difficult to determine the allocation of marketing processes. Products, salesmen, advertising, distributors—all contribute to sales but in ways which are difficult to quantify. Similarly additional cost in manufacturing is likely to yield a given output, but it is much more difficult to estimate the effect on sales revenue of hiring extra salesmen or increasing an advertising appropriation. Marketing costs can only be viewed in terms of absolute accuracy in total; individual activity costs provide a basis for revision of the balance of these costs.

23. Cost and profit analysis: methods. Nevertheless measurement depends on being able to examine both cost and revenue. Margins, for example, might be increased either by increasing sales more than expenses, or by reducing expense more than sales. It is difficult to adjust margins or to use budgets to regulate specific marketing activities unless, therefore, there is an attempt to break down marketing expenses. Cost and profit analyses are consequently carried out in three main ways:

(*a*) *By calculating gross margins for specific managerial units.* Gross margins are what remain after the cost of goods sold is deducted from sales revenue. Lower gross margins on certain products or in certain markets point to a need to investigate. Falling margins may, for example, indicate that there is something wrong with the marketing plan and marketing efforts may be badly directed.

(*b*) *By breaking down expenses into normal categories* such as salaries, rent, supplies, and comparing the expense against the gross profit of a profit centre.

(*c*) *By allocating all direct and indirect costs* to specific managerial units and setting these against profits. The units may be territories, customer groups or product groups. There are very considerable problems of allocation, e.g. when one salesman handles products from two or three different product groups or calls on two or three different customer groups. Similar problems arise in the case of corporate product advertising, billing, or mixed product-customer-type deliveries. Where product groups, outlet types, sales delivery arrangements and so on are reasonably well separated, it is possible and often very worth while to carry out this kind of analysis. The major consideration is to ensure that the benefits of undertaking the exercise exceed the costs.

24. Cost and profit analysis: interpretation. Interpretation needs care since most cost allocations are arbitrary. Direct costs are simple, e.g. cost of salesmen or advertising directly associated with a product, but costs of space, management salaries, taxes, corporate advertising present considerable difficulties. Distribution cost analysis in its purest state can rarely be the basis for an immediate decision. It is a yardstick—to some extent arbitrary—measuring relative performance and should be regarded as a guide to areas requiring further investigation.

It may be found, for example, that by measuring total sales achieved against quotas there seems to be one star salesman in a team. A gross margin analysis by product may reveal that the salesman's effort and expense have been devoted mainly to an easy selling line which yields a lower gross margin than other products. If sales targets and expense budgets have been set on the basis of anticipated market demand and an expectation of balanced sales across the range of products, and if direct costs have been allocated on the basis of actual expense incurred by having the salesman in his territory, the unbalanced selling could result in both a low gross profit and a small contribution to profit. This kind of analysis would indicate, in this case, the need for more balanced selling effort; in other cases there might be pointers to the need for purely increased sales volume or reduction of selling expense.

25. Advertising analysis and mark-up. Advertising evaluation has been covered previously (*see* VII, **13–15**) but attention should be drawn to the fact that the costs of advertising are frequently given unfavourable publicity while little mention is made of the costs of effecting distribution and sales through conventional channels by offering suitable margins of profit. While there are very considerable variations, and generalisations in terms of all goods marketed are impossible, it would not be unusual to find that the advertising of strongly promoted foodstuffs may account for 5% of the final retail price against 20% for retail margins. Wholesale margins are far lower and this explains why it sometimes is not only more effective in terms of sales revenue but also cheaper in cost to arrange terms direct on a single margin with large retailers. Sums spent on research and development, too, are frequently insignificant compared with mark-up allowances.

Marketing costs are mainly fixed regardless of the level of the flow of goods—unlike the variable cost of manufacturing. Margins to intermediaries may be regarded as an economic cost, but they are not an accounting burden. If their role was taken over by company-owned wholesale warehouses and retail outlets, then rents, salaries and running expenses generally would become a fixed cost or overhead.

26. Determining marketing expenses. Companies find it difficult to assess whether they should increase or decrease marketing expenses—or indeed at what level they should be fixed at all. It might be simple to consider the costs of each marketing activity—selling, advertising, market research, channel costs, order processing, product planning. The problem here is that each reacts on the other. A method of isolating functions has been described under advertising as the sales-task approach (*see* VI, **6–7**). Other possible ways of investigating expense and effectiveness are as follows:

(*a*) Analysis of resources, results, marketing methods and expenditure of competitors.

(*b*) Analysis of customer attitudes and behaviour.

(*c*) Analysis of non-accounting statistical data, e.g. difference in results of advertising carried out under controlled experimental conditions.

(*d*) Analysis of the relative importance of marketing activities in relation to sales. Similarly analysis of expense within an activity should be measured, e.g. who is the least productive salesman (in terms of contribution to profit); which is the least productive form of advertising. This kind of approach would be used if profits were falling; it is a useful guide—but only a guide—when profits *and also* expenses are rising. Some attempts to reduce cost are unlikely to have any really significant effect, e.g. general requests to cut down on telephone calls or stationery.

27. Budgets and flexibility. From what has already been said (**10–14** above) it will be clear that, although sales budgets are essential and central to the company operation, variations in the constituents of the total marketing expenses have no inevitable consequence in terms of sales revenue. There is, therefore, room for flexibility in the light of unexpected happenings. It is important that a measure of flexibility in the constituents be maintained since there will always be some unexpected developments in market situations. Often these developments will require adjustments in the way marketing expense is used in order to reach the planned marketing objectives; sometimes unexpected opportunities to exceed planned objectives will arise. Production expense may be affected by changes in wage levels or materials cost, for example, but the budgetary changes necessary are less complex and more predictable than in marketing. Indeed, production budgets are most likely to be affected by changes in sales.

Flexibility in sales budgets should not lead to thinking in terms of immediate reduction of constituents such as advertising, as demand falls. A fall in demand would affect the production budget and it may indeed be necessary to *increase* sales effort beyond the point of marginal return on sales cost in order to absorb uneconomic production capacity. One budget must be seen in relation to another and none is more critical in its interrelated effect than the sales budget. An apparently high selling cost might be justified if the volume of sales generated were sufficient to enable high productivity machines to be installed in the factory leading to reduced manufacturing cost, thus greatly improving the contribution to overall profit.

28. Fixed costs and revenue. Most marketing costs are fixed, but variable costs are involved in activities such as short-term promotions, sales commissions, temporary salesmen. If a high fixed cost in selling is combined with a high fixed cost in manufacturing, the dangers of a fall in profit (resulting from increased wages, rents, reduced demand, falling prices) are clear; diversification, rigorous product development policies, and a drive to differentiate products might be expected in circumstances of this kind.

29. Market development and investment. Although emphasis has been laid on the importance of comparing performances of products, of sales personnel, and of channels on the basis of profit contribution, it should be stressed that low contributions may arise because of the need to invest in sales training, or in cultivating certain intermediaries, e.g. voluntary group wholesalers, just as much as from the need to invest in product development and market introduction.

30. Financial reports and relevance. The rapid speed of punched card and computerised systems means that sophisticated information can be made available quickly. Consider the range of data which could be obtained from drawing up a product and a customer code for computer processing on the following lines:

    (*a*) *Product.*

        (*i*) Product line, e.g. filter paper.
        (*ii*) Product size, e.g. 3 cm.
        (*iii*) Product type, e.g. circles.
        (*iv*) Product grade, e.g. 4.
        (*v*) Product price, e.g. £0.055.
        (*vi*) Product quantity, e.g. 12×100.

    (*b*) *Customer.*

        (*i*) Name and address, e.g. Bryce and Co. Ltd., 29 Warren St., Tonbridge TN3 4BC.
        (*ii*) Industrial or business classification, e.g. chemical and allied industries.
        (*iii*) Size by potential sales revenue, e.g. £10,000 p.a.
        (*iv*) Sales department, e.g. 4.
        (*v*) Salesman, e.g. 6.

The possible combinations of information would be too much

for an individual to digest and it is, therefore, important to provide the right data for the right level at the right time.

The product manager concerned with product profit contribution may require summary reports by size, design, quality, revenue and margin. From this he might see slow-moving lines, uneven spread of sales, unexpected margins. More detailed reports may be necessary to follow through on significant variations from anticipated results.

The field sales manager is concerned not so much with profit contribution on single products as with volume or revenue targets and controllable expense. He may, therefore, need information on sales progress by territory and a considerable range of individual expense items such as office and equipment depreciation, salesmen's cars, stationery supplies, hotel bills, clerical salaries. The salesman, on the other hand, would be unable to control variable expenses apart from his own travelling, hotel and entertainment bills. His area manager may need a regular record of these expenses, but the salesman himself is primarily concerned with a record of sales and deliveries on his territory—in total by product and by individual account—plus, perhaps, records of outstanding customer debts.

31. Reports from field sales forces. Two problems arising from the various information systems described are, firstly, that there is a *time lag* between the event and the reporting of the event; and secondly, that the information is in *quantitative* terms. Supplementary verbal information may be necessary.

To remedy these defects salesmen are usually asked to make periodic reports on their field activities to area managers who similarly may provide reports for more senior executives. The frequency and detail of such reports must be carefully considered in the light of their value as evaluation and decision-making aids. Not infrequently very detailed daily sales reports from representatives contain information which is not really required or is available from other sources—and the compilation of these reports reduces the time available for selling and/or planning selling calls.

Well-planned field reports may, however, provide faster or more extensive information on such matters as the following:

(a) Number of calls made on particular days.

(b) Sales made or not made, with some explanation.

(c) Economy of routing.

(d) Localised competitive activities.

(*e*) Significant customer or potential customer developments.

(*f*) Details of complaints on, for example, product performance, delivery.

32. Possible effects of sales reports. Field sales reports may lead to more effective operation in the following ways:

(*a*) By indicating the need for urgent training, motivation, or other remedial action.

(*b*) By acting as a constant reminder to the salesman or field sales executive that each day or week or month targets must be met if the annual target is to be reached.

(*c*) By providing fast information on the progress of special presentations or campaigns or on sales tactics which are proving particularly successful.

(*d*) By giving information on such matters as the progress of product tests, special display activities, technical servicing.

33. Communication, evaluation and control. It will be seen that much of the information required for evaluation and control is passing along formal organisational channels. An inherent danger here is that information can be misunderstood or distorted, giving rise to suspicions, conflict and low morale. Marketing is an activity involving a particularly large number of informal groupings and personnel with wide individual differences. A purely bureaucratic, mechanistic approach to objectives, control and evaluation is, therefore, likely to lead to low morale and failure to meet imposed objectives. In a bureaucratic control system sales reports, for example, can become mainly alibis—means of protecting the individual or the group. The purpose of control and evaluation must, therefore, be understood and accepted by the participants in the system so that they constructively participate in achieving and setting objectives which satisfy not only the company and its executives' hierarchy, but the needs and aspirations of informal groups and individuals.

34. Marketing, information and microelectronics. The possibilities of microelectronics in terms of new product development are clear. In this chapter it is important to comment on the effect of the new technology on marketing information systems. Inside the company the automation of order processing and production scheduling provides the opportunity for faster access to sales results and these can be displayed and assessed at distant locations through terminals or telephone line links providing, for example, a sales representative with stock/delivery data while with a customer—or a negotiator with cost data for the purpose of price calculations. External information, always expensive, will be easier and cheaper to capture, e.g. by obtaining immediate access to distributor data or by conducting consumer questionnaires by means of interactive terminals. A revolution will just not happen by acquiring hardware —or indeed software. Positive steps will have to be taken to create the climate for processing and decentralising the relevant decision marketing information. A programme of education, training and persuasion will be required if change is to be managed.

PROGRESS TEST 8

1. What are the reasons for the development of formal marketing plans, and what elements do they consist of? **(5, 6)**

2. What are profit centres? **(7, 8)**

3. How might a company express its overall objectives? **(12, 13)**

4. What are the main types of marketing control analyses? **(16)**

5. Why are there special problems in the allocation of costs to marketing activities? **(22)**

6. What are the three ways in which cost and profit analyses are carried out? **(23)**

7. In what way might information for product managers differ from information for field sales managers? **(30)**

8. What is the purpose of field sales reports? **(31)**

CHAPTER IX

Channels of Distribution

DEFINITION AND TYPES

1. Channels defined. The term "channels of distribution" refers to the system of marketing institutions through which goods or services are transferred from the original producers to the ultimate users or consumers. Most frequently a physical product transfer is involved, but sometimes an intermediate marketing institution may take title to goods without actually handling them.

2. Marketing institutions: types and functions. There is a very wide range of marketing institutions which carry out a variety of functions along the distribution channels. Amongst the most important are the following:

(*a*) *Retailers*. Independent traders operating outlets selling "at retail" to household consumers.

(*b*) *Wholesalers*. Independent traders who sell "at wholesale" to other business organisations either for the purpose of resale or for business use. The terms "distributor" and "jobber" are frequently used in American literature to describe an exactly similar type of trader. (Occasionally the terms have a different meaning, e.g. American jobbers dealing in automobile components and packed-meat products frequently buy from distributors who own warehouses and then sell to retail outlets.)

(*c*) *Agents and brokers*. Organisations which buy or sell on behalf of a firm without buying anything from the firm, in a manner defined by agreement. They normally earn their profit from commission payments made in return for their part in negotiating business transactions.

(*d*) *Distributors*. Organisations which contract to buy a firm's goods and services, and sell to third parties.

(*e*) *Facilitating institutions*. Organisations which neither take title to goods nor negotiate purchases or sales but assist the marketing activities of manufacturers and the institutions mentioned in (*a*) to (*d*) above. Examples include:

144

(*i*) commodity trading exchanges;

(*ii*) trade associations;

(*iii*) advertising and marketing research agencies;

(*iv*) credit service organisations and finance companies;

(*v*) freight carriers.

BASIC CHANNEL DECISIONS

3. Direct selling. Some producers sell direct to end users. This type of operation is found more frequently in the marketing of industrial goods and services than in marketing to domestic consumers. Door-to-door selling and mail order, however, are examples of direct consumer marketing.

4. Reasons for the use of direct selling. Factors which stimulate direct marketing are as follows:

(*a*) The need to demonstrate a technical product, to supervise tests, to undertake complicated and perhaps lengthy negotiations, or to provide specialised after-sales service.

(*b*) The lack of active selling by intermediaries.

(*c*) Inability to persuade existing channels to carry or merchandise stock.

(*d*) Unduly *high intermediary profit margins* which might give rise to cost and price advantages under a direct marketing system.

(*e*) Inability of intermediaries to effect physical transportation.

(*f*) Industrial market structures with comparatively few potential buyers—often geographically concentrated.

5. Reasons against the use of direct selling. Factors which inhibit direct marketing are as follows:

(*a*) *Lack of financial resources.*

(*b*) *The need to use capital* to provide a better *return on investment*; e.g. a manufacturer of a range of games would under most circumstances utilise available capital more efficiently in ways other than by engaging large numbers of salesmen to call on thousands of potential occasional domestic purchasers buying in small quantities.

(*c*) *Lack of "know-how"* in effecting final distribution. Retail store management calls for special skills, e.g. in buying for resale, in shelf-space allocation, in organising a predominantly female and often part-time labour force.

(*d*) *Lack of a sufficiently wide assortment* of own products to operate economically. Sales of individual items at retail are affected markedly by the assortment available.

(e) The existence of channels which are designed specifically to deal in *assortments and to break bulk*.

(f) A consumer market structure with *large numbers of potential buyers geographically scattered*.

6. Basic marketing processes. Marketing involves various basic processes:

(a) Bringing buyers and sellers into *contact*.

(b) Offering a *choice of goods* sufficient to gain the interest and meet the needs of buyers.

(c) Persuading potential buyers to develop *favourable attitudes* to particular products.

(d) Maintaining an *acceptable price level*.

(e) *Physically distributing goods* from manufacturing points to buying or use locations with the possible provision of additional storage points.

(f) Effecting an *adequate flow of sales*.

(g) Providing *appropriate services*, e.g. credit, technical advice, spare parts.

7. Channel decisions: effectiveness and cost. Channel decisions must, therefore, ultimately be based on the realisation that failure to delegate the functions listed in **6** above to intermediaries will increase costs, and that increased costs must be justified by appropriate economic advantages in terms of profit, market penetration or other company objectives.

There is a noticeable movement towards more vertically integrated production-marketing systems. The integration does not necessarily take the form of complete ownership of channels. Producer co-operatives are appearing more commonly in some markets, e.g. agriculture.

8. Multi-channel decisions. A producer may decide to use more than one channel system in order to reach his market. A large-scale manufacturer of soaps and detergents may, for example, decide to market products to both domestic consumers and industrial users. To reach domestic markets most effectively and economically the following decisions may be taken:

(a) Terms of sale for large chain groups will be negotiated by senior management direct. Delivery will be made to individual stores. Salesmen will have access to individual stores to arrange displays and to take orders under conditions negotiated centrally.

(b) Other large retail outlets will be sold to direct by salesmen allocated to particular territories.

(c) Salesmen will sell to wholesalers whose main resale activity will be concentrated on smaller retail outlets.

To reach a wide range of industrial users it may be decided to effect distribution by various channels. Certain sectors of the market, e.g. restaurants, canteens, will be reached through well-established wholesalers. Other sectors, e.g. textile manufacturers, will be sold to on a direct basis, perhaps because of a need to demonstrate technical superiority of specialised products or because a major share of the total market can be obtained by calling on a relatively small number of outlets in a limited number of geographical concentrations.

9. Physical distribution: logistics and the total systems approach. The increasing costs of physical distribution have attracted considerable attention, and operational research methods are being used in connection with the logistics of warehouse location and transportation utilisation. There is, however, a great need to explore in greater depth the complexities of existing and potential consumption systems. Vertically integrated ownership theoretically leads to greater control over—and more aggressive handling of—final markets which, in turn, should stimulate derived demand. Control has to be bought, however, and the total investment has to be measured against the total resultant increased return and set against alternative opportunity investment. Each point in the channel system, however, has its own "service package" offered to its own customer constellation at varying levels of effectiveness, cost and profit. There is growing interest in the total systems concept of physical distribution whereby all aspects of the physical handling and distribution of goods and services are examined in close detail and linked to channel strategy. Specialised distribution contracting is also increasing.

RETAILING

10. The functions of retailing. Retailing is the final link in the chain of distribution of consumer products. The functions retailers perform are the consequence of the separation of distance, time and information between producers and consumers (*see* I, **13**). Hence all retailers are involved in assisting in the physical movement of goods and in effecting a change of ownership. Retailers also hold stocks so that goods are available when required by the consumer, thus contributing to the reduction of the time separation. Retailers pass information on products to consumers and back to producers, so reducing the information separation.

11. Methods of retailing. The manner in which retailing functions are performed differs widely; e.g. some retailers have van delivery services, some rely on counter selling, others on self-service; some retailers hold wide stock assortments, others hold very limited ranges; some retailers advertise in the press and run their own sales promotions, while others rely on personal service.

Retailing functions are performed by non-store (*see* **12–14**) and store establishments (*see* **15–35**).

NON-STORE ESTABLISHMENTS

12. Types of non-store establishments. Examples of non-store establishments are mail-order houses, vending machines, door-to-door sales organisations, mobile shops, market traders and credit traders, but these outlets only account for a very small proportion of retail business. The most significant developments in non-store retailing are considered in **13** and **14** below.

13. Mail order. Over 4% of total trade is now conducted by mail order and the six largest mail-order organisations account for two-thirds of mail-order business transacted. Household textiles, soft furnishings and footwear represent their greatest volume of business. The following may be included among the reasons for growth:

(*a*) *Increased trading in branded goods* known and accepted by potential customers.

(*b*) *Congestion in major shopping centres*, with parking and transport problems for shoppers.

(*c*) *More married women in employment*, with less time to spend on shopping or unable to visit shops during opening hours.

(*d*) *Improved organisation* by mail-order companies—central buying, better stock control, more effective use of advertising—and, particularly, improved catalogues. This has led to higher operating margins.

(*e*) *More large organisations* entering this form of trading.

14. Door-to-door selling. The most interesting developments in this type of operation are associated with specific companies, e.g. the "Tupperware" party-selling system and Avon Cosmetics, which use home selling by part-time women representatives paid on a commission basis. In both cases major contributory factors to success have been the development of a leisurely social climate during the selling process and the provision of ample opportunity for the demonstrating and testing of products.

RETAIL STORES

Store establishments account for the major proportion of retail business; their organisation and operation is considered in some detail in 15–35 below.

15. Methods of classification of retail stores. Retail stores may be classified as follows:

(a) *By type or range of goods offered.* Some stores offer only goods in a highly specialised category, e.g. furniture, millinery, meat; others offer a wide range of different types of goods, e.g. a combination of food, drapery, hardware.

(b) *By the functions performed.* Some stores offer goods only by self-service; some offer delivery as well as self-service; others offer counter service and delivery.

(c) *By size.* Measurement of this may be based on the number of employees or the sales turnover.

(d) *By ownership*, e.g. independent, co-operative.

(e) *By location*, e.g. rural, urban.

These classifications are all important in specific marketing situations, but the present purpose is to examine general trends in retailing. The majority of shops in Britain are small in size and unincorporated, i.e. owned by one individual or a partnership. The share of total retail trade transacted in shops which are part of an incorporated business, i.e. owned by private or public companies, is, however, constantly growing. The position of the independent (unincorporated) tradesman is first examined (**16**) and there follows a more detailed treatment of the developments in incorporated retail establishments (**17–34**).

16. The independent trader. The majority of shops in Britain are small and independently owned, but the percentage of total trade these small establishments transact is constantly diminishing. Loss of market share is most outstanding in the case of grocery products.

(*a*) *Difficulties* encounted by the small trader include the following:

(*i*) Price competition from multiple organisations, who enjoy bulk-buying advantages as well as other organisational economies of scale. There is no longer the protection of resale price maintenance.

(*ii*) Lack of specialist expertise in the various functions of retailing, e.g. buying, display, accounting, stock control.

(*iii*) Lack of capital to invest in modernisation, e.g. provision of self-service facilities, accounting machines.

(*iv*) Location. Small traders usually lack the advantage of being in a major shopping centre where the customer is free to exercise choice over a wide range of purchases (but *see* (*b*)(*ii*)).

(*v*) Increased car ownership and the involvement of husbands in both buying and transportation tends to draw shoppers to the larger stores in the major shopping centres.

(*b*) *Advantages* the small trader can offer customers include the following:

(*i*) Personal relationship with customers.

(*ii*) Convenience in being located near customers' houses or place of work.

(*iii*) Stock not necessarily limited to fast-moving items but catering for more individual needs.

(*iv*) Greater flexibility in arranging shopping hours.

(*v*) Overheads can be kept small because of siting, low labour costs, etc.

(*vi*) Greater flexibility in offering credit.

(*vii*) More flexibility in providing delivery service.

INCORPORATED RETAIL BUSINESSES

Incorporated businesses are retailing establishments owned by public and private companies; their organisation and the main trends in their development are examined in **17–34** below.

17. Multiple organisations: chain stores. Chain stores are groups of retail stores of a similar type with a common ownership and some degree of centralised control. Multiples normally concentrate on a limited range of merchandise, e.g. groceries, furnishings, clothing, shoes. Variety chains are exceptions, e.g. Woolworths, British Home Stores: retail chains handling a diversity of goods.

The major multiples have, in fact, been actively developing stores

with sales areas of over 25,000 ft² (2,300 m²) and it is these superstores which account for larger and larger shares of retail business
(one-sixth of all commodity turnover through grocery outlets in
1980). Productivity in terms of sales per head soars. Nevertheless,
it is interesting to note that one of the big retail successes in the
seventies and eighties has been Kwik Save, which concentrates on
smaller stores. Superstores are sited on the outskirts of towns and
have excellent parking facilities, but 30% of households do not
have a car and few housewives, anyway, would drive six miles for,
say, a piece of fish—especially at today's petrol costs. The organisational fragmentation of the Co-operative movement, however,
has not been solved and market share losses continue.

A further current problem relates to the range of items carried
by multiples—how specialised should they be? Woolworth is
currently disposing of over 30 major outlets carrying highly diversified ranges to re-invest in more specialised areas of activity, e.g.
"do-it-yourself" items. Tesco and Asda are officially classified as
"large mixed businesses with food". Sainsbury are moving into
the cosmetics field.

Multiples have flourished particularly in central shopping areas
and their location, as well as price advantages and stock arrangements, has probably contributed greatly to their success. Supermarkets are defined as self-service shops with a sales area of over
400 m². Note also the spread of hypermarkets, which have been
defined by the following characteristics:

(a) Each has a selling area of at least 5,000 m² on one level,
offering a wide range of foods and a more general range of non-
foods.

(b) They apply self-service methods with payments at one point
by means of 15 or more checkouts.

(c) They are usually located 2–4 miles from a town centre.

(d) Each has an adjacent free parking area at least three times
the selling area.

The number of hypermarkets in the UK at present is growing;
there are over 400 in Germany (F.R.), over 200 in France, and
over 50 in Belgium.

18. The battle for shelf space. As multiples grow into regional and
national organisations they present new problems to the manufacturers whose products are handled by them. Their large share
of business transactions means that major manufacturers may be
able to restrict very considerably the number of actual selling calls

made, but the need to acquire shelf space and display becomes more vital. So much are ultimate movements of goods (and profit) associated with shelf space that major retailing organisations—especially supermarket operators—are turning more and more to assessing stock assortments in such terms as sales per square (or linear) metre of space, or gross margin per unit of space per unit of time. Advertising and sales promotion schemes—particularly the latter—are becoming more necessary to gain appropriate space allocation and accelerate movement of goods out of retail stores (*see* II, **19**; III, **27**; and VI).

In the final resort, however, the multiple organisation is concerned with long-run profit, and margins are as important as stock turnover. The more dominant multiples become in trade share, the more likely it is that they will be able to exert pressure on manufacturers' margins.

19. Private branding. Pressure on margins may be increased by the introduction of retailers' own private brands. Privately branded products are almost always sold on the basis of price. These private brands are rarely manufactured by the retailer organisation but are supplied by both small and large manufacturers frequently in addition to their own branded products. Manufacturers may decide to supply privately branded goods on the argument that spare capacity can be utilised or larger runs operated, margins being kept low by selling at prices sufficient to cover or slightly exceed marginal costs. Unless the retailer has a quality control organisation there may be the temptation to lower quality standards; many private brands are certainly variable in quality. The argument of lower costs incurred by the manufacturer does not apply to all types of products, however, and is generally only valid in the case of products where there is a very large margin allowed normally for advertising and promotion. A manufacturer may also be prepared to supply private brands on the argument that, if he doesn't, a competitor will. The potential dangers to his own brands are, of course, obvious.

20. Marks and Spencer: the St Michael brand. In some cases, private brands were developed to overcome the problems of uniform pricing imposed by resale price maintenance, but the practice has grown since the abolition of R.P.M. The outstanding example of private brand marketing with rigid specifications and quality control is the Marks and Spencer operation. The "St Michael" label has been used to create a distinctive quality/value for money image. No competing brands are sold and marketing policy is not based on providing the cheapest product but on satisfying the needs of a large but well-defined market segment.

21. Principles of chain store operations. Significant general principles of chain store operations include the following:

(*a*) *Large volume movement and a high break-even point.* Success, therefore, depends largely on siting.

(*b*) *Uniformity*—store fascias, layout and operational policies.

(*c*) *Concentration on fast-moving lines*—popular manufacturer's brands or private brands.

(*d*) *Centralised buying.*

NOTE: Multiple domination clearly reduces the number of buying points, i.e. the points into which the manufacturing organisation can actually sell. It is, for example, estimated that in the UK the 43% of retail grocery business transacted by multiples involves only 10% of the total number of retail grocery outlets (107,500) and that the buying points are fewer than 170. The number and type of salesmen required for "selling in" is therefore reduced drastically, but there is an increased need for promotional activity at retail outlets.

(*e*) *Minimum customer service* (cf. departmental stores, **22**).

(*f*) *Group advertising and promotional activities.*

(*g*) *Low prices.*

DEPARTMENTAL STORES

22. Characteristics of departmental stores. The departmental store is really a collection of "shops," under one roof and ownership, each shop or department specialising in selling a special range of goods, e.g. clothing, furniture, footwear, cosmetics, electrical goods. Each department normally buys separately, exercises its own stock control and sets its own merchandising policy. There are, therefore, few economies of scale in terms of supply. The advantages must lie in providing service and convenience to customers under a general "house image."

23. Customer service. Customer service advantages may include the following:

(*a*) Provision of wide range of specialised goods in one location.

(*b*) Freedom to move around store to view.

(*c*) Provision of special services such as restaurants, telephones.

24. General principles of departmental store operations. Significant general principles of departmental store operations also include the following:

(*a*) *Siting* in major shopping centres in urban locations.

(*b*) Fairly extensive *local advertising* and specialised promotions, frequently in the form of special "sales."

(*c*) *Delivery services.*

(*d*) *Staff trained* in handling specialised merchandise.

(*e*) *Provision of house services,* e.g. carpet laying, curtain fitting.

(*f*) *Increased leasing of space* for "shops within shops"; space leased to manufacturers, e.g. Berkertex and Jaeger.

(*g*) *Trading-up in price* to compensate for services provided and high overhead structure.

25. Characteristics of variety stores. A variety store is one which handles a wide assortment of goods not necessarily related to each other, e.g. toys, cosmetics, sugar confectionery, hardware. It may be independently owned but is usually owned by a private or public company. A group of variety stores may, therefore, constitute a chain or multiple. Characteristics of variety stores include the following:

(*a*) *Handling of a wide range of unrelated goods* with customer opportunity to walk round store freely.

(*b*) *Preponderance of "convenience" or "impulse" goods* of low unit price.

(*c*) *Absence of credit and delivery service.*

(*d*) *Siting* in major shopping centres.

(*e*) *Counter service* and counter display.

(*f*) *Very limited direct advertising.*

26. Recent trends. Originally variety stores such as Woolworth operated mainly on the principle of low prices—the "bargain" store. More recently, there has been some evidence of extension of the lines stocked to include higher-priced items such as cameras, radios, clothing, kitchen furniture. In some cases there are indications of trading-up. Stocking of more expensive items and trading-up can be seen in the Woolworth operation but more particularly in such chain variety outlets as Littlewoods and British Home Stores. The Marks and Spencer variety chain, as has been previously indicated (**20**), is unique in its adherence to a single brand with rigid control of specification and quality.

In order to reduce operating costs, many variety stores have introduced "cash-and-wrap" operations. Individual counters are unattended and customers take their intended purchases to cash-and-wrap desks located at various points in the stores.

27. Buying practices. The variety chain invariably has a centralised purchasing organisation but there are wide differences in the delegation of purchasing power to individual stores. The Woolworth central buying organisation, for example, may negotiate contract prices and keep store managers informed, but the individual store and district managers are free to make their own purchasing decisions and to negotiate with manufacturers. Marks and Spencer store managers do not have this negotiation freedom and are concerned only with the regulation of quantity and assortment of specified goods from specified sources.

CO-OPERATIVE SOCIETIES

28. Early developments in the UK. The Co-operative movement began in Rochdale in 1844 and was based on the notion that consumers should themselves control production and distribution in order to eliminate the waste of a competitive capitalist system. Dividends were to be paid out from trading surpluses in proportion to purchases made. Each retail society was to have its own area of trading free from competition from another retail society.

29. Later difficulties. The movement progressed fairly well up to the 1930s, but has more recently encountered great difficulties. As the members control the societies there have been tremendous differences in the attitude to change. Consequently many retail societies have stagnated while others have made notable progress. Attention is drawn to the *Co-operative Independent Commission Report* of 1958. It should be noted that Co-operative Societies were pioneers in the two most significant changes which have occurred in the pattern of retail trading, viz. the introduction of self-service and the rise of supermarkets.

Failure to keep pace with competition, however, may be attributed to the following factors:

(*a*) *Poor management.* This stems first from the inefficiency of many management committees consisting of members with no business expertise—committees which are difficult to change because there is usually insufficient organised voting power to replace ineffective members. There is also often a lack of managerial skill in executive store managers because of poor selection, lack of training facilities and inadequate financial incentives.

(*b*) *Poor service*, which stems from poor management.

(*c*) *Lack of integrated policy* between production and distribution. Individual societies have not always supported the Co-operative factories distributing the product through the Co-operative Wholesale Societies in England and Scotland. In turn, there has been a lack of marketing policy and direction in manufacturing and wholesaling organisations. Steps are now being taken to recruit more highly paid experienced marketing experts, and as the C.W.S. has increasingly become involved in the financing of many retail societies a greater measure of control of goods handled at retail is becoming possible.

(*d*) *Lack of member loyalty*. The original notion that members would shop exclusively from Co-operative Stores was impracticable. The increasing attractions of competitive retail outlets have shattered any remaining illusions of large-scale exclusive store loyalty. The attraction of a dividend paid annually has decreased and only recently have quickly redeemable "Divi Stamps" been introduced.

(*e*) *The high degree of decentralisation* has made the economies of scale and improved efficiency techniques of more closely-knit large retail organisations difficult to effect.

(*f*) *Problems in relation to pricing policy and dividends*, provision of capital reserves and accounting procedures generally.

MANUFACTURER-OWNED OUTLETS

30. Arguments against vertical integration. Vertical integration—complete control from production through to ultimate distribution—is comparatively rare for the following reasons:

(*a*) Most companies prefer to utilise limited assets—of skill as well as finance—in specialised activities from which they have the greatest opportunity of profits.

(*b*) Rarely is it possible to provide a satisfactory assortment of goods in retail outlets from a single manufacturer's range.

(*c*) Selling to other (now competitive) retail outlets becomes difficult and the rate of retail growth must therefore correspond closely to the rate of manufacturing growth.

(*d*) The number and range of retail distribution points is inevitably curtailed.

(*e*) It is very difficult to adapt the level range and style of manufacturing output to the fast changing requirements of the consumer market place. The difficulties of integrated tailoring operations, such as Burtons in the late 1970s, demonstrate this problem.

31. Arguments for vertical integration. Arguments in favour of an integrated manufacturing/retailing organisation include the following:

(*a*) Possible cost savings. The elimination of middlemen margins may provide the opportunity for pricing advantages.

(*b*) Provision of more effective service. This argument might apply particularly in the case of certain technical products or "do-it-yourself" items, e.g. Singer sewing machines, Marley tiles.

(*c*) More effective merchandising and broad line stocking. The problems of introducing new or slow-moving items to large retail outlets have been previously mentioned (*see* **18** above).

(*d*) The growth of large-scale integrated organisations dominating distribution of a product range, e.g. footwear, petrol, alcoholic drinks, pharmaceuticals. If a manufacturer has difficulty in gaining adequate retail distribution because many retail outlets are owned by his competitors, he may have to protect his interests by investing in retailing, e.g. Rank's flour is used in shops owned by British Bakeries, Spillers' flour in United Bakeries shops.

DISCOUNT STORES AND FRANCHISING

32. Characteristics of discount stores. Discount stores which began to develop in the USA in the early 1950s became a significant factor in European channel systems in the seventies. Basic features are as follows:

(*a*) *Low price* is the major appeal.

(*b*) *There is a low mark-up* with minimum customer service (mainly self-service). Gross margins on durable items and clothing may, for example, be up to 10% below those operated in departmental, variety or multiple stores.

(*c*) Purchases are mostly for *cash*.

(*d*) *Stores are usually very large* (in the USA normally over 5,000 m² and sometimes exceeding 10,000 m²).

(*e*) *"Hard" goods* are the major lines stocked, but some discount houses have added foods and other "soft" goods.

33. Recent trends. It is interesting to note that there is already evidence in the USA that many discount houses are departing from the original warehouse-like, self-service, cash-down operation, and moving towards the provision of credit financing arrangements, sales attendance and more attractive furnishings. In the UK, Comet already offer servicing guarantees for electrical equipment as well as financing arrangements. Discounters also use very many local media promotions.

34. Difficulties in classifying retail stores. It will now be evident that classification in terms of size, service and range of products carried may be possible in general terms but there is a great deal of overlap. There are small and large co-operatives, there are independent traders who provide counter service while others have self-service, and there has been a reduction in the number of stores carrying a limited range of highly specialised items. The dairy sells sausages, the off-licence sells confectionery, the multiple food store, perhaps, sells paint and kitchenware.

35. Franchising. One of the most interesting distribution developments of the seventies is franchising. The franchisor supplies a name, products, services and general know-how and the franchisee contracts to use all or a major part of the franchisor's services in an agreed manner within an agreed territory. What might be called "first generation" franchising, e.g. tied petrol stations, public houses and car distributors, have been around for a very long time. The present significant factor is the rapid growth to new trading areas, e.g. the restaurant and food industries, home cleaning, printing and copying, car rustproofing etc. Franchising may be attractive to manufacturers in that it offers some of the advantages of forward vertical integration without the risk of capital investment; to the franchisee it offers a degree of independence in operating a business of a size which may otherwise not be feasible.

WHOLESALING

36. The economic purposes. Wholesalers may be said to provide the economic utilities of time, place and possession which may lead to economies in distribution—adequate stocks to be available at the right time in a convenient location.

37. Merchant wholesalers. Most wholesalers fall into this category —they buy and sell goods, taking title to the goods, then deriving profit from the marginal difference between the price at which they buy and the price at which they sell. Most merchant wholesalers undertake the following additional functions:

(*a*) They store goods.
(*b*) They undertake some advertising or promotional activity.
(*c*) They fix selling prices.
(*d*) They arrange credit terms.
(*e*) They make delivery.
(*f*) They offer advisory services.

38. Trade margins. Buying and selling margins vary widely, fluctuating in general with the risk carried and the range and effectiveness of functions performed. If a wholesaler, for example, stocks expensive durable goods which require technical service, his margins must be sufficiently high to compensate for these activities. It would, therefore, be reasonable to expect that the manufacturer of refrigerators who expected a wholesaler to carry high stocks and provide servicing facilities would give much higher margins than a manufacturer of fast-moving canned food products. Sometimes, however, margins remain at a traditional level when original functions such as stocking and servicing are no longer carried out. This state of affairs may occur either because manufacturers are slow to recognise changed circumstances or because they are reluctant to take action in case they lose ground to competitors offering more favourable terms.

39. Size and specialisation. Some merchant wholesalers handle a wide range of general merchandise, but the majority specialise to a greater or lesser extent. Many are small and operate within a comparatively small geographical radius, but a number (particularly in certain trades such as grocery) are large and have regional and even national distribution. Examples of the various types of specialised wholesalers with a limited range of functions are described in **40–45** below.

40. Cash and carry wholesalers. These are at present mainly concerned with grocery products. They offer neither credit nor delivery services and, as a result, operate on lower margins.

41. Rack jobbers. This is a recent development of truck wholesaling, previously limited mainly to perishable goods which may be collected from producers and delivered direct to retailers without the need for storage facilities. Rack jobbers are beginning to carry out a truck wholesaling function in supermarkets, where they may take over responsibility for maintaining stocks and display of particular lines on particular shelves.

42. Brokers. Brokers negotiate sales between sellers and buyers. They take neither title to nor possession of goods. Profits are derived either on the basis of an average commission on value, on a commission on volume, or on a pre-determined fee based on sales. Brokers usually specialise in narrow ranges of products, e.g. sugar, tea, cotton piece-goods. Specialisation is to be expected since their value lies in the deep knowledge of particular markets and market conditions.

43. Factors or commission merchants. Factors do not buy goods, nor do they take title, but they do take possession and provide warehousing and handling facilities. Payment is normally by fixed commission. Whereas the broker represents buyer and/or seller, factors represent the seller only. Factors are most commonly found where there are many small producers and a few large central markets through which products are resold, e.g. agricultural products.

NOTE: The factors here described should be distinguished from factors who specialise in finance and who are really credit wholesalers. Credit factors may buy outstanding debtors' accounts and in doing so take over the function of a credit department. They also sometimes advise on customer selection and debt collection. Some finance factors have entered the business of stock financing, e.g. in the case of car distributors, the dealer could take possession of cars in stock but these would in fact be owned by the finance company to which sales revenue would go. Finance factoring is a growing business.

44. Selling agents. Selling agents are most commonly found where small manufacturers wish to be relieved of marketing responsibility so that very limited financial assets may be devoted exclusively to production. The selling agent usually works closely, therefore, with the manufacturer over long periods, having complete responsibility for all sales. He accordingly sometimes supplies advice on style and design. Some sales agents work for one principal but the majority carry a range of manufacturers' products, normally of a complementary kind. Selling agents sometimes carry the risks of credit loss and have considerable discretion over selling prices.

45. Manufacturers' agents. A manufacturers' agent differs from a selling agent in the following ways:

(*a*) He handles products in a limited geographical area only.

(*b*) He usually handles several manufacturers' lines, although these are normally by terms of the agreement non-competitive.

(*c*) He has little if any freedom to negotiate terms of sale and price.

(*d*) He has usually little control of product-styling design.

(*e*) He is rarely involved in credit collection and risk.

Manufacturers' agents commonly have warehousing facilities from which local deliveries are made, goods being held on consignment. Commissions are normally much smaller than in the case of selling agents since the functions performed and risks involved are smaller. Agency organisations vary in size, although most are comparatively small. They flourish particularly in circumstances where small manufacturers are endeavouring to tackle complex or widespread markets, e.g. industrial supplies and overseas markets. Automobile distribution is, however, conducted mainly through large-scale agencies who have exclusive area selling rights and usually, in return, act for one manufacturer only.

46. Wholesaler-sponsored voluntary groups or chains. The growth of large-scale retail operators is a threat to small independent traders and to wholesalers alike. To counter the threat a number of wholesalers have combined to provide a central staff, while retaining control of the individual business. The central staff provides various services to all retailers who subscribe to the group. Members are expected to purchase a high percentage of their goods from a group wholesaler. Services provided by the central staff may include the following:

(*a*) *Advertising and promotional support* under a group name, e.g. "Mace," "Spar," "Centra," "V.G." Special promotions are arranged with manufacturers.

(*b*) *Advice on merchandising*, layout, equipment.

(*c*) *Advice on retailing efficiency techniques*, stock ranges, accounting, capital utilisation.

(*d*) *Access* to private label products.

(*e*) *Financial assistance* for shop improvements.

(*f*) *Preferential insurance* coverage terms.

(*g*) *Special buying terms* resulting from negotiation of bulk-buying contracts.

It should be noted that the voluntary group wholesaler movement lays great emphasis on assisting members to sell more effectively and enhance profits by greater all-round efficiency, and is not merely or primarily offering goods at cheaper prices. This movement has so far been most prominent in the grocery field, but may well spread to other retail outlets.

47. Retail-sponsored buying groups. Attempts have been made in various retail trades to establish group-buying arrangements on a voluntary basis in order to obtain advantages of larger-scale purchases. Groups are usually formed on a very local basis, sometimes with a central warehouse and office being acquired. The progress of the movement in the UK has been much slower than in some European countries and it seems unlikely that this form of group buying will become a major factor in the foreseeable future.

48. Producers' co-operatives. Producers' co-operatives are at present strongest in agriculture. They aim to provide a more planned and aggressive approach to marketing by:

(*a*) improving the quality of goods offered, through more rigid sorting procedures associated with the grading of produce according to set standards;

(*b*) undertaking co-ordinated promotional activities;

(*c*) regulating output levels in order to avoid the producer disadvantages of inelastic demand.

Producer co-operatives may be formed by the producers themselves and the profit be returned to the owners. The function of producer co-operatives, on the other hand, may be absorbed by government-sponsored marketing organisations.

CHANNEL-CHOICE PROBLEMS FOR THE MANUFACTURER

Channel choice must be considered in the light of market coverage and control, product characteristics and market characteristics.

49. Market coverage and control. Distribution policy can be based on the following systems:

(*a*) *Intensive distribution.* This is a term used in different ways: viz. limited geographical distribution as opposed to national distribution; maximum distribution to all outlets of a specific type, e.g. chemists, grocers; maximum distribution to every possible type of outlet.

(*b*) *Selective distribution.* This involves selection by the producer of the types of retail outlets through which the product may be bought. The decision may be made because of special services required, e.g. television sets, or because of the need to create an appropriate prestige image, e.g. certain cosmetics available from chemists only.

(c) *Exclusive distribution.* This is a further development of selective distribution. Particular outlets are granted exclusive handling rights usually within prescribed geographical areas. Wholesalers are given exclusive distribution rights more frequently than retailers. Sometimes exclusive distribution or franchise rights are coupled with special financing arrangements for land, buildings or equipment, e.g. petrol station agreements.

50. Product characteristics. Those affecting channel decisions are as follows:

(a) *Frequency, value and quantity of purchases.* In general, low-value items bought in large quantity and frequently are widely distributed, using various channel combinations, whereas high-value items infrequently purchased are sold by selective or exclusive distribution, or direct to the consumer.

(b) *Value in relation to weight and density.* The usefulness of intermediaries in the case of large, heavy items of low unit value may lie in their provision of local storage and bulk-breaking facilities.

(c) *Product life or seasonal demand.* Products which deteriorate rapidly or are affected by seasonal demand involve special problems of risk and inventory control which have a bearing on channel selection. Speed of movement is essential and channels tend to be shorter. Special storage, e.g. refrigeration, or transport, e.g. air cargo, may be necessary.

(d) *Product service requirements,* e.g. repair facilities, spares.

51. Market characteristics. Those affecting channel decisions include the following:

(a) *Market size.* If the market is large the cost of performing all the marketing functions will probably be higher and manufacturers may prefer or be forced to use intermediaries extensively. Cost could be reduced, of course, by limiting geographical distribution.

(b) *Market structure.* Consumer markets are inevitably dispersed. There are, however, differences in the concentrations of the potential users and distributors of products. Industrial customers require services of different types, e.g. technical advice, ready availability of spare parts, and although they are fewer in number they may be widely scattered and have very different financial resources.

(*c*) *Market exposure.* Some products are bought almost on impulse and sales are affected by exhibitions and special displays. Others require much more personal selling.

52. Decisions connected with channel selection. After consideration of basic channel problems (**49, 50, 51**) manufacturers are faced with more specific problems such as the following:

(*a*) *Organisation of selective selling.* In most types of business there are many outlets but there is a disproportionate concentration of business in a small number of large units. This leads to "selective selling" and use of more than one channel, e.g. direct sales to large outlets, small outlets being supplied through wholesalers. Nevertheless, profitable operation may depend on securing wide distribution and/or promoting sales of slower-moving lines.

NOTE: Selective selling should not be confused with selective distribution (**49** (*b*)). By selective selling a manufacturer may succeed in obtaining intensive distribution.

(*b*) *Pricing structure.* (*See* V, **14, 15.**)

(*c*) *Terms of sale.* As distinct from price, special credit arrangements, guarantees, and arrangements for return of goods may be necessary.

(*d*) *Organisation of sales forces.* Sales forces may have to be organised partly by territory, partly by product type and partly by outlet size. Centralised buying has led to the creation of "special outlet sales managers" in many companies.

(*e*) *Telephone selling.* The rapid growth of telephone selling must be mentioned. In-house operations in, for example, classified advertising, frozen foods and repeat subscriptions are not new, but there are now specialised telephone selling companies of which the leading six have been established within the past two to three years. Advantages are:

(*i*) quick advertising and assessable results;

(*ii*) rapid contact over a wide market;

(*iii*) cost advantages *vis-à-vis* personal selling calls.

Telephone selling companies have been linked with mailing in campaigns by large British and multi-national plastics manufacturers.

(*f*) *Promotional support.* Channel choice will determine to what extent advertising should be used to *pull* products through the channels and to what extent sales effort will be needed to *push* products through the channels (*see* VI, **10**). It may be necessary to supply private label brands (*see* VII, **21–24**).

(*g*) *Motivation and control of intermediaries.* Intermediaries are frequently order-takers and problems of motivation and provision of sales training may arise. In selective or exclusive distribution systems it will be necessary to evaluate the performance of intermediaries following careful selection. Replacements will have to be considered from time to time. Both intermediaries and channels which are the most suitable or feasible in the early stages of development of a business may cease to be so later on. In general, the further the manufacturer is removed from the ultimate consumer by links in the channel chain, the more difficult it is for him to control the flow of goods.

(*h*) Costs of stock holding.

(*i*) Costs of extending credit.

(*j*) Costs of invoicing, order processing, etc.

(*k*) Costs of transportation.

PROGRESS TEST 9

1. What are the five main types of marketing institutions? **(2)**

2. What are the seven basic processes in marketing? **(6)**

3. What are the main reasons for growth in mail-order business? **(13)**

4. What are the advantages and disadvantages of the small independent retailer? **(16)**

5. Define supermarkets. **(17)**

6. What are the main general principles of chain store operations? **(21)**

7. What have been the main difficulties of retail co-operative societies in recent years? **(29)**

8. What are the main characteristics of discount stores? **(32)**

9. What services do wholesaler-sponsored voluntary groups offer? **(46)**

10. What is meant by "intensive," "selective" and "exclusive" distribution? **(49)**

CHAPTER X

Sales Management

SALES FORCES: TASKS AND ORGANISATION

1. The role of sales forces. Sales forces are concerned with some or all of the six basic steps of the sales process (*see* VI, **7**). The closing of the sale may be the most important contribution to the process which most salesmen make, but some may not be in a position to take orders, e.g. "detailmen" who call on hospitals and general medical practitioners to convey information about the products of pharmaceutical companies. The five other steps involve a salesman, however, in many activities. Amongst these are the following:

(*a*) He may provide merchandising services to speed up the stock turnaround (vital in retailing).

(*b*) He may act mainly as a specialist adviser, e.g. on the installation of telecommunication systems.

(*c*) He may provide after-sales service and advice.

(*d*) He may actually deliver goods—van salesmen, bread roundsmen, etc.

(*e*) He may collect payment for goods delivered.

(*f*) He may be expected to advise on stock levels.

(*g*) He may train and motivate other salesmen, e.g. overseas agents, retail sales staff.

(*h*) He may report back on customer needs and reactions or on market conditions.

(*i*) He may progress orders and handle complaints.

(*j*) He may have a missionary or pioneering role, i.e. locate and open up new business accounts.

(*k*) He may be part of a telephone sales team, e.g. advertising space selling, stock selling of frozen goods.

NOTE: Many salesmen are concerned with the sale of intangible services, e.g. insurance.

2. Selling and status. The range of products and services offered and the range of customer categories upon which salesmen might call are both enormous. Aircraft have to be sold to governments; milk has to be sold to housewives. Some products are bought repeatedly; others very infrequently.

The low status which attaches to the word "salesman" in Britain derives partly from a popular ignorance of the diversity of personal selling tasks. Companies often attempt to overcome the status problem by using job designations such as representative, technical consultant. This is unfortunate since all salesmen are concerned to a greater or lesser extent in actively persuading and educating prospective customers to reach the point of deciding to buy or to continue buying the company's products or services.

COMPANY OBJECTIVES AND SALES FORCE DECISIONS

3. Sales force decisions. A company must decide why it is employing a sales force, what role the sales force is to perform in the marketing mix. This basic decision will affect other decisions:

(a) What is to be the size of the sales force?

(b) How should the sales force be organised; e.g. by products, by geographical territories, by customer categories?

(c) What is to be the comparative importance of the various activities of the sales force, e.g. actual selling, providing technical service, display?

(d) What kind of men (or women) are required?

(e) What levels and systems of payment should be adopted?

(f) What structure, e.g. levels of management, is required?

4. Sales force size. The size of the sales force will depend mainly on the following factors:

(a) *The resources available to the company* and consideration of returns in relation to alternative forms of investment at particular times under particular conditions. A company with small financial resources will clearly be restricted in employing salesmen, who inevitably carry a high burden of expense. A company may decide it can meet its objectives by other means, e.g. investment in advertising, and therefore may rely entirely on mail-order selling.

(b) *The value of potential orders.* The expense of operation must be measured against the returns. The key factor is profitability. In some cases a company may be selling a particular piece of capital equipment at a price which covers easily the cost of direct sales representation. However, where unit margins are low and varied, a key consideration becomes the potentially profitable assortment of products which the salesman has to offer. It is, therefore, logical to consider the minimum potential order value which will warrant the expense of personal representation.

(c) *The location and number of potential customers.* All other things being equal, consumer sales forces are larger than industrial sales forces since there are far more potential customers for consumer goods, scattered more evenly across wider areas. Industrial salesmen may, however, waste travelling time in visiting widely scattered accounts if too small a force is employed.

(d) *The buying habits and characteristics of potential customers.* Existing efficient channels of distribution, e.g. good wholesalers and retailers, may mean that fewer salesmen are required. Lack of efficient channels and need for demonstrations and technical information—as in some industrial markets—may mean that the ratio of salesmen to potential end users should be high. The *frequency of call* rate must also be taken into account here.

(e) *The product and customer range.* Different products may sometimes be handled effectively by one salesman calling on similar types of outlets—or sometimes even on different types of outlets. The depth and breadth of product range may, however, lead to a position when salesmen become ineffective because they have too many products to handle or products which require different technical knowledge or sales journeys which are uneconomical.

(f) *Marketing policy.* The company may decide to concentrate on selective distribution or to attempt the widest possible distribution.

5. Sales force organisational patterns. Sales forces are normally organised on the basis of:

(a) geographical areas;
(b) product types;
(c) customer types;
(d) customer sizes; or
(e) a combination of geography, product and customer types.

These five patterns are described in **6–10** below (*see* also **13**).

6. Allocation by geographical area. The possible advantages of a single salesman assigned to cover all company products in a particular territory are:

(a) savings in travel expenses;
(b) better local and customer knowledge;
(c) avoidance of multiple calling on the same customer.

The products offered, however, must be fairly homogeneous and within the technical competence of the salesman to handle. In addition, the need for frequency of call must be judged against the number of calls which have to be made, when determining the extent of each salesman's area.

7. Allocation by product types. Sales force structures built around product specialisations have the advantage that highly qualified salesmen can be employed to deal with technical explanations and problems, e.g. pharmaceuticals, lifting equipment. This type of structure is favoured by larger companies who have highly diversified specialised product lines, each making substantial profit contributions.

8. Allocation by customer types. Product specialisation selling may lead to duplication of calling on the same customers, whereas a specialised knowledge of different kinds of customers, their organisations, attitudes and product applications, may be just as important as a specialised knowledge of the product. Sales forces may, therefore, be organised to call on particular market segments, e.g. on laundries, on retail outlets. The development of systems selling, e.g. of a range of items to furnish an office—carpets, curtains, filing cabinets, tables and chairs—often leads to customer type organisations.

9. Handling large outlets. The significance of large outlets in relation to total market size has given rise to the practice in some companies of creating a sales force to handle key accounts. In some cases key accounts, often termed "House Accounts," may be handled by the sales manager himself or by other sales executives.

10. Mixed selling systems. A combination of the above four basic types of structure is increasingly found in large organisations offering diversified products to wide-ranging markets. The combination approach leads to inter-company communication problems, e.g. the relationship between product managers and sales managers. Not only is there a staff-line organisation problem, but also a problem of co-ordinating the objectives and plans of different product managers competing for the attention of sales managers responsible for the field selling operations.

The overall role of the sales force as a part of the promotion sales process (*see* VII, **5**) must be determined in order that the sales manager may be given a clear definition of his objectives and the standards by which his performance will be judged. The objectives will determine the responsibility and authority assigned to him.

SALES MANAGEMENT TASKS

Sales management is concerned with the planning, direction and control of sales forces. Objectives may differ, but there are certain tasks common to almost all sales management roles.

11. Selection. Good selection presupposes a knowledge of the requirements of the particular job. It is, therefore, desirable that jobs should be analysed and at least that a detailed job description is drawn up. The job description might lay down the overall objectives, detailed duties and responsibilities, limits of authority, organisational relationships and minimum standards of qualifications, experience and personal qualities required. Job analysis is desirable not only for selection but also for training, performance evaluation, and motivation.

Good selection also demands interviewing skill and a knowledge of personality, intelligence and aptitude tests which may guide judgment.

12. Manpower planning. Selling is an activity which, in general, is associated—particularly in the early years of employment—with high turnover rates. Some sales managers would even argue that a reasonable rate of turnover is desirable on the grounds that injections of new personnel bring in new enthusiasm or new ideas. It is also sometimes asserted that turnover is inevitable, since promotion opportunities are often inadequate in sales organisation. It should be remembered that turnover is expensive in terms of the time and money spent on advertising, interviewing and retraining. It can also have damaging effects on general morale. In recent years turnover in some sales forces has reached a level which has disturbed even the most cynically minded sales managers, and it is clear that more consideration must be given to overall manpower policies and career planning. Questions which need to be raised and answered include:

(*a*) Is it company policy to open up avenues of promotion in marketing careers other than selling to selling recruits? Some marketing executives would appear to take the line that over-long experience in selling with its encouragement of a subjective persuasive way of thinking is an insurmountable barrier to career transfer to marketing positions calling for an objective, analytical approach to problems. This kind of thinking seems to be more prevalent amongst executives concerned with the marketing of consumer goods and services than those concerned with industrial markets.

(b) Are personnel specifications set too high in relation to the job description and career prospects? Is it wise to seek the "best" prospects for a routine merchandising task with little in the way of progressive career opportunity?

(c) Are selling organisation structures too flat? Is there not some opportunity of introducing structures which permit greater promotional opportunity in selling—quite apart from other marketing avenues?

(d) Is it not important to distinguish between those selling tasks which require considerable time for the establishment of the appropriate level of confidence amongst a wide range of people influencing the buying decision, e.g. capital projects and those where sales development appears to be comparatively little affected by changes in sales personnel, e.g. strongly branded mass consumer products?

13. Training. New salesmen should be provided with a period of induction and organised training. Special refresher courses will be required from time to time, and there should be a continuous programme of planned development. Training is essentially the responsibility of line management and not of personnel departments who act in a "staff" capacity. Decisions have to be made on the length of training periods required, the content of the training (product knowledge, market knowledge, selling skills, administrative procedures, etc.) and the method. Method is extremely important and, as most training will be given on the job, it is important to select and train instructors.

14. Design of sales territories and allocation of salesmen. A sales territory may be part of a larger unit, e.g. a salesman's area which is part of a sales manager's district.

Basic considerations in designing sales territories are as follows:

(a) To divide work loads equitably.

(b) To provide adequate sales potential for motivation purposes.

(c) To reduce travel and expense as much as possible.

(d) To provide for simple administration and control.

The establishment of sales potential in a given area provides a basis against which performances can be assessed, but it is often more difficult to achieve sales in some areas than in others. Again, a sales manager may decide that, even if it were possible to equalise opportunities to sell, some inequality should be preserved to allow for the introduction of new men and means of motivating more highly skilled or more senior men. The problems of territory design and allocation are linked inextricably with the problems of target setting and reward (*see* **15**).

Once a territory is defined it is important to consider how best coverage may be achieved and routing plans in relation to the salesman's home base can make enormous differences to operating efficiency.

15. Allocation of targets and financial consideration. Salesmen are paid in three main ways:

(*a*) *Payment by straight salary.* This method is commonly used in sales situations either where the role of the salesman involves many considerations other than actual orders received, or when orders are very infrequent, e.g. in many industrial markets. The method does not, of course, preclude the setting of targets as indirect non-financial motivation.

(*b*) *Payment by salary and commission or bonus.* This method is to be found regularly in sales situations where orders are frequently taken or credited to salesmen, e.g. in consumer products or industrial materials.

(*c*) *Payment by straight commission.* This method is increasingly rare and is normally associated with speciality selling, e.g. of encyclopedias or specialised capital equipment by agents.

Financial incentives have a very profound effect on the performance of sales forces, but they must be devised in such a way that the additional payments are geared to an appropriate increase in company profitability and so that the basis on which rewards are given is seen to be as fair as possible. The sales manager, therefore, has a considerable problem in taking a complete sales target and allocating it among individual areas and territories.

While individual financial incentives are considered by many to be the most effective, it is often impracticable to allocate the reward for a particular sale to one specific salesman. One man may have taken a central order, others may have provided displays, others may have provided technical services. *Group bonus schemes* are, therefore, sometimes applied to areas or districts. It is sometimes argued that the group bonus has other advantages over individual incentives in developing the group spirit which is necessary for more effective total sales performance.

Under purely commission systems of payment the company loses direct control and unless commissions are based on very sophisticated lines it is difficult to develop business systematically, e.g. by introducing new accounts, or by spreading sales across products or customer types. Once established, it is difficult to adjust commission rates; sales targets and bonus systems to salaried sales forces require regular revision.

16. Fixed and variable elements in financial rewards. Salesmen often enjoy a number of fringe benefits which, unlike bonuses, become a fixed cost. These benefits may include provision of a company car with special concessions for private motoring, or an allowance for mileage for use of a personally owned car, garage allowances, lunch allowances, safe driving rewards, entertainment expenses and so on. The problem is to determine compensation in the light of the task to be performed, the supply of suitable men, the conditions in the particular country, and practices of competitors. This includes:

(*a*) The system of compensation;

(*b*) the level of compensation; and

(*c*) the constituent parts of the total compensation.

Few generalisations are of any value, but, where actual selling is a frequently performed and major role of the salesman, a combination of fixed and variable compensation elements seems to be ideal. The fixed element has to be sufficiently high to provide for basic security and living standards; the variable element has to be sufficiently meaningful to both salesman and company. A combination of fixed and variable remuneration has advantages in adjusting potential earnings according to changes in costs of living, changes in the company's profit record and various combinations of seniority and selling achievement. The problems are to devise equitable systems and to set equitable targets.

17. Direction and control. Important factors are as follows:

(*a*) *Economy in the use of time and effort.* The maximum amount of time should be spent on the outlets of major profit to the company. Waiting and travelling time should be kept to the minimum.

(*b*) *Arranging call frequency and rating.* Some outlets will require longer or more regular calls than others.

(*c*) *Development of business.* This includes increasing the business transacted with existing customers as well as locating and opening new accounts.

(*d*) *Reporting*. Reports will be required daily, weekly or monthly on calls made. Salesmen should also learn to report back significant field intelligence, e.g. competitive activity, future developments by major customers. Reports on lost business or complaints will be required.

(*e*) *Evaluating the performance of salesmen*. Salesmen's performance should be evaluated on quantitative factors, e.g. progress towards targets, comparison with past performance, business development in relation to territory potential. Qualitative assessment will also be necessary since the salesman will have to undertake part of the selling process other than closing sales (*see* VI, 7). It is increasingly common to find that salesmen are appraised formally on their performance once or twice each year. Appraisal forms are frequently used and these often indiscriminately list quantitative and qualitative factors, e.g. attainment of target sales, condition of car, expenses against budget, initiative, etc. The primary assessment should be on achievement of quantifiable objectives weighted according to their importance. Many of the qualitative factors on appraisal sheets refer to subjective assessments of personal characteristics or methods, and these should be considered only in so far as they may affect individual performance or company reputation and be susceptible to change by training or practice. A good appraisal scheme should be viewed by the salesman as a mutually open exchange of view between himself and his manager, a frank analytical performance check and, when necessary, a basis for agreeing on personal development action plans (*see* 19).

MOTIVATION

18. Special problems of motivating salesmen. Motivation of field sales forces provides special problems, for the following reasons:

(*a*) A salesman meets frustration very regularly—every time he fails to make a sale or gain a favourable buying reaction. He can quickly lose confidence and his future performance suffers.

(*b*) A salesman works alone and lacks the immediate moral support of company colleagues. Sometimes he feels he lacks company backing if deliveries are late or invoices are incorrectly made out.

(*c*) A salesman has irregular hours and sometimes is away from home. This may lead to special personal tensions.

(*d*) Few people are always self-motivating and high morale and a sense of reward or achievement are necessary for a man to sustain effort if left entirely to his own devices.

19. Means of motivation. The need for a favourable working climate is, therefore, obvious. This can be stimulated in various ways:

(*a*) By providing helpful direction, e.g. assistance in field operations, by personal visits rather than perpetual written communications.

(*b*) By arranging sales and social meetings periodically.

(*c*) By arranging special sales contests.

(*d*) By making special efforts in writing and by telephone to keep men in the picture about company or area developments and progress.

(*e*) By encouraging positive suggestions for improved personal or company operation.

(*f*) By devising fair performance evaluation schemes, assisting men to develop their own capabilities, and providing a route to promotion or increased financial reward.

(*g*) By reducing unnecessary administrative procedures.

(*h*) By providing equipment and information to assist in the selling operation, e.g. sales manuals, sales literature, samples, demonstration models.

MARKET AND SALES FORECASTING

20. Basic forecasting considerations. Market and sales forecasting methods and procedures vary very considerably from company to company but there are really three basic considerations to be taken into account:

(*a*) The general economic environment and outlook.

(*b*) The particular industry environment and outlook.

(*c*) The outlook for the particular company and its products.

(*d*) Company and competitive marketing plans.

The above considerations should be related specifically to every product-market segment in which the organisation operates. For a company concerned with the marketing of tyres, for example, there would have to be a breakdown in terms of demand by tyre type, size and price bracket; by demand from original equipment manufacturers as opposed to replacement demand; by distributor size and type; by geography. Products and services should also be considered in the light of the stage they have reached in the product-market life cycle. New products in markets where demand is mainly dependent on innovators should be distinguished from products on sale in mature, developed markets. Companies marketing similar products and services to a range of different industrial and commercial end-users will find considerable variations in end-use demand trends and structure.

21. Forecasting time periods. Forecasts cover different time periods:

(*a*) *Short term.* The operating budget forecast covers the immediate financial year and is used to determine standard costs, prices, cash flow and similar matters.

(*b*) *Long term.* Forecasts are required for varying periods of time ahead, to provide for items such as major capital requirement, new market or product developments.

22. Basic forecasting methods. Three basic methods are used for short-term forecasts—often in combination:

(*a*) Estimates (or guesses) by executives.

(*b*) Internal analysis of company data, e.g. using regression analysis (*see* V, **27**).

(*c*) Analysis of company data related to other external performance criteria, e.g. economic conditions, industry trends. This form of analysis normally involves the use of statistical techniques such as correlation analysis (*see* V, **27**).

In any attempt to predict future demand from historical data, great attention should be paid not only to absolute levels of demand in specific product-market segments but to monitoring rates of change. Key decision points occur where there are major directional changes in the typical S-curve of demand.

23. Sources of additional forecasting information. In order to supplement the information gained from various forms of statistical analysis, companies sometimes undertake the following exercises in addition to use of marketing research data:

(*a*) *Surveys of buyers' intentions.* It would obviously be impracticable to approach every potential buyer or even to identify every one. Consequently a sample is normally taken (*see* III, **18–25**). Enquiries may be carried out by market research personnel, but sometimes sales forces are asked to co-operate. This method is more often practised when there is a comparatively small number of significant purchasers, e.g. in some industrial markets. Difficulties arise if:

(*i*) buyers are unwilling to give information (salesmen may find this a major problem);

(*ii*) buyers give deliberately false information;

(*iii*) buyers themselves do not really know.

(*b*) *Seeking the opinion of salesmen and sales executives.* The advantages should be:

(*i*) that men in touch with actual buying conditions should know what is likely to happen;

(*ii*) that the forecasts will be readily available by products or areas;

(*iii*) that the sales force will support the forecast more readily because it has participated in the process.

This practice also has its greatest validity in highly technical selling fields. Adjustments have to be made to compensate for the over-optimism of some salesmen and the low estimates of others who fear that targets will be increased if sales estimates are high.

24. Problems in the analysis of internal data. Analysis of company data should take into consideration the following:

(*a*) Variations in demand—resulting from seasonal factors, cyclical changes in consumption and cyclical changes in inventory.

(*b*) Secular change—long-term trends of growth or decline in demand brought about by substitution or obsolescence.

(*c*) Random factors—chance or temporary changes in sales.

(*d*) Changes in the company's own market share position.

25. Statistical processes. Once seasonal factors are removed, random factors can be eliminated by the use of moving averages to produce a trend line (*see* NOTE (*i*) below). The problem now is to project the trend. Sometimes statistical means are used, e.g. the use of the *least squares method* (*see* NOTE (*ii*) below). There still remains the problem of allowing for changes in the business cycle which affect some types of industry (e.g. textiles) more than others (e.g. food). Sometimes it is possible to use *correlation analysis,* i.e. to establish a relationship between specific materials or products, and demand for a company's own products. Thus a change in demand for retail products may be seen to have direct relationship to a change in demand for packaging, or a change in population to *per capita* demand for food.

NOTE:

(*i*) A moving average is a moving total divided by the number of periods constituting that total. A moving total for twelve-monthly periods, for example, would be determined by dropping out the earliest monthly total and substituting the latest monthly total as it becomes available. For short-term forecasting many organisations are now using exponentially weighted moving averages, following a technique devised by Professor Holt of the Carnegie Institute of Technology. The weightings applied to a series of moving averages form a geometric progression. The latest data is thus given the greatest weighting and the diminishing weightings of previous data are systematically reduced by the use of a smoothing constant determined from examination of the nature of the demand curve.

(ii) It is most unlikely that the figures to be plotted on a graph will fall in a straight line which would show immediately the trend. The trend has, therefore, to be established by finding the line which would most nearly fit, i.e. where the values shown on the line (the trend) would be nearer to actual values than any other line. The method of least squares is based on the mathematical concept that the best line is the one that minimises the total of the squared deviations.

26. Forecasting accuracy. The extent of forecasting error should be considered in the light of the cost of excessive stock-holding or out-of-stock situations and delivery hold-ups. It may not be economically justifiable to incur the cost of reducing errors by plus or minus 1 per cent, but it is certainly important to know the likely limits of error and few companies are really satisfied with the reliability of their present forecasting procedures. If inaccuracy is seriously affecting profits, greater attention must be paid to preparing the basic economic assumptions, securing relevant and reliable data and applying sound statistical techniques, and to analysing more closely the effect on demand of product policy, pricing and promotion.

27. Sales forecasting and sales targets. Sales targets are derived from a consideration of sales forecasts, i.e. levels of sales anticipated at various levels of marketing expense. Sales targets do not necessarily coincide exactly with the finally accepted forecast, since targets are motivational tools (**15**) and may be set at a slightly higher level than the forecast in order to stimulate salesmen to greater effort. Where salesmen are involved in the forecasting process it should be noted that there is a real problem in practice in dissociating the idea of a forecast from that of a target. The experienced salesman may well realise that his future earnings will be geared to his estimate of sales and make suitable downward modifications. Another source of possible distortion in a salesman's estimates may arise in the form of upward modifications where there has been a history of delay or shortfall in deliveries on his particular territory (*see* 23).

28. Marketing plans and forecasting—the link. Forecasting and marketing planning are complementary activities. Marketing plans are part of the corporate strategic and tactical decision making process. The first stage is normally the identification and quantification of marketing opportunities, but consideration of resource availability, overall company objectives, risk, etc. enter into the picture. Before plans are put into action they will require top-level approval and the participation of those also concerned with forecasts, e.g. accountants, production managers, purchasing officers, personnel controllers, etc. Marketing specialists take the lead in the forecasting process, involving sales personnel at various levels according to task and situation.

PROGRESS TEST 10

1. What are the various functions which might be performed by sales forces? **(1)**
2. What consideration might determine the size of a sales force? **(4)**
3. On what bases might sales forces be organised? **(5)**
4. What are the problems of providing financial incentives to sales forces? **(15, 16)**
5. How might salesmen be motivated? **(19)**
6. What are the problems in interpreting company data for the purpose of forecasting? **(24)**

CHAPTER XI

Marketing Industrial Goods and Services

The main principles of marketing as set out in earlier chapters apply to the marketing of all types of goods and services. The special characteristics of industrial markets, however, lead to special problems in the application of those principles.

BASIC MARKET CHARACTERISTICS

1. Definition. Industrial goods and services are those bought by manufacturers, distributors, institutions (e.g. schools, government departments, extractive industries, agriculture and other commercial enterprises) for their own use rather than for resale.

2. Classification. There are four basic categories as follows:

(*a*) *Capital goods*. These goods include such items as factory structures, machinery, office furniture and materials-handling equipment. Capital goods are treated by accountants as capital assets of a business, their value being depreciated over given periods of time.

(*b*) *Components and materials*. These include basic raw materials and partly or wholly processed materials and goods which form ultimately part of the products which are sold to customers, e.g. copper, tyres, sparking plugs, packaging.

(*c*) *Supplies*. Supplies are goods which assist production and distribution but are not included in finished products and, unlike capital goods, are not regarded as a capital investment. Examples include lubricating oils, stationery, cleaning materials.

(*d*) *Business services*. These cover a wide range of intangible services, e.g. business consultancy, office cleaning, advertising.

3. Special features of industrial products. There are certain common features distinguishing industrial and consumer products as follows:

(*a*) *Product similarity*. Industrial products have frequently to conform with national or international standards. This limits the extent to which a producer can differentiate his products from those of competitors. Again, buyers often lay down their own specifications. In general, the more a product is processed or fabricated the greater is the possibility of differentiation: cf. steel and office furniture.

(b) *Technical complexity.* Many industrial products call for a high level of technological skill and precision, e.g. electric motors, paper-making machinery. This factor means that not only is there often a need to maintain high investment in research and development activities and manufacturing processes, but it is frequently essential to supply technical assistance and advice. Provision for after-sales maintenance and for the supplying of spare parts is also frequently necessary.

(c) *High unit values.* Industrial goods, e.g. capital equipment, are frequently highly expensive items. The unit value of components and materials may be comparatively low, but the quantity required usually means that the value of total sales to individual customers is high.

(d) *Irregularity of purchase.* Materials which are used as part of finished products must be bought fairly regularly, but many other items, e.g. equipment, have a long working life and their purchase can be deferred. Components and materials are also frequently bought on a contract basis and the opportunity to obtain new business may arise infrequently.

4. Technological forecasting. Since traditional products and processes with high levels of committed investment are facing more rapidly the challenges of technological obsolescence, it is not surprising that considerable attention is being paid to a comparatively new type of forecasting—technological forecasting. Key questions which have to be answered include:

(a) What are the particular demand factors which promote the development of particular technologies?

(b) What are the total potentials for new technologies and at what speed will they be adopted in particular markets? The direction and speed of technology transfer is indeed a significant problem. The impact of nuclear and computer technology and satellite communications, for example, falls on government and private undertakings over a wide range of activities.

One of the techniques associated with technological forecasting is the *Delphi* method whereby a panel of specialists is invited to express views on the probabilities of major technical changes taking place along a future time-scale. The method involves a series of carefully planned sequential investigations and further details of this and other methods at present being explored are outside the range of this HANDBOOK.

The importance of these developments should be stressed, however, since it has been estimated that, by the year 2000, for every £1 spent on successful research in heavy industry, £25 will subsequently be spent on development work and £500 on commercialisation.

5. Special features of industrial demand. The following considerations are particularly important:

(a) *Derived demand.* The demand for industrial products is dependent on the demand for consumer products. A fall in consumer demand would quickly affect the demand for materials used in consumer goods, and a lack of buoyancy in consumer markets would lead to reluctance on the part of producers to buy new equipment or replace existing equipment. Because of derived demand, industrial markets are subject to greater irregularities in demand pattern than consumer markets and the problems of forecasting are greater. Not only are there annual fluctuations; demand levels also often vary enormously from month to month.

(b) *Inelasticity of demand.* From the above it will be seen that lowering prices cannot be expected to have the same effect as in many consumer markets. If there is not ultimate consumer demand the price of industrial goods and services is irrelevant. On the other hand, if there is a lowering in total demand, price reduction might provide an important advantage in the case of an individual company. Nevertheless, large price differences are unlikely since producers will be often using similar materials from similar sources and competitors will probably react by reducing their prices. The greatest price fluctuations are to be found in markets for materials and components, where there are more suppliers competing for business than in capital goods markets.

6. Special features of industrial market structures. There are a number of marked structural characteristics of industrial markets. The most important are as follows:

(a) *Number of potential buyers.* It is clear that there are fewer potential industrial than consumer buyers. These buyers also have more specialised needs. Thus industrial markets consist of a number of special segments. The demand for certain products will be limited to one specialised segment, e.g. agricultural machinery.

The demand for other products may be spread across a number of segments, e.g. industrial oils. The total number of potential buyers in different segments will vary tremendously: cf. distributive services and aircraft manufacture. In all industrial market segments, however, a small number of buyers account for a very high percentage of the total market demand.

(*b*) *Geographical concentration.* Many industries are concentrated in particular geographical areas, e.g. paper making, car manufacture. On the other hand, the demand for certain products and services is geographically widespread, e.g. industrial cleaning materials.

7. Special features of industrial buying. Attention must be drawn to the following:

(*a*) Economic motives (*see* **8**).
(*b*) The group-buying influence (*see* **9**).
(*c*) Professionalism (*see* **10**).
(*d*) Reciprocal buying (*see* **11**).
(*e*) Supplier loyalty (*see* **12**).

8. Economic motives. Industrial buyers are essentially concerned with the acquisition of goods and services which will provide measurable benefits in terms of ultimate profit. This, combined with the fact that the cost of purchase is often high, means that rational economic motives are much more significant than purely emotional considerations. Although industrial products are bought on a performance and benefit basis, however, it should be remembered that industrial buyers are subject to human emotions. Emotional aspects of buying may be seen, for example, in the following:

(*a*) Differences in attitudes of buyers towards features such as colour and design which may have no obvious economic value.

(*b*) Differences in attitudes of buyers towards particular salesmen, sales literature, supplying companies.

(*c*) Differences in attitude towards salesmen in general which may have a sociological or psychological basis. The position and status of a professional buyer in the formal organisation structure, for example, will affect his attitude to sales approaches. One buyer with low company status may wish to bolster his ego by adopting a militant manner to salesmen; another may be anxious to learn of new developments in order to gain a benefit for his company which might improve his own standing.

9. The group-buying influence. The final purchasing order for industrial goods and services may be signed by one man, but the decision to buy is usually the result of the opinions of a number of people. These people may be motivated in different ways. The benefits seen by a manufacturing specialist may be minimised by an accounting specialist, for example. Again, persons who influence the buying decision may have different formal and informal status in their organisations. In general, research has shown that, the larger the organisation, the greater is the number of people who influence buying decisions.

Robinson, Faris and Wind, in an important American research report *Industrial Buying and Creative Marketing*, have drawn attention to the differences in the "decision-making unit" according to whether the purchasing decision is:

(a) a new buy;
(b) a modified re-buy;
(c) a straight re-buy.

Modified re-buy situations differ from routine straight re-buy situations in that some pressures exist to depart from routine, e.g. a cost/profit squeeze; an existing supplier having to stagger deliveries. Modified re-buy and, particularly, new-buy situations open up the real opportunities for a potential supplying company to contact a wide range of decision-makers and to offer creative ideas.

10. Professionalism. Industrial buyers are often not only familiar with technical and basic cost requirements, they may be specialists in such matters as evaluating sources of supply and deciding on the appropriate level of investment in stocks. Buying organisations are more and more concerned with setting basic standards of product and delivery performance, service requirements and so on, which must be met before a potential supplier can be seriously considered. The level of buying expertise varies tremendously. In general, the larger the buying company and the greater the expenditure involved, either in terms of capital equipment or in terms of cost of materials and components in relation to total costs, the greater is the professionalism of the actual buyer.

11. Reciprocal buying. This may be an informal arrangement whereby a buying organisation tends to favour suppliers who are customers. On the other hand, there may be strictly formal agreements.

Formal agreements are not particularly widespread and have the great disadvantage of preventing buyers from obtaining the best value. It should here be pointed out that many large industrial organisations have highly diversified interests in different types of businesses. Sometimes there is complete control of capital; at other times there is a considerable percentage share-holding. Formal and informal reciprocal or transfer buying arrangements might be anticipated in such circumstances. Transfer arrangements apply to systems whereby one company or department buys components or processed materials from another, each unit operating as a profit centre. Sometimes when transfer arrangements are possible, buyers are still free to obtain supplies from outside sources if there are special advantages.

12. Supplier loyalty. Amongst industrial buyers there is frequently much greater loyalty to traditional suppliers than is the case in consumer markets. The reasons may be essentially emotional, e.g. the establishment of a personal relationship between buyers and sellers. Another important reason is that a new piece of equipment or new materials in industrial processes frequently affect total performance. Industrial buyers are, therefore, reluctant to change. Large organisations may have research and pilot plant facilities where prolonged testing can be carried out and the period of negotiation for a major purchase may be quite lengthy.

SPECIAL FEATURES OF THE MARKETING MIX

13. Industrial selling. Direct selling, i.e. from producer to user, is a feature of many industrial marketing operations. The main reasons for this shortening of the channels of distribution are as follows:

(*a*) There are fewer customers and these may be geographically concentrated. The potential size of orders is large. Thus fewer salesmen are necessary to establish direct contact and the cost in relation to potential business is normally lower than in the case of direct personal selling to domestic customers.

(*b*) Considerable technical knowledge and demonstrations may be required in the selling process. The manufacturer's salesmen can be expected to be more effective, therefore, than salesmen of intermediaries who may handle a wide range of products.

(*c*) Many industrial items are bought to individual specifications and involve direct negotiation between buyer and seller on a technical level.

(*d*) Items of high unit value may require special credit arrangements which are more easily negotiated on a direct basis. Some items may be leased or rented.

(*e*) The importance of servicing and after-sales technical advice leads many buyers to prefer direct dealings with manufacturers.

(*f*) Industrial buyers need a much more individual approach than consumer buyers. It would be impossible in most cases to arrange for a standard monthly presentation of a drive brand, for example. Individual benefits have to be sold to meet the needs of particular organisations and people within those organisations.

NOTE: It is important that industrial salesmen should combine appropriate technical expertise and selling skill. There is a danger that industrial salesmen may be appointed on the basis of the technical qualifications alone and there is frequently insufficient training in selling skills provided.

14. Industrial advertising. Advertising is a much smaller constituent of marketing costs than in consumer marketing. Apart from the fact that advertising budgets are lower, there are many distinguishing features of industrial promotion, including those considered in **15–18** below.

15. Use of mass media. As industrial markets are highly segmented it is usually wasteful to use mass media. Some companies do advertise in the national press for the following reasons:

(*a*) To build up a corporate image of a large progressive organisation. Large companies whose products may be used in many market segments, e.g. I.C.I., are more likely to derive direct advantage from mass communication media than smaller companies offering a limited product range. Corporate images also serve to attract investment and personnel.

(*b*) To attract the attention of executives who may influence the buying decision but rarely have the opportunity or inclination to read specialised journals.

(*c*) To stimulate consumer demand for products which will reflect on industrial demand. Consumer campaigns for man-made fibres and plastics are good examples of this. The industrial manufacturer may have much greater resources than the distributors along the distribution chain. In some cases, therefore, industrial manufacturers bear the whole cost of such advertising; in others they may make a contribution towards the cost of advertising.

NOTE: Consumer campaigns organised by industrial manufacturers are often associated with branding, e.g. Terylene, Acrilan.

16. Specialised media. Industrial advertising is usually concentrated in the following media:

(*a*) *Trade press.* The range of journals is extremely wide; some are aimed at highly specialised readers, e.g. *Photographic Abstracts*, while others have a more general appeal, e.g. Purchasing. There are also considerable variations in costs of space, frequency of publication, circulation (often an estimate and not subjected to audit) and so on. This leads to specially acute problems in media scheduling and planning.

(*b*) *Business and professional journals.* These are ever changing in number, format, circulation and influence. Professional journals often have a guaranteed circulation to members, e.g. *Work Study*, *Marketing*.

(*c*) *Direct mail.* There is evidence of the growing use of planned direct mail campaigns. In many industrial markets where prospective customers can be identified, are relatively few in number, and can be mailed at different times, use of this medium can bring valuable results, e.g. in stimulating enquiries to be followed up by salesmen; in keeping companies constantly informed of developments between sales visits.

(*d*) *Films.* Expenditure on documentary films for cinema showing could be justified by very few companies, but the specialised use of films is particularly appropriate in industrial markets. Industrial products are often large and difficult to demonstrate, specially if complex industrial processes are involved. Films can be used at trade shows, at national and international exhibitions, and at private company demonstrations. The use of special equipment for the showing of films by salesmen on customer calls should lead to the stimulation of greater attention and interest.

(*e*) *Sales aids.* The provision of catalogues, price lists and sales literature is a vital part of any industrial advertising programme. Insufficient attention is often paid to the design and use of this material and salesmen are inclined to rely too much on verbal descriptions and means of persuasion.

(*f*) *Exhibitions.* These are a feature of industrial marketing, but the large investment involved in participating in many national exhibitions is often unjustified except on the basis of keeping in line with competition. The case for arranging mobile exhibitions, e.g. in vans and special trains, is usually much stronger, as is that for participating in important international exhibitions (*see* XII, 55).

17. Advertising agencies. Large agencies often concentrate on consumer goods campaigns because of the higher total expenditure and often better media discounts (15% as opposed to 10% offered by many trade publications). There are sometimes, therefore, difficulties in finding agencies willing and able to undertake campaigns suitably geared to industrial users. Some smaller agencies specialise in this kind of work.

18. Establishing advertising objectives. Because of the range of specialised needs and buying motivations and the relative infrequency of buying, it is more difficult to establish clear objectives for a promotional programme than in consumer markets. The relatively low budgets and wide range of media available complicate the issue and advertising expenditure is frequently wasted. It is particularly important that objectives should be clarified when resources are so scarce. Too many industrial advertisements attempt to communicate too much at one time and too many campaigns are spoilt by attempting wide coverage at infrequent intervals.

NOTE: Publicity (*see* VII) is a specially powerful industrial marketing tool.

19. Trends in organisation and negotiation. There is a real decline in purely geographically structured sales forces and the following trends are clearly to be seen:

(*a*) More key account salesmen specialising in large customers.

(*b*) More "new account" salesmen requiring special qualities of enthusiasm, patience, ingenuity—pioneer selling as opposed to maintenance selling.

(*c*) More market- or product-centred sales forces geared to particular industries, specialised applications etc.

A great deal more attention is also being given to developing negotiating skills and providing the appropriate background knowledge skills to assist, e.g. financial, product demonstration.

20. Conclusion. The total value of industrial goods and services bought in the United Kingdom exceeds the total value of consumers' expenditure. This fact together with the special complexities of industrial marketing covered above should emphasise the importance of the adoption of the marketing philosophy by all companies involved. Yet the process of change from production orientation to marketing orientation is slow. Vast sums are being spent on research and development of products while the amount of money invested in analysis of the markets to be supplied is infinitesimal.

PROGRESS TEST 11

1. Industrial markets are varied and complex. How might they be classified in order to examine broadly common characteristics of purchasing behaviour? **(2)**

2. What is the special significance of demand elasticity in industrial marketing? **(5)**

3. What are the special features affecting the industrial buying process which create selling problems quite different from those usually encountered in selling consumer products? **(7)**

4. Why is "direct selling" such an important factor in many industrial markets? **(13)**

5. What are the special difficulties in devising advertising campaigns for industrial goods and services? **(14–18)**

CHAPTER XII

International Marketing

THE SIGNIFICANCE OF INTERNATIONAL TRADE

1. The principles of comparative advantage. There is nothing new in the notion of international marketing. The *theory of comparative advantage* derives from the idea that nations will tend to capitalise on the possession of special natural resources or special skills, so that they can offer to other nations advantages in terms of price or special product qualities. They will import products which they themselves cannot produce as economically or as well. The theory is complicated in practice by shifting variables—wage levels, material costs, transportation costs, production methods and costs, scientific and technological development, educational standards and so on. In addition, financial and legal problems complicate the issue and various restrictions on free trade are imposed by governments. Again, there is a natural tendency to satisfy an unsaturated home demand before entering international markets.

2. The balance of trade. Nations lacking essential materials are compelled to import and must attempt to balance their trade by exporting.

The United Kingdom, lacking valuable raw materials and being highly industrialised, is particularly dependent on international trade. To maintain a balance of trade it is necessary to earn sufficient from visible and invisible exports to meet international obligations and finance imports and the outflow of capital.

3. Recent trends in international trade. The factors which have led to an accelerating rate of change in the pattern of international business are as follows:

    (*a*) Social and economic factors (*see* **4**).
    (*b*) Technological factors (*see* **5**).
    (*c*) Legal and political factors (*see* **6**).

These factors are, of course, interacting.

4. Social and economic factors (*see* I, **3**). Among major considerations are the following:

(*a*) Industrialisation.
(*b*) Education.
(*c*) Distribution of wealth.
(*d*) Life expectation.
(*e*) Population size.
(*f*) Social and physical mobility (*see* I, **3** (*c*), (*d*)).
(*g*) Urbanisation.
(*h*) The development of economic trading blocs (*see* **6** (*d*)).

5. Technological factors. Changes are taking place almost at an exponential rate. Examples are very evident: the use of atomic power in generating electricity, the increased speed of air transport, automation and increasing mechanisation in industrial processes. International trade in manufactured products is increasing at a greater rate than trade in primary commodities. The need for primary commodities, however, does not increase in direct proportion to the growth of population or income. Countries which are industrialised tend to trade with one another more and more and so the gap between the economic development of industrially developed and non-developed countries tends to intensify. More and more countries are becoming industrialised, however, and seek to develop their economies by international exchange. Even those countries which are comparatively self-contained, e.g. the USA, are increasingly involved in international marketing.

6. Legal and political factors. National and international bodies have been working towards the removal of economic and financial barriers. Examples can be seen in the following:

(*a*) *The General Agreement on Tariffs and Trade* (GATT). Set up originally in 1948, there have been various rounds of negotiations involving the USA and major industrial countries—the most important in the 1960s—the result of which has been to reduce hundreds of tariff barriers.

(*b*) *The International Monetary Fund.* This organisation came into being in 1945 to devise and operate a system which would give stability to exchange rates and expand international liquidity —so necessary for the growth of international trade. Despite occasional difficulties, a system of fixed exchange rates geared to the American dollar held fairly well until the late sixties, and world trade developed amongst the industrialised countries at an unprecedented rate. A major slowdown in the development of international trade has been a feature of the seventies and early eighties. This, together with the widespread use of monetarist policies to stem inflation, has also slowed down national growth rates in most industrialised countries while unemployment levels have risen.

(*c*) *The Organisation for Economic Co-operation and Development.* This organisation was set up in 1961 with a membership of twenty countries including the United States and Great Britain. Its aim is to foster the growth of the national income of its members through co-operation.

(*d*) *Economic trading groups.* One of the prime aims of these groups is to remove trade restrictions (e.g. tariffs, quotas) amongst members. The European Economic Community was established under the Treaty of Rome signed in 1957. It came into existence in 1958 and Britain became a full member in 1973. Full membership in 1982 comprised Belgium, Denmark, France, West Germany, Greece, the Irish Republic, Italy, Luxembourg, the Netherlands, and the UK. Associate membership, with limited rights, was also possible. Full members of the European Free Trade Area were Austria, Iceland, Norway, Portugal, Sweden and Switzerland, with Finland as an associate member. All EFTA countries have signed or are negotiating agreements with the EEC to eliminate mutual industrial tariffs. Other groups are emerging, e.g. in South-East Asia, Latin America, Africa. At the same time there are the centrally planned economies of groups of communist countries with external selling and buying conducted by state agencies.

(*e*) *Various forms of assistance* provided to exporters by national governments.

7. Significance of recent trends.

(*a*) *The emergence of multi-national companies.* As a consequence of these changes truly multi-national companies are developing. Multi-national companies may be defined as those which have manufacturing or other substantial investment overseas and which make management decisions on the basis of global opportunities and global resources. Few companies have reached this situation but many have found the need to effect economies of scale and by doing so have become more dependent on world markets; others have realised the increasing global opportunities now being opened up.

(*b*) *The emergence of regionalism and nationalism.* The emergence of multi-national companies has led many governments, urged on by organised labour, to re-consider forms of national protection of trade. In particular, the spread of American multi-national operations is regarded as politically and economically dangerous in many quarters. At the same time, new independent national states have been formed and countries which are considered less developed in an economic sense are pursuing policies which will transform them as quickly as possible from poor agricultural areas, with the majority of the population living at a mere subsistence level, to fully-fledged industrialised societies, with total national and *per capita* wealth greatly enhanced. Amongst the schemes for some degree of economic integration, the formation of the following six regional markets is significant:

(*i*) East African Economic Community (Kenya, Uganda and Tanzania).

(*ii*) Central African Customs and Economic Union (Congo, Gabon, Cameroon and Central African Empire).

(*iii*) Maghreb Common Market (Algeria, Tunisia, Morocco and Libya).

(*iv*) Central American Common Market (Guatemala, Nicaragua, Honduras, El Salvador and Costa Rica).

(*v*) Latin American Free Trade Area (all South American republics and Mexico).

(*vi*) Regional Co-operation for Development (Turkey, Iran and Pakistan).

(*c*) *The Third World.* One of the great problems is the disparity in wealth and population between the so-called developed and industrialised countries, e.g. members of the OECD, and the diverse essentially agricultural Third World countries, where over 1 billion people live in extreme poverty.

The conflicts between regionalism, nationalism, and multinational private enterprise were well illustrated in the exercise of economic power in the mid-seventies by oil-producing and exporting companies, and the consequent policies and actions of multi-national oil companies, oil-importing regional groups and national states.

THE POSITION OF THE UK

8. Productivity and international trade expansion. Britain's share of an increasing volume of world trade is falling. The decline is more marked in some industrial groups than others—notably in the more traditional industries, e.g. textiles.

Various reasons may be advanced, but all amount really to a

failure to maintain a marketing advantage in increasingly competitive conditions. Sellers' markets have almost invariably become *buyers'* markets and, where attention has been paid to the specific needs of customers, companies and industries have been relatively successful, e.g. those that manufacture specialised paints, high-quality woollen goods, sports cars. Often exports have been increased in spite of pricing disadvantages. In general, however, the prices of German, Japanese and Italian goods have not risen so sharply as those of British goods. It could be argued that the Japanese have had the advantages of lower labour costs, but a similar argument is not completely true of Germany. Where price advantages have been gained by Germany, Italy, France and Japan, they have been achieved by marked improvements in productivity rather than by simple differences in wage rates. Improvements in productivity have been matched by, and to a large extent made possible by, aggressive overseas marketing and a philosophy of global growth.

9. Changes in demand patterns, markets and products. Apart from considerations of prices, productivity, and increasing competition, it is clear that many of Britain's traditional markets have become self-sufficient and, indeed, are exporting some products in competition with Britain. It is also evident that world demand for the kind of products on which British international trade was mainly dependent before the Second World War has declined, or expanded at a much slower rate than the demand for other types of products. It may be argued that government policy, often aimed at damping down home consumption to stimulate exports in post-war years, has had a dampening effect on industrial activity. It does not follow that a restriction of spending power in home markets will lead to increased attention on the part of manufacturers to export business. Home and overseas business are not mutually exclusive and a healthy home market may well be a condition for competitive overseas operations—and in some cases, unless trade barriers are erected, a condition for survival at home.

10. Major opportunities for British trade. The greatest opportunities for British exports in the near future would appear to be in five main areas, viz. Western Europe, the USA, Commonwealth countries, the Middle East, Latin America. It is the more highly industrialised countries which generate the highest level of world trade and these countries lie within the areas specified, with the exception of communist countries. Communist countries are relaxing controls to some extent and limited opportunities for trade exist.

East–West trading calls for new types of economic relationship based on special co-operative agreements of various kinds, e.g. joint manufacturing operations under which the partners supply components for assembly into a finished product with provision for technical assistance, training, joint marketing—as in the case of tractor manufacture by Hungary and Rumania in association with Steyr-Daimler-Puch of Austria and Fiat of Italy respectively.

11. Analysing opportunities in world markets. It is likely that success or failure in world markets will depend more on marketing expertise than on manufacturing or financial resources. The first consideration is to discover what the market wants and is likely to buy. It is therefore necessary to obtain the following basic information:

(*a*) *Population details:*

(*i*) Total population.

(*ii*) Growth rate.

(*iii*) Geographical concentrations.

(*iv*) Income levels, distribution and trends.

(*v*) Consumption trends.

(*vi*) Family size and number of households—solidity of family groupings.

(*vii*) Language, religious, cultural and social groupings—buying patterns and attitudes.

(*viii*) Educational standards.

(*b*) *Economic resources:*

(*i*) The existing structure of economic wealth—minerals, agriculture, manufacturing.

(*ii*) Likely changes in the economic structure and rate of change.

(*c*) *Communications:* Availability and cost of transport to and in the overseas territory—road systems, ports facilities, railways, airports, telephones, etc.

(*d*) *Location, climate and topography:* Possible effects on resources and productivity.

(*e*) *Government policy and political philosophy:*

(*i*) Attitude to foreign trade and investment.

(*ii*) Taxation policy.

(*iii*) Economic planning and control; attitude towards particular products or industrial development.

(*iv*) Foreign exchange policy.

(*v*) Military demands on economic resources.

12. World demand: basic systems. Analysis of world markets on the above lines will reveal certain basic similarities and differences arising from basic systems, viz. social, economic, technical, political and legal.

13. The social system. Nations develop social attitudes and customs which derive from their peculiar pattern of cultural development. Attitudes towards the family, social class structure, class mobility and material values, for example, have a basis in the moral and ethical standards of a community, standards often rooted in religious beliefs. Some of the effects on social systems caused by very different religions, e.g. Hinduism and Christianity, will be obvious; other attitudes, e.g. those towards colour, require close investigation. Significant differences in attitudes and customs are to be found in Christian countries. Attitudes towards certain products and advertising copy are quite different in France from those in Holland.

It should be noted that attitudes and beliefs tend to strengthen over time and thus countries are often associated or associate themselves with special abilities or characteristics. The German, for example, considers himself technically superior but is prepared to buy a Ford car combining German technical achievement and American styling. "Image" associated with particular countries persists long after the basis for the "image" has disappeared. It is, therefore, more difficult to remove a reputation for poor delivery service than to create it. Changes can be effected, however. The Japanese reputation for shoddy workmanship is fast disappearing, but major technological changes have been aggressively marketed.

14. The economic system. Differences in market opportunities are frequently the result of differences in the following:

   (*a*) Standards of living.
   (*b*) Cost of labour, materials, capital and equipment.
   (*c*) Rate of population growth.
   (*d*) Distribution methods.
   (*e*) Spread of industrialisation.
   (*f*) Availability of credit.
   (*g*) Communications.

Market similarities spring from economic similarities, the influence of mass consumption societies, international companies and international advertising. Patterns of consumption and income distribution follow similar trends according to broadly defined stages of economic development. The pyramid pattern of income distribution, with wealth concentrated in a few hands, moves through various stages until an ovoid pattern denotes a high level of industrialisation, with incomes of the majority narrowly dif-'ferentiated and well above subsistence level. Thus countries with a high *per capita* income level have an ever-increasing demand for consumer luxury goods while the demand for necessities remains fairly stable. The difference lies in the type of luxuries, e.g. telephones, refrigerators, washing machines, cars.

15. The technical system. The development of technology depends on economic factors, e.g. the availability of capital and professional and skilled labour, and on political factors, e.g. high investment in defence projects as in the USA. One of the major problems is that the "technological gap," the difference in technical knowledge and its application, between the less developed economies (the Third World) and the developed economies of Europe, the USA and Japan is widening as a result of these economic and political factors (*see* **4, 6, 11** above).

16. The political and legal system. Political philosophies and government actions based on these philosophies affect the pattern of international trade. Moves towards liberalisation have been mentioned earlier (**6**), but amongst major differences are the following:

(*a*) The extent of state intervention in the control of the economy, e.g. complete state control in communist countries, national planning as in France.

(*b*) The attitude of governments, e.g. towards the import and export of goods and currency, the investment of foreign capital, the use of foreign labour.

(*c*) Political stability. Frequent changes in government, e.g. in Latin America, give rise to economic and financial instability.

(*d*) Business law and legislative procedures.

(*e*) Efficiency and integrity of civil servants.

17. Distribution patterns. The major differences between distribution patterns in various countries are due to the following factors:

(*a*) Economic factors (*see* **18**).

(*b*) Social factors (*see* **19**).

(*c*) Geographical and communication factors (*see* **20**).

18. Economic factors.

(*a*) *Ownership.* In communist countries, for example, there is complete state control of the distribution process. In some other areas state-owned enterprises or co-operatives co-exist with private institutions.

(*b*) *Number, physical size and turnover of retail outlet.* In general, the more developed economically a country is, the larger is the size and turnover of major retail and wholesale outlets. Average retail store sales in the USA are thirty-five times higher than in India, for example.

(*c*) *Functions performed and services offered.* Self-service, for example, is a feature of more highly developed Western economies. Other differences occur in the provision of credit, after-sales, stock-holding and risk-carrying, promotional and display facilities. These activities may require financial support from manufacturers or wholesalers where retailers are notably short of capital.

(*d*) *Assortment of products.* In general, the less developed the economy the greater the degree of specialisation in channels.

(*e*) *Productivity and manpower.* In more highly developed countries great attention is being paid to the economies of operation. This may lead to lower margins and a decline in personal service.

(*f*) *Industrial product distribution.* Where there is a lack of industrialisation, industrial goods are frequently handled by importers who carry a wide range of products. This presents difficulties in providing for technically competent after-sales service.

19. Social factors

(*a*) In many countries manufacturing is considered to be more socially useful than distribution. The low status of wholesaling in many underdeveloped countries has, for example, led to the dominance of distribution by immigrant populations.

(*b*) In all countries various types of outlets have greater appeal for particular strata of society than for others.

(*c*) There are considerable differences in the extent to which buying is regarded as a social activity by both industrial and domestic customers.

20. Geographical and communication factors. In a large country with a comparatively underdeveloped economy and communication system, historical trading patterns and dispersion of customers may lead to a greater number of links in the distribution chain. One of the problems in this kind of situation is that there is often a marked difference in attitudes and objectives of traders in the distribution chain. Lack of advertising media intensifies the problem.

METHODS OF EXPORTING

Once a company has decided to enter overseas markets it has to make decisions on the extent to which it should become financially involved and exercise control over various aspects of distribution.

21. Distribution: control considerations. Major factors to be considered are as follows:

(*a*) The physical distribution of products including the maintenance of stock.

(*b*) Establishing contact with buyers.

(*c*) Providing information to buyers.

(*d*) Negotiating sales.

(*e*) Providing technical advice and after-sales service.

Every country has its established channels of distribution and the principles governing their selection are set out in Chapter IX. It is always wise to study the use of channels by competitive organisations. Various marketing institutions, however, provide specialist services in the field of international marketing in order to reduce the separation between producers and consumers (*see* I, **13**).

22. Specialist marketing institutions. The following marketing institutions may be used because they have had expertise not possessed by the producer organisation or because they enable the producer to enjoy many of the opportunities afforded in overseas markets at a low level of financial investment and risk:

(*a*) *Export merchants.* Goods are purchased outright by the merchant in the country of origin. The merchant then takes over the task of re-selling abroad. Use of merchants means that the manufacturing organisation has no control over marketing operations. Merchants usually handle many lines and may not attempt to sell aggressively a particular company's products. Non-differentiated commodities, e.g. raw copper, may be handled more successfully in this way than products which have distinctive benefits and company and brand identification. Export merchants do, however, offer advantages to small companies lacking resources or knowledge to export directly, or to large companies in small market potential areas. Many export houses provide a wide range of valuable services, e.g. information on markets, agents, advertising, finance. Merchants sometimes are also able to carry out more effectively barter arrangements which may be necessary in dealing with countries in the Eastern bloc.

(*b*) *Overseas company buying offices.* Many large companies establish buying offices abroad. Once an order is placed with an overseas supplier he normally makes arrangements for transportation, invoicing, documentation and so on.

(*c*) *Export commission houses.* These organisations act as buyers on behalf of overseas companies. They try to locate suitable supply sources, putting buyers and sellers in contact. They are paid in the form of commissions from the foreign firms they represent on the basis of sales ultimately negotiated.

(*d*) *Overseas agents or distributors.* The appointment of overseas agents or distributors has traditionally been a major method of exporting. Historically, British export success has been based very largely on the notion of finding distributors to stock, advertise and sell products and to develop markets at a reasonable margin of profit. Personal contact on the basis of exchange visits was rare and business was transacted almost entirely by correspondence. Unfortunately, this original tenuous arrangement often persists. Agents can still frequently perform a most valuable export selling operation at the minimum risk, but great care must be taken in selection and very considerable attention must be paid to training, motivation, direction, and support (*see* IX, **2** (*c*)).

NOTE: Licensing (**29, 30**) also has the advantage of limited investment and low risk. Methods of international marketing involving much risk and investment are examined later (**32–41**).

23. Important factors in selecting agents. Because agents are so widely used it is appropriate to examine in closer detail problems of agency selection, agency agreements (**27**) and methods of motivating agents (**28**). When the decision is taken to use agents it should be realised that these agents will carry the major burden of effective selling, however much support (e.g. advertising and technical assistance) they may receive from the company engaging them. Careful selection is, therefore, absolutely essential. Factors to be considered in making the selection are examined in **24** and **25** below.

24. Business standing, reputation and policy. The following points must be taken into account:

(*a*) *Financial strength and reputation* with bankers and suppliers: credit policies.

(*b*) *Business success* or prospects of success. The record of sales growth over the past few years is a valuable selection pointer. Again, the significance of business with a new company would have to be considered. A fairly new agency with the right resources and development potential might sometimes sell more aggressively.

(*c*) *Integrity*. Agents must have a favourable reputation with the trade and be trustworthy in conforming to the spirit of agreements and plans made with the company they represent.

(*d*) *The number and type of products handled.* An agent will be more readily motivated if business with a particular company represents a significant part of his profits. Handling of competitive products or a very long portfolio of products would be most undesirable.

(*e*) *Business and technical competence*. It is important for agents to be able to take decisions quickly and efficiently without constant reference back to the manufacturer at home.

25. Marketing organisation and expertise. The agents' ability must be evaluated through careful consideration of the following:

(*a*) *Marketing strength*. This may be seen in the size and quality of the sales force, the quality and location of warehousing and office facilities, reputation with customers, customer coverage, pricing and advertising policies, knowledge of market and market requirements.

(*b*) *Ability to undertake market research* and to feed back reliable information on market development. The ability to communicate in appropriate languages is of great importance.

(*c*) *Provision of after-sales service*. This also covers the stocking of spares. Ready availability of replacements, supply continuity and maintenance arrangements are often the key to success.

(*d*) *Marketing training*. An agent should be willing to co-operate with the home manufacturer in providing suitable training.

26. What agents want from the company. Some of the best agents may already have arrangements with competing companies. They will certainly look for readily marketable products and favourable conditions, e.g. commissions, credit, product guarantees, delivery reliability of product and spares, training, advertising support, technical support.

27. Agency agreements. Agreements should normally be kept as simple as possible but very careful consideration must be given to defining certain essential rights which otherwise will possibly lead to dispute.

(*a*) Duration of the agreement. There may well be advantages in having the initial trial period reasonably short.

(*b*) Exclusiveness or otherwise of representation. Agents will naturally aim at exclusive representation; suppliers will have to consider the longer-term implications of exclusive rights over wide territories if business develops beyond the capacity of original agents.

(*c*) Payment, discount, tax conditions.

(*d*) Delivery conditions.

(*e*) Rights to additional or new products.

(*f*) Pricing policy.

(*g*) Use of trade names, trademarks, etc.

(*h*) Advertising, promotion and sales literature requirements.

(*i*) Inventory holding.

(*j*) Reports and information exchange.

It should be noted that often the law affords greater protection to the agent than to the overseas supplier.

28. Stimulating agents. Personal visits by home company executives to sole agents should be arranged on a fairly frequent basis. These should not be purely a matter of courtesy but be sufficiently long to measure progress and offer help and suggestions—generally to motivate and tactfully control. Some companies engage field forces (not always large—but highly mobile) who work with, train and motivate agents. Return visits by agency personnel not only create a sense of belonging but provide opportunities for technical and sales training. Some companies have found that sales conferences of agents have generated tremendous enthusiasm and provided an invaluable means of exchange of ideas. Many companies find that sales targets provide a major incentive. Rewards can take various forms, e.g. special pricing structure, additional promotional support. One problem is to establish and agree realistic targets. Potential must be taken into consideration—not simply past performance. If precise market data is lacking, potentials can often be established with adequate accuracy by using combinations of indicators, e.g.:

(*a*) *per capita* Gross National Product;

(*b*) percentage of Gross National Product accounted for by wholesaling and retailing;

(c) economic development status;

(d) literacy rate;

(e) percentage of population in towns and cities;

(f) industrial output;

(g) average household size;

(h) import volume and pattern;

(i) population statistics.

A regular flow of well-planned bulletins, letters, publicity (*see* VII, **40**) and promotional ideas should be maintained to keep interest high.

29. Licensing. (*See* **22**, NOTE.) Licensing takes various forms, e.g. patent design or process licence contracts, trademark contracts, technical information contracts, franchising contracts.

The exporting of expertise, which can be extremely rewarding, is a very underdeveloped area of British international trading. It is often the fastest way of entering overseas markets—sometimes the only possible way, e.g. in centrally planned economies. It is clearly a method involving little expense, avoiding all distribution cost. On the other hand, it may not be the best way of maximising on overseas opportunities in the long run and there is a risk of creating potentially serious competition. At this point it should be noted that, frequently, successful international operations depend on a combination of the exporting methods best suited to particular markets at particular points of time in relation to company policy and development plans.

30. Major reasons for entering into licensing agreements. A major reason for entering into licensing agreements is that no capital risk is involved. There are, however, other considerations as follows:

(a) Licensing arrangements normally involve close collaboration and, at a later stage, more direct involvement may be possible and desirable.

(b) Cross-licensing arrangements may be easier to negotiate. This is particularly important in view of the high cost of specialised research and development and the speed of scientific and technological change. Licensing arrangements can be used to obtain a higher return on the costs of research investment.

(c) Currency advantages exist as foreign currency is saved and there are few exchange difficulties.

(d) Some markets are too small or too risky for any serious consideration of capital investment.

(*e*) Licensees often have well-developed marketing organisations.

(*f*) Licensing may overcome the barriers of trading with nationally owned enterprises or of trading in countries with strong nationalist tendencies. Newly established or developing countries, for example, may accept licensing agreements as a means of stimulating economic development without the risk of foreign domination of industries and markets.

(*g*) The customer reputation created through some licensing arrangements may assist in the marketing of other company products currently or later.

(*h*) There are advantages in diversifying the methods of receiving income from overseas.

31. Problems to be considered.

(*a*) *Long-term risks.* Apart from the obvious problem of weighing risk against opportunity, licensing involves a number of potential dangers which must be seriously considered. It is important, for example, that there should be adequate safeguards for the maintenance of quality standards if a company's reputation is not to suffer. Companies with large financial resources must consider the long-term position most carefully. Patents and trademarks are valid for a limited period of time only and, if the real long-term aim is to enter more directly into overseas operation, the licensing period may have provided just the necessary time for the licensee to acquire the skills and marketing position with which it would be difficult—and certainly costly—to compete.

(*b*) *Legal factors.* Licensing agreements require specialist legal advice. They will often, in any case, require the approval of governments, but in the final analysis there has to be complete mutual confidence. It is now very rare for a company simply to agree to a set fee; almost invariably royalty payments based on the value of the business are built into the agreement, which may also contain provisions for the possibility of acquiring equity, termination arrangements, minimum volume conditions, renewal conditions, taxation and accounting procedures, degree of exclusiveness, subcontracting rights.

32. Joint venture.
Joint venture involves a capital partnership and may be arranged in connection with manufacturing activities, marketing activities or both. The cases for and against joint venture are considered in **33–36** below.

33. Advantages of joint venture.

(*a*) *Political*. Like licensing, this is frequently a method which is acceptable to governments who strictly limit imports or the operations of wholly-owned foreign companies. Local conditions may regulate the extent of such co-operation but, once established, joint ventures usually receive favourable treatment in matters of import licences, taxation and exchange control.

(*b*) *Financial*. Joint ventures are often regarded as the safest, easiest and least expensive method of engaging in international business. It may be possible to obtain local capital which is a safeguard against the risks of political and economic instability.

(*c*) *Commercial*. These may include acquiring new knowledge on manufacturing methods or research information. Access to new markets may be gained through a well established distribution system.

34. Problems of joint venture. The most important ultimate consideration is probably the amount of control which can be exercised over the vital decision-making processes. Some companies will not enter into joint venture agreements unless they have a majority financial interest. Differences in management philosophy, cultural attitudes, development plans or dividend policy, for example, may lead to considerable strife and possible deadlock. Legal agreements have to be supplemented by a tremendous amount of mutual confidence.

35. Major preliminary requirements. To minimise the risk of later difficulties there should be:

(*a*) a thorough investigation of the contributions the parties can make to research, manufacturing or marketing expertise, plant facilities and equipment, and so on;

(*b*) a clear understanding of exactly what is required from the partners;

(*c*) a clear understanding of profit pay-out policy, e.g. long-term investment at low returns or high immediate returns.

36. Decision-making in joint venture. Companies operating on a world-wide basis may find special problems in joint venture arrangements, particularly in relation to pricing and supply. Single ownership allows for the setting of corporate company objectives, profit standards and use of resources. Joint venture decisions cannot be based on the same premises.

37. Wholly-owned subsidiaries. Overseas companies may be involved in the whole commercial process from design through to
manufacturing and marketing, or they may concentrate on a particular operation, e.g. purchasing, marketing or manufacturing,
or the manufacture or assembly of parts. Whatever the extent
of the operation, there is complete capital commitment and
control.

The decision to invest in overseas establishments is normally the
result of either failure to find a suitable alternative or belief that
complete company control is essential for the most effective and
profitable operation. It is large companies who usually move in
this direction, but small and medium-sized companies might be
wise to consider the possibilities since the investment need not
necessarily be very high. The recovery of initial investment, however, may be comparatively slow and it is the long-term advantages
which should be taken into account. Statements that exporting
is unprofitable often arise from short-term thinking. A substantial
world business may be highly profitable, but time for build-up
will certainly be needed.

38. Establishing overseas companies. There are two basic methods:
acquisition, and starting from scratch. Special factors which may
lead to foreign ownership include the following:

(*a*) *The volume of business expected.* This is very frequently the
principal criterion in establishing overseas sales branches.

(*b*) *The need to provide specialised facilities.* It may be very important to establish adequate servicing, by way of spare parts,
repair facilities and so on.

(*c*) *The strength of nationalistic feeling.* This may be reflected
in official government policy by the provision of financial incentives, tax or exchange benefits, but it may also be a matter
of potential buyer sentiments. Customers may sometimes react
more favourably to products which are produced in their own
country. In consumer goods in particular, customers are frequently
unaware that the producing company is foreign.

(*d*) *Reduction of manufacturing overheads.* Domestic plant capacity may be of such size that it is essential to have large world
markets and the establishment of overseas sales branches may lead
to a more profitable total operation, even if these branches are
not highly profitable in their own right.

(*e*) *Legal restrictions.* Prohibitive import duties or conditions,
severe exchange restrictions or heavy tax burdens can sometimes

be overcome. Sometimes it is necessary to establish an overseas operation in order to exercise a patent.

(*f*) *Rationalisation.* Ownership may lead to more profitable over-all global operations by rationalisation of manufacturing, research, servicing and/or marketing activities.

(*g*) *Capital availability.* Overseas development may offer advantages in the re-investment of profits or the raising of capital from local sources. In many cases long-term credit is easier to finance—and this is particularly important in the marketing of capital equipment.

(*h*) *Advantages in acquiring particular currencies* which may be transferable to other overseas operations.

39. Risk factors. The extent of risk will obviously depend on the size of the investment, which may be small in the case of establishing sales, purchasing or warehousing facilities, or very large in the setting up of a large assembly or manufacturing plant. A major consideration will be the possibility of loss in the case of nationalisation. A marketing operation may incur a high running cost in terms of salaries, but large-scale investment in fixed assets—manufacturing installations and equipment, for example—is a much greater cause for investigation of stability of government policy. Nationalisation is not the only problem. Currency and exchange-rate stability are important considerations.

40. Problems of acquisition. Although acquisition may seem an attractive means of developing overseas trade on a large scale quickly, it is important that any acquisition should be preceded by the formulation of a clear policy and a thorough investigation of the business to be acquired:

(*a*) *A clear acquisition policy.* In order to develop a truly international business most profitably it will often be necessary to co-ordinate policy and rationalise resources. Heterogeneous acquisitions make these steps virtually impossible. The American General Foods organisation encountered enormous difficulties after acquiring businesses in many parts of the world on the very general basis of involvement in convenience foods markets. Convenience foods are difficult to define on a global basis. This raises problems of product policy which have direct repercussions on development and research. Many other problems arise from divergencies in accounting systems, personnel policy, business philosophy and so forth.

(b) *A careful investigation of the business to be acquired.* Investigations must be made to discover the following:

(i) Financial standing and profitability record.

(ii) Market standing and marketing organisation and methods.

(iii) Personnel policies and, in particular, wage and salary structures.

(iv) Research and development strengths or weaknesses.

(v) Patents and licensing agreements.

(vi) Plant and depot facilities and values.

(vii) The strengths and weaknesses in the existing management structure. This is a particularly important issue since a great deal will depend on the ability and adaptability of the local management team.

(viii) Government regulations and controls.

Many companies use the services of brokers or consultants in locating suitable companies for acquisition. Really good prospects are difficult to find and an extensive search may well be necessary. The use of legal and financial specialists will clearly be necessary in evaluating possible acquisitions, but other management personnel, e.g. research, manufacturing, marketing, will usually be needed to carry out a complete investigation.

41. Organisation structure. It is usually impracticable—and unwise—to think in terms of setting up an organisational structure which is a replica of the home operation. There may be very real differences in market conditions, effective manufacturing methods, administrative procedures, growth rate and personnel capability. There are very few companies which have as yet succeeded in creating a fully integrated international operation—one which has no dominant domestic roots, but which is fully international in ownership, financing, management and operation. There is little doubt that such companies will increasingly emerge in the future.

The problems of corporate organisational structure are enormous. It is clear that there must be some degree of central control—but the problem is to determine the extent of that control, to establish the appropriate relationships between central staff and line management and decentralised managements.

The following are some of the questions that need to be posed:

(a) To what extent, for example, does central planning and direction conflict with the development of a decentralised profit-responsibility concept? What type of reporting system is needed?

(b) How is it possible to utilise the best managerial talent in the right place at the right time? To what extent is it possible to think in terms of truly multi-national management structures? How can the problems of differences in standards and cost of living be overcome if management is to be moved from one operation to another?

(c) What should be the basis of evaluating the performance of different companies, considering the wide differences which exist in, for example, government taxation systems, currency stability, market structures and development problems, and cost factors?

(d) What special qualities are needed in the international manager and how can he be trained and developed?

(e) To what extent should immediate or local considerations outweigh long-term and corporate considerations in determining the allocation of resources?

42. The international manager. Special qualities and/or qualifications are needed in the personnel selected to carry out operations. Far too little consideration has been given to providing the training and development programmes needed for British personnel working in overseas territories.

Overseas operations demand the following qualities:

(a) *The capacity and authority to make prompt decisions.* Overseas buyers are not likely to react favourably to men who have constantly to refer back to headquarters. Even an overseas representative will need to be much more capable of assuming responsibility of a managerial kind than his counterpart in home markets. He may well be responsible for guiding agency operations as well as for direct customer dealings.

(b) *Adaptability.* This characteristic is needed to cope with the wider range of unusual conditions surrounding the transaction of business.

(c) *Knowledge of languages.* The importance of language is too often underrated because of the ability of other nations to communicate reasonably well in English.

(d) *Acceptance of the need for mobility.* The distances which may have to be covered and the possibility of international transfers makes it essential that wives and families are prepared to adjust to a particular way of life. It may be necessary to provide special incentives to cover the possible additional cost of education, travel, home visits.

(*e*) *Health and energy*. Overseas operations are usually more demanding physically than domestic operations.

(*f*) *Knowledge of local customs*, culture and current events.

(*g*) *Tolerance*—a willingness to recognise that people with different cultural backgrounds have different points of view which to them are as valid as any other; an ability to work with and through people with diverse attitudes, beliefs and motivations.

(*h*) *Persistence*. It may frequently be necessary to pursue a line of action for a long time in face of difficulties before success is finally achieved.

(*i*) *Reliability and attention to details*. Irritations and business loss may spring from slow, inaccurate or vague transmission of information. Weaknesses in administrative procedures leading to delivery delays, excessive correspondence or slow reaction to complaints intensify the doubts an organisation may have of doing business at all with overseas companies.

Whatever the form of overseas operations it is clear that success depends to a very large extent on the calibre of the personnel involved, and there must be an acceptance that this usually means that top-level executives must themselves be more mobile and more directly in touch with the market place.

43. Organisational evolution. It is beyond the scope of this book to cover all the various organisational structures to be found in practice. A small export operation run entirely through agents may, at the outset, be organised by a small section of the home marketing department. This may develop into a separate export division with responsibility for market investigations, distribution systems, service, advertising and promotion. The establishment of overseas sales offices, assembly points and warehouses may follow. As the organisation develops, problems of communication and the relationship with the home operation will have to be resolved. The final step is the creation of a fully international corporation.

MARKETING SERVICES AND GOVERNMENT SUPPORT

44. The need for international marketing research. The differences in social, economic, technical, political and legal systems (**12–16** above) and in distribution patterns (**17–20** above) clearly point to the need for particular attention to be paid to marketing research and promotion. The geographical separation of producers and consumers adds to the normal marketing problems of separation of time and knowledge or information (*see* I, **13**).

45. International marketing research: the basic steps. There are really four major steps in an investigation. These are as follows:

(*a*) Basic data concerning the market.

(*b*) General factors relating to the product.

(*c*) Specific factors relating to the market for the product.

(*d*) Specific factors which would influence the operation of the particular company.

46. Major problems to be resolved. The first two steps of this investigation are required for top-level policy decisions in connection with involvement in overseas areas. The third and fourth steps are required for decisions on distribution outlets, prices, terms and so on, but, more important, on the specific products to suit specific markets. For product decisions information on the following will be necessary:

(*a*) The effect of differing legal requirements.

(*b*) The advantages and disadvantages of standardisation of complete products or components.

(*c*) The need to adapt existing products to suit local conditions, functional or aesthetic design changes, packaging, branding and advertising, quality standards, and specifications.

47. Special problems in conducting overseas surveys. The techniques covered in Chapter III apply but the following are some of the special problems which may arise:

(*a*) *The choice of the means of undertaking investigations:* e.g. overseas agencies, British agencies, agencies with international associations, company staff. The major problem is to weigh up the frequently conflicting considerations of efficiency, time and cost. A provisional estimate of a market may be prepared by experienced researchers in two or three days whereas a more detailed investigation may require two or three months, including time for preparation of the survey, for execution, and for analysis and interpretation. Field interviewing can clearly involve high travelling expenses.

(*b*) *The value of published information.* Information from every possible source should be utilised, but it varies in reliability and statistics are often constructed on differing bases.

(*c*) *Language problems.* Large companies' executives may speak

English, but surveys may need to cover respondents who are not bilingual. If the researchers cannot speak the particular language, interpreters have to be used, raising questions of additional cost and communication difficulties.

(*d*) *Terminology*. Definitions and technical specifications in connection with similar products may be widely divergent.

(*e*) *Differences in culture and traditions*. These may affect the willingness of respondents to co-operate and the reliability of the answers they give.

Overseas surveys are likely to be carried out in a series of stages. There are so many markets to examine and so few on which a company can concentrate that a screening process is essential. The first stage is likely to be primarily desk research aimed at eliminating countries and products offering inadequate profitable potential. Stage two research might require field investigations of the more promising product-markets and a third stage might be concentrated on depth study of a limited number of critical issues in the "short-listed" product-markets.

48. Selection of advertising agencies and media. Important matters to consider are the following:

(*a*) *Choice of agency*. As in marketing research there are very large international companies and local companies of various sizes; there is also the possibility of using a British-based agency. The range and efficiency of services offered require most careful consideration.

(*b*) *Differences in the quality and quantity* of media available. Contrast the availability of commercial television, national daily press, magazines and trade literature, for example, in France, the USA, Germany and Britain. Accurate statistics on circulation and readership are often difficult to obtain.

(*c*) *Direct mailing*. This is a form of presentation which is receiving increasing attention. Obvious difficulties arise in obtaining full and classified lists of potential overseas customers. Direct mailing can often be most effectively organised in co-operation with local agents.

49. Economic and social problems in promotion. Differences in economic and social systems (*see* **13, 14** above) create individual promotion problems. Some of these problems are considered in **50–54** below.

50. Level of expenditure. The stage of economic development reached has a direct bearing on the extent of advertising. Highly developed economies, as might be expected, show a higher level of advertising expenditure than underdeveloped economies but the level of expenditure is not directly related to either national income or *per capita* income. In general, however, companies should be prepared to spend comparatively more on advertising in overseas than in domestic markets since both they and their products will usually be less well known and have less intensive direct selling effort.

51. Distribution patterns. Differences in distribution patterns (*see* **17** above) may mean that there should be a totally different allocation of advertising expenditure; e.g. if final distribution is mainly in the hands of small retailers it may be difficult to obtain effective displays but profitable to concentrate on promotions to large wholesalers.

52. Differences in customer motivations. Buying habits will be conditioned by income and assets available but there will be differences in priorities and values. European countries with strong Protestant traditions tend to resist appeals based on labour saving, for example. Reports from many sources show that Swiss housewives reacted much more favourably to dish-washing machines promoted essentially on the basis of high water temperatures and sterilisation than on the basis of ease and convenience.

53. Differences in decision-makers. The influence of women and children differs tremendously in consumer goods markets. In industrial markets, management structure and styles have to be considered in determining the form and direction of communications.

54. International "images." There are obvious advantages in terms of both cost and effectiveness if a company can use the same kind of advertising copy and visual material all over the world. It is, however, rarely possible to reproduce identical promotional material for different markets. As well as problems in translation, illustrations must often be modified or completely changed; e.g. a Smarties advertisement showing children physically handling the sweets and examining their different colours was completely unacceptable in Holland because of the Dutch attitude towards hygiene. Agents and distributors can often provide invaluable help in advising on idiomatic usage and appropriateness of copy and visual appeal.

NOTE: Legal regulations differ. Particular attention will need to be paid to restrictions in the advertising of food and drugs.

55. Exhibitions. The decision to participate in home exhibitions is not infrequently based on the notion of keeping in line with competitive practice rather than on calculated objectives in regard to communications and sales. Overseas exhibitions often attract much more serious buying attention and may be one of the most effective ways of communicating with potential customers. It is important to plan for exhibitions well in advance. The most important should be carefully selected and a timetable not only of the events themselves but of preparatory work must be drawn up. Apart from important matters of stand design, location and size, it will be necessary to prepare special literature and exhibits and to allocate responsible executives. The Department of Trade provides valuable advice and assistance to British companies wishing to take part in international exhibitions. In addition, through its overseas Fairs Directorate, the Dept. Of Trade organises British Pavilions and Information Stands and All-British Trade Fairs. British Weeks are also organised and financed by the Dept. of Trade and assistance is given in promoting British goods through special store promotions.

56. Co-operation in exporting. The cost of overseas marketing operations sometimes prevents companies from undertaking activities in which they could effectively participate if they were to look more closely at the possibilities of collaboration. Manufacturers' associations or voluntary groupings of firms could achieve great economies by co-operative effort in organising exhibitions, advertising, selling missions or visits by buyers. Co-operation in industrial markets may be necessary to supply a complete system, e.g. the building of oil refineries and power plants. Special consortia are sometimes set up for combined tenders. The Dept. Of Trade can assist and/or advise in all these matters and, for the smaller manufacturer, there is the "pick-a-back" scheme which enables firms to contact successful exporting organisations who are willing to assist by offering certain selling facilities. The Institute of Marketing has established a company, Marketing Ltd., specifically to arrange for co-operative export marketing efforts.

The Department of Trade now offers valuable help to companies wishing to carry out research in overseas markets. This includes advice on research methods, costs, agencies, etc., as well as financial assistance.

57. Credit and insurance. Exporters face not only normal commercial risks of payment default but the additional risks of shifting political circumstances, currency exchange and import restrictions. There is also, in increasingly competitive world markets, the problem of providing long-term credit. Most exporters have, therefore, to obtain finance from outside sources which themselves require reasonable guarantees against risk. Various national schemes have been developed in most industrialised countries to assist in the problems of credit and risk. Some schemes are private; others are state controlled (cf. Hermes Kreditversicherungs A.G., Hamburg—a private company—and the Export Risks Insurance Corporation Ltd., Bombay—a government-owned corporation).

58. The Export Credit Guarantees Department. The Export Credit Guarantee Dēpartment is a government department set up to encourage the export of UK goods and services. It has two main functions, viz. to provide insurance cover for exporters against the risks of non-payment by overseas customers and to provide security so that banks will lend money to finance exports. *British Overseas Trade Board Export Handbooks* set out the main features and conditions of the scheme. It is possible to insure from the date of contract acceptance or from the date of the shipment. There are comprehensive policies covering the whole of a company's business or its export business, and specific policies for particular large individual export contracts.

(*a*) *Rates.* These vary according to the extent of risk involved and cover requested. Rates for special contracts, for example, are higher than those for comprehensive policies. Even special policy rates are, however, favourable! Basic cover ranges from 90% of loss due to insolvency or default by a buyer to 95% of loss arising from political or economic conditions. It is possible to take out policies to cover special risks such as cost escalation, contracts involving construction work and capital goods export on credit terms of two years or more. An ECGD guarantee paves the way to bank lending at preferential rates of interest to cover normally 80 to 100% of a contract's value.

(*b*) *Cover.* ECGD cover provides the necessary collateral for normal bank financing and various special guarantees to banks may also be negotiated. The main risks for which cover may be provided are:

(*i*) insolvency of buyer;

(*ii*) failure of buyer to pay within six months of acceptance of goods;

(*iii*) war, civil wars, revolutions;

(*iv*) cancellation of UK export licences or new export restrictions;

(*v*) delay in the transfer of sterling to the UK.

59. The Diplomatic Service. It should be remembered that the Diplomatic Service through its commercial services is increasingly devoting attention to the promotion of exports by providing market information, advising on overseas opportunities and assisting in liaison between British and overseas companies and trade organisations.

60. Conclusion. It is evident that increasing home competition, the profit squeeze, increasing world industrialisation and the formation of economic trading communities will all combine to bring pressure on the need for consideration of marketing on an international basis. The distinction between home and export business will tend to disappear and marketing strategies will be based on global rather than national patterns or segmentations.

The principles of marketing set out in Chapters I–X are as true of international as of home markets. Decisions have to be made on product policy, pricing, promotion, channels and organisation. Customers have to be understood, forecasts and targets have to be set and performance has to be measured. Special knowledge and means of obtaining that knowledge are, however, required. Thus special training and experience must be linked with appropriate adaptability to environment and linguistic ability. Not least important is the fact that company directors and top-level executives must become committed to accepting the marketing philosophy and to more personal involvement in the actual fields of operation.

PROGRESS TEST 12

1. What are the most significant recent trends in international trade? **(3–7)**

2. What basic information is needed to analyse world market opportunities? **(11)**

3. In what basic ways do international markets differ? **(12–20)**

4. What specialist marketing institutions might be used by a

company seeking entry to overseas markets at a low level of risk and investments? **(22)**

5. List the important factors to be considered in selecting agents. **(23–25)**

6. What are the major reasons for entering into licensing agreements? **(30)**

7. Why and how do companies establish wholly-owned subsidiaries? **(37, 38)**

8. What are the main problems involved in the acquisition of overseas companies? **(40)**

9. What special qualities does the "international" manager require? **(42)**

10. What are the special problems of international marketing research? **(47)**

11. What are the economic and social problems of international promotion? **(49–54)**

12. What is the function of the Export Credit Guarantees Department? **(58)**

External Sources of Marketing Information

There are many external sources of information; the more important can be categorised as follows:

GOVERNMENT PUBLICATIONS

Census of Population. The last full Census was carried out in 1981. The Census supplies details of population by age, marital status, occupation, social class, house ownership, sex, geographical area and a considerable amount of social and economic data. This can be supplemented by the annual statistics produced by the General Register Office.

Statistics on Incomes, Prices, Employment and Production. The Department of Employment publishes a bulletin several times per year and this is supplemented by the monthly *Gazette*. Details of employment and unemployment by industry and region, data on wage rates and retail prices, industrial disputes, etc., provide useful guides to purchasing potential by areas and income groups. More detailed analyses of incomes are available from Inland Revenue statistics.

Annual Family Expenditure Surveys. These are carried out by the Department of Employment and give details of consumer spending on individual items by income groups and geographical areas. The survey is based on a limited sample of some 3,000 households.

Census of Distribution. These were carried out by the Department of Trade in 1950, 1957, 1961, 1966, 1971 and 1981. The 1950, 1961, 1971 and 1981 surveys involved a complete analysis of distribution through retail outlets. The 1957 and 1966 surveys were only partial.

Census of Production. This census, carried out every five years, gives information on manufacturing organisations, mining and quarrying, building and contracting and public utilities. The information includes details of materials and fuel purchased, stocks at the beginning and end of a year, annual output and sales analysis, expenditure on services, plant, machinery and vehicles, and value of buildings and land. Calculations of gross output, net output and net output per person employed are made.

Monthly Digest of Statistics. This contains information collected by various government departments, e.g. Dept. of Trade, Dept. of Industry, Dept. of Energy. The information is summarised in the *Annual Abstract of Statistics.*

The Department of Trade Business Monitor Series. This gives monthly or quarterly data on production over a wide range of industries as well as comparisons with past figures.

Overseas Trade Accounts. These are published monthly by the Customs and Excise Department, showing, in detail, figures on imports and exports.

Statistical Classification for Imported Goods and Re-exported Goods.

Annual Statement of Trade of the UK with Commonwealth and Foreign Countries.

Trade and Navigation Accounts. These are published monthly by the Dept. of Trade.

The Export Service Bulletin. Published by the Dept. of Trade.

Department of Trade Journal.

UK Balance of Payments and the Economic Report.

Input-Output Tables for the UK. These are designed to show the flow of business from one industry to another, and cover industrial groupings.

Public Investment in Great Britain.

Directory of Employers' Associations, Trade Unions and Joint Organisations.

Company Assets, Income and Finance. This is published by the Dept. of Trade and shows the net assets, profits, reserves and new capital of over 2,000 companies.

National Income and Expenditure Blue Book. Although all the raw statistics appear elsewhere the data is processed in this annual publication to provide a particularly valuable source of social and economic information for both consumer and industrial marketing.

Special surveys published by the Social Survey Unit of the Central Office of Information.

The above publications are available from H.M.S.O. and students should consult the *List of Principal Statistical Series Available*, published by H.M.S.O.

OFFICIAL INTERNATIONAL PUBLICATIONS

United Nations Statistical Year Book.
United Nations Monthly Bulletin of Statistics.
United Nations Current Economic Indicators.
United Nations World Economic Survey.
United Nations Commodity Trade Statistics.
Bulletin of the European Economic Community.
EFTA Bulletin.

Statistics for Market Research in Europe and North America (Organisation for Economic Co-operation and Development).
Bulletin Générale de Statistiques (European Economic Commission).
International Monetary Statistics (International Monetary Fund).
GATT Compendium of Sources (International Trade Statistics).
GATT World Directory of Industry and Trade Associations.
GATT Analytical Bibliography of Market Surveys by Products and Countries.
International Bibliography of Marketing and Distribution (Staples Press).

OTHER SPECIALIST PUBLICATIONS

Quarterly Economic Reviews⎫
Retail Business   ⎬ *The Economist* Intelligence Unit.
Marketing in Europe   ⎭
A. C. Nielsen Indices—for food, drugs, pharmaceuticals, confectionery and tobacco.
Legion Publishing Company's *Statistical Review of Advertising Expenditure.*
Bradstreet Register.
Dun and Bradstreets's Guide to Key British Enterprises.
Kompass Register.
Stock Exchange Year Book.
Kelly's Directory of Merchants, Manufacturers and Shippers.
British Rate and Data.
Advertisers Annual.
Consumer Marketing Manual of the U.K.
Industrial Marketing Manual.

NEWSPAPERS, PERIODICALS AND JOURNALS (* = American).

The London and Cambridge Economic Bulletin.
The Times Review of Industry and Technology.

The Economist.
The Financial Times.
British Journal of Marketing.
Marketing.
Marketing Forum.
Commentary.
Scientific Business.
*Journal of Marketing.**
*Journal of Marketing Research.**
*Journal of Advertising Research.**
*Harvard Business Review.**
Campaign.
Retail Distribution Management.
Industrial Marketing Digest.
Which?
Anbar (*Marketing and Distribution Abstracts*)
Reviews published by the various banks.

INSTITUTIONS

The Institute of Marketing, Moor Hall, Cookham, Berkshire SL6 9QH.

The British Market Research Society, 39 Hertford Street, London WX 7PA.

The Advertising Association, Abford House, Wilton Road, London SW1V 1NJ.

The Incorporated Society of British Advertisers, 2 Basel Street, London SW3 1AA.

The Institute of Public Relations, 1 Great James Street, London WC1N 3DO.

The British Institute of Management, Management House, Parker Street, London WC2B 5PT.

The Confederation of British Industry, 21 Tothill Street, London SW1H 9LP.

The Institute of Export, Europe House, East Smithfield, London E1 9AA.

Council of Industrial Design, 28 Haymarket, London SW1Y 4SU.

British Export Houses Association, 69 Cannon Street, London EC4N 5AB.

British Standards Institution, 2 Park Street, London W1A 2BS.

Department of Trade, Export Intelligence and Statistical and Market Intelligence Library, Export House, 50 Ludgate Hill, London EC4M 7HU.

Department of Trade and Industry EEC/EFTA Information Unit, 1 Victoria Street, London SW1H 0ET.

Industrial Marketing Research Association, 11 Bird Street, Lichfield, Staffs WS13 6PW.

European Society for Opinion and Marketing Research, Raadhuisstraat 15, Amsterdam.

British Overseas Trade Board, 1 Victoria Street, London SW1H 0ET.

Central Office of Information, Hercules Road, Westminster Bridge Road, London SE1 7DU.

H.M. Stationery Office, 49 High Holborn, London WC1V 6HB.

Communications, Advertising and Marketing Education Foundation Ltd., Abford House, 15 Wilton Road, London SW1V 1HJ.

Trade Associations.

Chambers of Commerce.

Banks.

Embassies and Consulates.

Bibliography

BASIC GENERAL TEXTS

Basic Marketing: a Managerial Approach. E. J. McCarthy. Irwin, 1978

Basic Marketing: Principles and Practice. T. Cannon. Holt, Rinehart and Winston, 1980

Marketing: an Introductory Text. M. J. Baker, 3rd Edition. Macmillan, 1979

Glossary of Marketing Terms. N. A. Hart and J. Stapleton (for Institute of Marketing), 1977

Marketing in a Competitive Economy. L. W. Rodger. Assoc. Business Programmes, 1974

Marketing Management: Analysis, Planning and Control. P. Kotler. Prentice Hall, 1980

Principles of Marketing. P. Kotler. Prentice Hall, 1980

Effective Marketing Management. M. A. Christopher, *et al.* Gower, 1980

Marketing Techniques for Analysis and Control. P. Allen. Macdonald and Evans, 1977

SPECIALISED TEXTS

Market and Sales Forecasting: A Total Approach. D. Bolt. Kogan Page, 1981

Marketing: A Behavioural Analysis. P. M. Chisnall. McGraw-Hill, 1975

Marketing: The Management of Distribution Channels. M. Guirdham. Pergamon, 1972

Marketing: The Sales Manager's Role. A. Tack. Cedar Books, 1976

Marketing Decision Making: A Model Building Approach. P. Kotler. Holt, Rinehart and Winston, 1974

Research for Marketing Decisions. P. E. Green and D. S. Tull. Prentice Hall, 1978

Your Marketing Department: Its Organisation and Structure. B. Krief. Business Books, 1975

International Marketing. J. Fayerweather. Prentice Hall, 1970

Legal Aspects of Marketing. J. Livermore. Heinemann, 1978

Management Controls in Marketing. R. N. S. Wilson. Heinemann, 1973

Marketing Technological Products to Industry. R. W. Hill. Pergamon, 1972

Marketing: New Industrial Products. N. T. Baker. Macmillan, 1975

Marketing of Professional Services. A. Wilson. McGraw-Hill, 1972

Pricing Decisions and Marketing Policy. K. S. Palda. Prentice Hall, 1971

Bargaining for Results. J. Winkler. Heinemann, 1980

Pricing. F. Livesey. Macmillan, 1976

Methods in Marketing Research. K. Elliot and N. G. Christopher. Holt, Rinehart and Winston, 1974

Product Policy and Management. M. J. Baker and R. McTavish Macmillan, 1977

Strategy and Marketing. K. Simmons. Philip Allan, 1982

Spending Advertising Money. S. Broadbent. Business Books, 1980

Competition and Consumer Protection. D. Swan. Penguin, 1979

Examination Technique

1. Timing. Read most carefully the instructions relating to the question to be attempted. Be sure that you understand how marks are to be allocated. In some papers there is a compulsory question: in others questions are divided into sections in order to ensure that students attempt questions covering as wide a range of the pre-scribed syllabus as possible. Having understood the directions, read the questions through once fairly quickly. At this stage it is normal for students to become unduly worried. Remember this and read the paper again more slowly, "short-listing" those questions which you believe you can answer most satisfactorily. Then make your final selection in accordance with the instructions given. Deduct a time allowance for reading through your answers at the end of the examination and apportion the remaining time according to the mark contribution each question makes towards the maximum obtainable on the paper. Do not underestimate the cumulative danger of over-running your time allocation for individual questions. Essay-type questions are very rarely awarded full marks and there is almost invariably more to be gained by completing all questions as instructed than by adding small refinements to earlier questions attempted and having insufficient time for later questions.

If you are running out of time make the best of the situation by listing salient points in note form or by covering the over-all approach to a problem rather than by writing in full essay form or indulging in specialised calculations affecting a small part of the required answer.

2. Legibility. Examiners are usually marking large numbers of papers. They are not looking for copperplate handwriting but they will naturally be inclined to ignore or be irritated by writing which is difficult to read.

3. Logical presentation. Written examination questions may occasionally be devised to test knowledge of facts but more usually they are intended to examine the student's ability to use facts in investigating a problem or in analysing a line of argument. It is, therefore, of great importance to plan answers in such a way that they have a logical flow. Time spent on planning answers is time well spent.

4. Relevance of material. Read questions carefully and make certain you understand exactly what you are being asked. A lengthy answer is no guarantee of high marks. Students are apt to write down what they know rather than what they are asked. This leads to completely irrelevant answers or answers which are out of balance, with undue emphasis being given to particular aspects.

5. Generalisations. Avoid sweeping and vague generalisations. Be as specific as possible by quoting actual examples, e.g. of company organisations, of marketing campaigns, of the statements of writers and practising marketing specialists.

6. Lay-out. Whenever possible emphasise your key points by suitable paragraph construction, underlining, use of diagrams and statistics. Clear and accurate diagrams and statistics often enhance an answer and make points more lucidly and rapidly than words, but avoid these devices at all costs if you are unsure of your facts.

7. Style. If you are a mature student who has not undertaken written examinations for several years it is particularly important to practise written answers in advance of the examination as much as possible. Write in short, concise sentences, taking care to avoid ambiguous words and phrases. Define unfamiliar terms and make sure that your use of such terms is consistent.

Except in emergency, do not write in note form. A definite mark allowance may be made for presentation, but, if not, examiners will normally still expect students to show the ability to express themselves fluently.

8. Assumptions. In questions requiring analysis of problems it is not unusual for the information supplied to be incomplete. It is expected that assumptions will be made, but that the assumptions will be stated and be maintained consistently throughout.

Test Papers

Do not attempt these papers until you have thoroughly studied the text and can answer satisfactorily the questions in the Progress Tests.

TEST 1

1. By what criteria would you decide whether a company were production or marketing oriented?

2. To what extent would you consider that the purchasing of industrial goods and services is a rational process?

3. Comment on the methods used by companies in determining advertising expenditure. What problems are involved in arriving at a decision and to what extent can these be overcome?

4. Under what conditions is it desirable to eliminate a product? What problems may have to be overcome despite the logic of any arguments put forward?

5. To what extent might channel decisions be conditioned by: (*a*) the characteristics of the product or products; (*b*) the practice of competitors? Illustrate your answer by reference to specific companies and products.

6. What would you consider to be the main responsibilities of a field sales manager controlling ten salesmen calling on grocery outlets? What considerations would you have in mind in selecting a man to take up such a position?

7. What do you understand by behavioural sciences? Of what importance is an understanding of behavioural sciences to a marketing research specialist?

8. What political and economic factors would you expect to be examined by a company before a decision is made to invest in setting up its own manufacturing or marketing organisation in an overseas territory?

TEST 2

1. What do you understand by the term "marketing mix"? Comment on the main "mix" differences you might expect to find

in marketing plans relating to (*a*) baby foods and (*b*) scientific instruments.

2. It is frequently stated that, the longer a man spends as a sales specialist, the less likely he is to develop ultimately into a good marketing manager. What do you consider is the validity of this argument?

3. What are the main problems in determining the size and type of samples for marketing research purposes in (*a*) specialised industrial markets and (*b*) mass consumer markets?

4. Discuss the various strategic considerations to be examined in determining a pricing policy. What are the special problems in pricing (*a*) completely new and differentiated products and (*b*) minor modifications of existing narrowly differentiated products?

5. To what extent do you consider that existing voluntary controls in advertising provide adequate safeguards for the consumer?

6. What are the problems involved in evaluating the performance of salesmen?

7. What do you understand by the "product life cycle"? What are the advantages of understanding the concept in actual marketing situations?

8. Why do companies frequently appoint sales agents to represent them in international markets? Discuss the problems involved in the selection of agents.

TEST 3

1. "Marketing considerations must receive priority in company strategy and planning, but research and development, manufacturing and finance should have co-equal status with marketing." Discuss this statement.

2. Discuss the major changes which have taken place in the pattern of retail distribution during the last ten years and the effect these changes have had on the marketing policy of suppliers.

3. By what means is it possible to investigate purchasing behaviour and attitudes which are apparently irrational? What contribution might any findings make in devising a marketing campaign?

4. What procedures would you suggest for determining the priority which might be given to a nember of new product possibilities?

5. Comment on the problems of evaluating the effectiveness of

advertising. Discuss the significance and limitations of the most commonly used research techniques.

6. Discuss the advantages and disadvantages of licensing and joint venture in international marketing operations.

7. "Relevant timely information is vital for effective marketing control." Discuss that statement indicating the types, sources and frequency of data which might be required by (a) a marketing manager and (b) an area sales manager.

8. What are the special factors affecting marketing research investigations in connection with industrial goods and services?

TEST 4

1. "Marketing begins before production and ends after production." Discuss this statement, particularly in the light of company organisational structures.

2. Explain what is meant by the following: (a) selective distribution; (b) intensive distribution; (c) exclusive distribution. Illustrate your answer by discussing distribution strategy in the marketing of (a) television receivers; (b) surgical appliances; (c) shirts; (d) motor cycles; (e) cigarettes; (f) agricultural machinery.

3. "A matching of advertiser needs with media capacity is a prerequisite to the development of an effective advertising campaign." Examine this requirement in connection with the marketing of (a) cars and (b) fork-lift trucks.

4. "Cost, ultimately, sets the floor to price." Discuss this statement with particular reference to (a) the break-even concept and (b) discounted cash flow.

5. What are the objectives of branding products? To what extent is branding feasible and desirable in marketing industrial products?

6. What are the possible benefits of test marketing? What criteria might be used in (a) selecting areas and (b) determining the period of testing?

7. Why is it important for a company to know as accurately as possible the market share its product enjoys? How can the relevant data be obtained in the case of (a) cosmetics and (b) industrial detergents?

8. Distinguish between marketing research and marketing intelligence with special reference to the problems of overseas markets.

TEST 5

1. "Marketing calls for a combination of creative and analytical

ability." Discuss this statement in connection with the selection of staff in (a) a company marketing department and (b) an advertising agency.

2. Discuss the advantages and disadvantages of telephone interviews, mail questionnaires and personal interviews in marketing research investigations.

3. Comment on the most commonly practised procedures for forecasting sales. What factors would you consider in forecasting the sales of a new car model for a forward period of three years?

4. Discuss the problems of cost allocation in determining marketing budgets.

5. "The pack protects what it sells and sells what it protects." Comment on this double function of packaging with special reference to marketing cake mixes (a) to housewives and (b) to catering organisations.

6. Why is personal direct selling a marked feature of the "marketing mix" in the majority of industrial markets? How might advertising contribute to the accomplishment of the "sales task"?

7. "The more advanced a society, the more it counts the variety of its goods as an indication of the standard of living rather than the amount of those goods." Examine the validity of this statement and the implications it might have on the international marketing plans of a company manufacturing domestic kitchen ware.

TEST 6

1. "Where is our company going? Where should it be going? What is our business, anyway?" Consider the relevance of these three questions posed by T. Levitt of the Harvard Business School to company chief executives in connection with long-term planning and the marketing concept.

2. Discuss the reasons for the emergence of "product" and "brand" managers in larger multi-product companies. Would you expect similar advantages and disadvantages in introducing brand-product management in connection with industrial and consumer markets?

3. Why have many retail organisations promoted "private label" products? How is this development affecting the marketing policies of manufacturers offering products of a similar type?

4. "The fact that the industrial buyer seeks the best value is not tantamount to saying that a seller can never get a high price."

Comment on price elasticity in industrial markets and ways in which industrial salesmen may overcome price objections.

5. To what extent do you consider that ability and competence in marketing are transferable? Discuss this question with particular reference to the following suggested transfers:

(*a*) from industrial products to consumer products selling;

(*b*) from industrial market research to consumer market research;

(*c*) from marketing management of consumer goods to marketing management of industrial goods.

6. Examine the advantages and problems of discounts and credit as forms of buying motivation.

7. What free external sources of advice and information are available to the manufacturer who wishes to export from the UK?

8. "Because an individual's values are conditioned by the social class structure he perceives, consumer buying behaviour reflects class differences." Comment on the limitations of the conventional socio-economic class definitions most frequently used in defining market profiles in the light of this statement.

Index

Details of some other Macdonald & Evans publications on related subjects can be found on the following pages.

For a full list of titles and prices write for the FREE Macdonald & Evans Business Studies catalogue available from Department BP1, Macdonald & Evans Ltd., Estover Road, Plymouth PL6 7PZ

Advertising
DAVID SHELLEY NICHOLL

Written to portray accurately the nature and scope of the advertising industry, this book covers topics such as the need for, and organisation of, the industry; the anatomy of an agency; planning a campaign; the adman's arsenal; and a future in advertising. It is aimed at both practitioners and students, including those on CAM, BEC and professional courses. This edition makes particular reference to commercial radio, and takes account of changes in the media, customs, conditions and statistics.

"The most useful advertising textbook to be published in a long time." *Broadcast*

Advertising Law
R. G. LAWSON

Ideal both as a textbook and as a reference source. Dealing with all aspects of advertising law, this book appears on the CAM reading list.

Cases in Consumer Law
G.H. SAMUEL

The emphasis of this CASEBOOK is on the principles of common law and on how those principles have been adapted over the last 100 years to cope with the rise of a consumer society. It is aimed at all law students, both those with a direct involvement in consumer law and those interested in legal method and the common law in general. In addition it is hoped that the book will appeal to the enquiring lay person and to students of non-legal disciplines, particularly those following professional and Higher National Diploma courses in business studies. ". . . of inestimable value to the general reader, and to the student both legal and non-legal." *Justice of the Peace*

Consumer Credit
R.G. LAWSON
The Consumer Credit Act 1974 is one of the most important and most complicated pieces of legislation of recent years. This HANDBOOK provides the student with a concise and clear discussion of the subject, and will be useful both as an introduction and as a revision source.

Consumer Law
M.J. LEDER
This HANDBOOK provides a concise but comprehensive survey of the diverse elements of consumer law, a subject which is being included in an increasing number of courses. It is intended primarily for the use of undergraduates on law degree and mixed degree courses, and for prospective solicitors preparing for the new Law Society final examinations. In addition it should be of considerable interest to business studies and accountancy students, and to anyone whose studies or work involves a consideration of the legal aspects of consumer problems.

International Marketing
L.S. WALSH
This HANDBOOK is concerned with those aspects of marketing that are applicable only to the international field and those that require a special emphasis and a deeper knowledge than are necessary in the purely domestic environment. It is aimed at students of marketing and business studies in universities, polytechnics and colleges of technology, as well as students of professional bodies.

Introduction to Marketing
JOHN FRAIN
This book is a foundation study of the "marketing concept" and the business processes that the concept implies. Its commentary on the benefits of the marketing concept to the organisation, to its customers and to society in general will be especially helpful for readers intending to work in marketing or any of its associated functions (distribution, selling, research, etc.). The work has been designed with the requirements of BEC especially in mind but the author's style and content should also appeal to the more general reader. One of the BECBOOK series.

Marketing Techniques for Analysis and Control
PETER ALLEN
This book relates new techniques of analysis and control to the marketing function and will be ideal for students of marketing, management and business courses.

Marketing Research
TONY PROCTOR & MARILYN A. STONE
Industry's growing appreciation of the value of marketing research has created a demand for courses to provide students with a fundamental knowledge of what marketing research is, and its practical applications to business. This HANDBOOK presents the subject in a simple and concise manner, using examples from the authors' own considerable industrial experience. It is aimed primarily at university students, but will also be most useful to DMS, BEC, Institute of Marketing Diploma and MRS Diploma students.

Modern Marketing
FRANK JEFKINS

This new HANDBOOK about the techniques of selling at a profit what people want to buy has been written to dispel the mystique surrounding marketing, a subject which many students often find difficult to grasp. Covering specifically the syllabus of the LCCI Higher Certificate in Marketing examination, which is a compulsory subject for the LCCI Group Diploma in Marketing and an option for the LCCI Group Diploma in Public Relations, this book will also be useful for students taking the relevant examinations of CAM, the Institute of Marketing and at BEC Higher level. The author, through his extensive practical, teaching and writing experience throughout the world, is able to bring an international approach to the subject. Whilst appreciating the special value of advertising as part of the marketing mix, he also sees public relations as an integral part of the entire marketing strategy and as an essential part of the marketing manager's job specification. This he demonstrates by showing the PR implications of naming, branding, pricing and packaging, and warns of the bad PR which can result from thoughtless sales promotion and merchandising.

The author has had wide experience in marketing and has lectured in marketing research and international marketing for a number of years at Croydon College. In addition he is the principal of his own Public Relations School and has lectured in marketing, public relations and advertising all over the world. He is also the Examiner for Marketing for the LCCI and has prepared the syllabus for their examinations in that subject.

Public Relations
FRANK JEFKINS

The success of this popular HANDBOOK demonstrates the increasing interest being taken in public relations all over the world. The book should be of primary use to those undertaking communication and business studies courses for the BEC Higher National Core Module "Understanding Organisations" as well as for those taking the examinations for the RSA Diploma for Personal Assistants. It can also be used as supplementary reading for CAM Certificate and Institute of Marketing students. Indeed, for anyone whose daily work involves some aspect of public relations, this book should provide a useful insight into this complex subject.

The author approaches the subject from an international point of view to suit its worldwide market, and investigates the problems of modern communication techniques. In addition, the value of public relations is discussed in this new age of readily accessible information, heralded by viewdata, teletext and the numerous computer services, in which the consumer can be increasingly selective not only in his choice of the information he receives but also in his choice of entertainment. The final chapter is devoted to public relations in developing countries and can be as enlightening to UK students as it is sympathetic to those in the Third World.

This edition covers the syllabus of the compulsory subject Public Relations for the LCCI Group Diploma in Public Relations, examination papers being included as appendixes. Frank Jefkins has lectured at the City of London Polytechnic, the College for the Distributive Trades, the Polytechnic of Central London and Croydon College. He is presently Principal of the Frank Jefkins School of Public Relations and is Vice Chairman of the Education Committee of the Institute of Public Relations.

Public Relations – A Practical Guide
COLIN COULSON-THOMAS

Unlike most public relations literature, which is concerned with techniques rather than the broader management questions of problem-solving, this book sets out a practical approach to the solution of public relations problems, illustrated with examples drawn from a wide range of situations in both the public and private sectors. It will be of particular interest to students preparing for CAM and Institute of Marketing examinations or studying for the DMS, and for those following courses in communications, marketing and public relations at colleges, polytechnics and universities. Practitioners will also find this a most useful text. "Clearly laid out and easy to use, the book should be as useful to those actively involved in public relations as to those studying the subject." *Trade and Industry*

Retailing
ROGER COX

This HANDBOOK attempts to show in a simple and straight-forward way many of the problems associated with retailing and how they may be solved. It deals in turn with the organisation of the industry, the theory and practice of retail location, merchandising, and the administrative aspects of running retail firms. "The text can be recommended to distribution students working for . . . RMS and CRS examinations and to those who will take BEC Level III tests."
Retail and Distribution Management

Sales and Sales Management
P. ALLEN

This HANDBOOK is intended to bring together the theory and practice of management as applied to the selling activity. It covers the requirements of the various professional examinations in marketing and will also be a valuable source of information for students studying for certificate, diploma, BEC and "A" Level examinations in business studies.